# NEVER TOGETHER

In November 2020, the *New York Times* asked fifteen of its columnists to "explain what the past four years have cost America." Not one of the columnists focused on President Trump's racism. This book seeks to redress this imbalance and bring Black Americans' role in our economy to the forefront.

While all humans were created equal, economic history in the United States tells a different story. Reconstruction lasted for only a decade, and Jim Crow laws replaced it. The Civil Rights Movement lasted through the 1960s, yet decayed under the rule of President Nixon. The United States has been declining in the Social Product Index, where now it is the lowest of the G7 and 26th in the world.

For health and happiness, Peter Temin argues that we need lasting integration efforts that allow Black Americans equal opportunity. This book convincingly integrates Black and white activities into an inclusive economic history of America.

Peter Temin is Elisha Gray II Professor Emeritus of Economics at the Massachusetts Institute of Technology.

## STUDIES IN NEW ECONOMIC THINKING

The 2008 financial crisis pointed to problems in economic theory that require more than just big data to solve. INET's series in collaboration with Cambridge University Press exists to ensure that innovative work that advances economics and better integrates it with other social sciences and the study of history and institutions can reach a broad audience in a timely way.

**Recently published:**

*Macroeconomic Inequality for Reagan to Trump: Market Power, Wage Repression, Asset Price Inflation, and Industrial Decline* by Lance Taylor with Özlem Ömer

*How Novelty and Narratives Drive the Stock Market* by Nicholas Mangee

**Titles forthcoming in the series:**

*Money and Empire: Charles P. Kindleberger and the Dollar System* by Perry Mehrling

# NEVER TOGETHER

*The Economic History of a Segregated America*

**Peter Temin**

Massachusetts Institute of Technology

# CAMBRIDGE
## UNIVERSITY PRESS

University Printing House, Cambridge CB2 8BS, United Kingdom

One Liberty Plaza, 20th Floor, New York, NY 10006, USA

477 Williamstown Road, Port Melbourne, VIC 3207, Australia

314–321, 3rd Floor, Plot 3, Splendor Forum, Jasola District Centre, New Delhi – 110025, India

103 Penang Road, #05–06/07, Visioncrest Commercial, Singapore 238467

Cambridge University Press is part of the University of Cambridge.

It furthers the University's mission by disseminating knowledge in the pursuit of
education, learning, and research at the highest international levels of excellence.

www.cambridge.org
Information on this title: www.cambridge.org/9781316516744
DOI: 10.1017/9781009030977

© Peter Temin 2022

First published 2022

Printed in the United Kingdom by TJ Books Limited, Padstow Cornwall

*A catalogue record for this publication is available from the British Library.*

*Library of Congress Cataloging-in-Publication Data*
Names: Temin, Peter, author.
Title: Never together : the economic history of a segregated America / Peter Temin.
Description: Cambridge ; New York, NY : Cambridge University Press, 2022. | Series: Studies
in new economic thinking | Includes bibliographical references and index.
Identifiers: LCCN 2021024658 (print) | LCCN 2021024659 (ebook) | ISBN 9781316516744
(hardback) | ISBN 9781009015288 (paperback) | ISBN 9781009030977 (epub)
Subjects: LCSH: African Americans–Economic conditions. | Racism–Economic
aspects–United States. | Income distribution–United States. | United States–Race
relations–Economic aspects. | United States–Economic conditions–19th century. |
United States–Economic conditions–20th century. | BISAC:
BUSINESS & ECONOMICS / Economic History
Classification: LCC E185.8 .T3793 2022 (print) | LCC E185.8 (ebook) |
DDC 331.6/396073–dc23
LC record available at https://lccn.loc.gov/2021024658
LC ebook record available at https://lccn.loc.gov/2021024659

ISBN 978-1-316-51674-4 Hardback

*For my family:*
*My daughters, Elizabeth and Melanie;*
*and grandsons, Colin, Zachary, and Elijah.*

# Contents

*Color plates can be found between pages 166 and 167.*

# Figures

# Tables

# Preface

I have been interested in the problems that the United States has been having in the past half century for several years. I wrote several papers about this subject and a book, *The Vanishing Middle Class,* to which this book may be regarded as a sequel. I wrote an epilogue to that book after President Trump's first year in office, which I draw on in Part III of this book. I also draw on some of my papers, particularly on mass incarceration. But while there is an extensive discussion of race in my 2017 book, I decided to make race a focus of this new book.

This book has its origin in the 2019 annual meeting of the American Economic Association. I was invited to present my paper on mass incarceration and to chair a session on graduate programs of economic history. I had an afternoon free and thought about who I would like to see. Having met and liked Professor Trevon Logan at various previous conferences, I asked him if we could talk. We had a long, friendly, and fruitful conversation.

This book grew out of the article that Professor Logan and I wrote as a result of that conversation. I want to thank him for his insights in our paper and his other research on American economic history, which are cited throughout this book. I also thank Thomas Ferguson of the Institute for New Economic Thinking, who gave me comments on early drafts of this book. I also want to thank two anonymous referees, and very able copy editors. Finally, I thank Ruth Levitsky of Massachusetts Institute of Technology and Michael L. Temin, who were very helpful in my research. And I thank the Institute for New Economic Thinking for supporting my research and writing of the book. The book was completed in the midst of the coronavirus pandemic when we were all isolated, which is why this book is centered more on the references than on contemporary discussions.

# Introduction

## *The Statue of Liberty*

THE UNITED STATES IS A NATION OF IMMIGRANTS. It had its origin in British colonies along the Atlantic coast and grew over time into the interior of what is now the United States. There were many waves of immigrants from many different places, but one wave of immigration, African immigrants, typically is missing from the historical list. "For generations, the impact of slavery has been written out of American history – indeed, with a few fleeting exceptions, such has been the rule through the nation's existence" (Forbes, 2007, 2).

Most immigrants came to America because they wanted to come, but African immigrants were forcibly brought to America by their captors. They differed from other immigrants because both they were captives who could not choose their place of residence and they became enslaved people in the colonies and early United States. This book aims to bring those neglected immigrants into the mainstream of American economic history by describing what happened to them as the economy developed.

The Declaration of Independence said famously, "All men are created equal." This equality extended to the British immigrants who dominated the American colonies, but it did not include the enslaved African immigrants. They were considered property, not individuals who could find a place in the American economy by themselves.

The Constitution echoed the Declaration in proclaiming, "We the People of the United States." Again, enslaved African immigrants were not considered or included. In fact, the framers of the Constitution made great efforts to avoid mentioning them. The framers used euphemisms

1

like "other persons" to refer to them as they set rules for politics and economics in the new country.

The Statue of Liberty has stood in New York City harbor since 1886. The torch-bearing arm was exhibited at the Centennial Exposition in Philadelphia in 1876, but it took another decade for the statue to be erected in its current space. It bears the famous poem verses:

> Give me your tired, your poor,
> Your huddled masses yearning to breathe free,
> The wretched refuse of your teeming shore.
> Send these, the homeless, tempest-tost to me,
> I lift my lamp beside the golden door! (Lazarus, 1883)

Even this later statement is in question now. As one recent book frames our era: "Since the country's founding, immigration has been at the heart of the American ideal of freedom and democracy, diversity and inclusion, opportunity, and upward mobility. But it has also been at the core of the nation's struggles with its own identity, at time yielding darker moments in which leaders have turned inward in hopes of preserving a bygone era. [President] Trump is one of them" (Davis and Shear, 2019, 8–9).

This book attempts to adapt these well-known assertions to our times and recount more than two centuries of conflicts since the Declaration and Constitution were written. I integrate Black and white activities into an economic history of America. My premise is that all men – and women – of all colors are created equal. Their histories, as will become clear, are quite different, and the resulting tension still informs us today. And when I discuss the people of the United States, I mean all people independent of their origins and skin color. In short, we all are descendants of immigrants.

Kenneth Stampp declared over fifty years ago, following Gunnar Myrdal, "One fact is established beyond any reasonable doubt. This is the fact that variations in the capacities and personalities of the *individuals* within each race are as great as variations in the physical traits. Therefore, it is impossible to make valid generalizations about races as such" (Stampp, 1956, 10; see also Myrdal, 1944, chapter IV, with footnotes on pp. 1212–18).

Nonetheless, the European immigrants were incapable of seeing their captives as individuals. Blacks were enslaved people who helped white Americans expand before the Civil War. Indeed, the 1858 *Dred Scott* decision explicitly noted that the founders never considered Blacks, free or enslaved, to be persons with any rights in the American republic. Slavery was outlawed soon after this court decision by the Civil War and Thirteenth Amendment. These rapid changes reveal the contradictions within white people.

Blacks began to participate in American politics en masse for the first time during Reconstruction. This process met with white resistance, and Black inclusion in the growing economy fell sharply as the Gilded Age followed and white political will for Black participation faded. The Supreme Court, still conservative, negated the force of the Fourteenth Amendment on the rights of freedmen.

Marx said, "History repeats itself, first as tragedy, then as farce (Marx, 1852)." The tragedy after the Civil War Reconstruction was followed by the fleeting memory of President Lyndon Johnson's Great Society. The measures in the second attempt to integrate Blacks into the majority status of the United States induced a reaction that echoes the failure of Reconstruction a century earlier. The Supreme Court encouraged the growth of commerce and industry while it aborted efforts to include Blacks into political and economic activities in both the 1880s and 2010s. The Court promoted white economic progress and impeded the integration of most Blacks into this prosperity.

Poor whites often appear in this story along with Blacks. They can be seen suffering under slavery just as they suffer now in mass incarceration. There are two ways to include these unfortunates in this story. One way is to regard them as collateral damage to the anger directed at Blacks. A more accurate view is that the dominant whites – landowners in the antebellum South, postbellum industrialists, and financial moguls and internet wizards today – engage in class as well as racial prejudice.

Each time there was a partial move toward integrating Blacks into the white economy and polity or helping poor people advance, there also was a reaction that returned Blacks and poor whites to widespread subservience. This was true in the Gilded Age of the late 1800s, and it is true again in the new Gilded Age of the last several decades. Blacks made gains toward integration in Reconstruction and in the Civil Rights Movement during postwar prosperity. Some of these gains have lasted, as I will show, but full integration remains far off because policies even in good times exclude Blacks and benefit whites.

It is worth stressing how much the Gilded Age of the late nineteenth and early twentieth century looks like our current Gilded Age. Everyone remembers robber baron names from the first Gilded Age, from Carnegie to Rockefeller and J. P. Morgan. Their current analogues today are Jeff Bezos of Amazon, Tim Cook of Apple, Sundar Pichai of Google, and Mark Zuckerberg of Facebook who testified before the antitrust subcommittee of the House Judiciary Committee in late July 2020 about antitrust and big tech. To which we should add Charles Koch of oil, Robert Mercer of finance, and Rupert Murdoch of FOX TV. The other similarity of course is that the robber barons of both periods created conditions for the establishment of Jim Crow laws then and the growth of mass incarceration, also known as the New Jim Crow, today.

Between these similar periods came the disturbances of world wars and depression in the early twentieth century. Everyone suffered, but Blacks tried peacefully to alleviate their fortunes in the Great Migration. Whites struggled through the violence and created economic and political foundations for the following prosperity ranging from interstate highways to personal computers. But while some educated Blacks have joined white society today by getting a good education, the cost of keeping many Blacks imprisoned and disenfranchised reduces economic growth in the United States.

The following chapters reveal that each time there was a concerted move toward integrating Blacks into the white economy and polity, there was an adverse reaction that returned Blacks to widespread subservience. Blacks made gains toward integration in Reconstruction and in the Civil Rights Movement, but they suffered reversals in the Gilded Age and in the new Gilded Age of today. The new Gilded Age is based on services instead of manufacturing, and demand for workers has fallen. The new robber barons inflame racial prejudice to maintain their political hegemony, while neglecting investment other than prisons for Black and brown people.

Isabel Wilkerson, whose research I cite and quote later in this book, recently championed the use of caste in understanding the role of Blacks in the United States. She equated racism and casteism, arguing, "Through no fault of any individual born to it, a caste system centers the dominant caste as the sun around which all other castes revolve and defines it as the default-setting standard of normalcy, of intellect, of beauty, against which all others are measured, ranked in descending order by their physiological proximity to the dominant caste" (Wilkerson, 2020a). And she quoted Andrew Hacker saying, "White Americans of all classes have found it comforting to preserve Blacks as a subordinate caste: a presence that despite all its pain and problems still provides whites with some solace in a stressful world" (Hacker, 1992).

Wilkerson defined the difference between racism and casteism in her book: "Any action or institution that mocks, harms, assumes, or attaches inferiority or stereotypes on the basis of the social construct of race can be considered racism. Any action or structure that seeks to limit, hold back, or put someone in a defined ranking, seeks to keep someone in their place by elevating or denigrating that person on the basis of their perceived category, can be seen as casteism." Simply put, accusing people of being inferior is racism, while acting to keep those people inferior is casteism (Wilkerson, 2020b, 70).

This book chronicles two episodes of dominant racism and casteism. Two Gilded Ages cannot make a rule, but the history described here and the analyses of Hacker and Wilkerson suggest that the future may be very much like the past.

The ensuing chapters provide a chronological survey of an inclusive American economic history in the nineteenth and twentieth centuries. The chapters start with slavery and the Civil War, Reconstruction, and the Gilded Age of the late nineteenth century. They continue with chapters on the world wars and depression, postwar prosperity, a new Gilded Age, and economic decline in our day. Each chapter integrates Black economic history into the conventional white economic history of the United States. Including Black people in this narrative provides a complete description of our history and suggests some paths by which we could integrate Blacks entirely in mainstream economic progress.

# PART I

# THE NINETEENTH CENTURY

# CHAPTER 1

# Slavery and the Civil War

## 1.1 REVOLUTION AND FORMATION OF THE UNITED STATES

This book incorporates the history of Black and other disadvantaged minorities into our accepted narratives to provide an inclusive American economic history. Three important events in 1776 initiated developments that are important in this inclusive American economic history: Adam Smith published *The Wealth of Nations*, James Watt patented the steam engine, and the American colonists signed their Declaration of Independence. One event was economic, second historical, and the third American. Together, they laid the foundation of American economic history with cumulative progress for whites and slavery and segregation for Blacks. I describe these three events in turn to reveal their implications and their omissions.

Adam Smith published *The Wealth of Nations* in 1776. This book is the bible of the new religion known as economics. Smith argued that the division of labor was the source of productivity. As he expressed it at the start of *The Wealth of Nations*, "It is not from the benevolence of the butcher, the brewer, or the baker, that we expect our dinner, but from their regard to their own interest." In other words, the purchase of dinner is a commercial activity of mutual benefit, not a charitable gift. Smith illustrated his mechanism with a pin factory and then with dinner. He implicitly extended his argument to national wealth, but not in this explicit form (Smith, 1776, Book I, Chapters 1–2; Skidelsky, 2019).

Adam Smith's writing highlighted the income inequality typical of many agricultural economies. While we cannot pin down the exact numbers, it is likely that only the top 10 percent of people in Great

Britain could read his book. Smith noted that he was conscious of the rest of the population in his discussion of investment: "When the stock which a man possesses is no more than sufficient to maintain him for a few days or a few weeks, he seldom thinks of deriving any revenue from it." However, as with the founding documents of the United States, Smith concerned himself primarily with the educated class. He was typical of his age in ignoring slaves. But he was prescient in his description of what freedmen and then segregated Blacks would face (Smith, 1776, Book II, Chapter 1).

James Watt patented the steam engine in 1776. This was the start of the British Industrial Revolution, and many English cotton factories powered their machines with steam power. American cotton factories were powered mostly with waterpower, as the New England ports were close to the fall line of several rivers. In both countries, steam power led to railroads in the course of the nineteenth century, making overland transportation competitive with water transport for the first time in history. African Americans were brought from Africa by sea, and some of them later would be porters on Pullman cars.

The invention of the steam engine relegated Smith's observations about the division of labor to a lesser part of economic history. Gains from the division of labor now are spoken of as "Smithian growth," in contrast to the economic growth deriving from steam-powered energy, initially in mines and factories prevalent during the Industrial Revolution. This is not a criticism of Adam Smith, who could not have forecast the future, but a reminder that he wrote in the late eighteenth century. Nevertheless, his insights into the productivity effects of the division of labor are still cited and utilized today.

The American colonists issued their Declaration of Independence in 1776. As noted in Introduction, "all men are created equal" did not include African immigrants. When Southern farmers first began to expand farming in the seventeenth century, they employed white and Black workers equally, subject to restrictions held over from medieval practices of lords and their dependent farm workers. The farmers' problem was not Africans, it was lack of labor to work their abundant land. (A few Northern areas, like the Hudson River Valley, had similar problems.) American farmers encouraged European immigration by loaning immigrants the money to get to America with their farm labor obligations as security. European workers became indentured servants, who would regain their freedom of action when they had paid back their loan and their indentures were over.

The farmers did not apply this approach to African immigrants because the Africans did not come to America voluntarily. English and Dutch migrants mostly came because they wanted to come, while African migrants were purchased and brought to America against their will. As Oscar and Mary Handlin stated in a classic article, "To raise the status of Europeans by shortening their terms would ultimately increase the available hands by inducing their compatriots to emigrate; to reduce the Negro's term would produce an immediate loss and no ultimate gain" (Handlin and Handlin, 1950).

The expansion of the African slave trade at the end of the seventeenth century provided Southern planters with abundant labor in a framework that developed to differentiate between whites and Blacks. The difference that had opened up between European and African immigrants led to landowners' fears of plots and conspiracies among the Black immigrants and to restrictions on Black workers. The Handlins concluded, "At the opening of the eighteenth century, the Black was not only set off by economic and legal status; he was 'abominable,' another order of man" (Handlin and Handlin, 1950).

Edmund Morgan, another respected colonial historian, asserted more recently that Southern planters adopted racism to justify their use of slavery. In other words, he reversed the causation in these early events. Racism was not the result of economic choices, but invoked to justify and defend economic decisions made on other grounds: "Racism thus absorbed in Virginia the fear and contempt that men in England ... felt for the inarticulate lower classes. ... And by lumping Indians, mulattoes, and Negroes in a single pariah class, Virginians had paved the way for a similar lumping of small and large planters in a single master class." Morgan closed his book with the assertion that this slavery mentality outlived the Civil War, asking, "Was the nation of equals flawed at the source by contempt for both the poor and the Black? Is America still colonial Virginia writ large?" (Morgan, 1975, 386–87).

The answer, alas, is yes. Morgan's recreation of colonial thought seems more accurate than the Handlins'. Colonial farmers adopted slavery and then borrowed from their English compatriots the same divisions Adam Smith adopted in his books. The illiterate and poor of eighteenth-century Britain were prosecuted for small crimes or vagrancy and imprisoned or sent abroad. They were ignored or mentioned only briefly by the colonial elite. They were the abhorred poor. In the American colonies they were predominantly but not exclusively Black. Native Indians and later Latinos also were abhorred.

Education reveals the severe nature of American slavery because American slave owners discouraged the education of slaves in order to minimize revolts. Roman slaves, who similarly were captives of war but often were freed, had owners who encouraged slaves to be educated and perform responsible economic roles. Adam Smith appreciated Cicero's able speeches because Marcus Tullius Tiro, his slave and secretary, recorded and published them. Cicero freed Tiro as he was so useful to him. Education increased the value of Roman slave labor to the owner and the probability that the slaves would be freed; manumitted slaves became Roman citizens (Temin, 2013, Chapter 6).

Slavery in antiquity and modern times can be classified as open and closed systems. In open slavery, slaves can be freed and accepted fully into the free society. In closed slavery, slaves are seen as a separate group, not accepted into free society, and to marry among the general population. Roman slavery was open; freedmen were Roman citizens, and marriages with widows were common. "By contrast, American slavery [was] perhaps the most closed and caste-like of any [slave] system known" (Watson, 1980, 7).

Think of a continuum of incentives among workers. Modern jobs are near, but not at, the open end; one can be fired or demoted for nonperformance. American slavery was near the opposite end; the threat of punishment was ubiquitous, while rewards for good service were rare. Roman slavery, by contrast, was more like modern jobs, although rural and unskilled slaves in ancient Rome may have experienced something like American slavery (Temin, 2004).

Education shows a mechanism repeated time and again in our history. The ruling class decides that the pariah class has an uncomfortable trait.

The ruling class in fact often projects some of its own uncomfortable traits onto the pariah class. Then the ruling class sets up conditions to create or sustain these traits in the pariah class. So, if Blacks – or other immigrants – were uncivilized, then make it illegal to educate them. Then Blacks can be condemned for their ignorance. American slavery was outlawed by the Fourteenth Amendment, but the master class still impedes the education of the pariah class by direct and indirect means.

The three events of 1776 foretell the story ahead. They concerned economics (Smith), history (steam power), and America (independence). Ironically, the American event overlooked the role of enslaved persons in the South. And that is the point here. This book describes the history of Black and other disadvantaged minorities to present an inclusive American economic history. While there are extensive libraries of Black history and white economic history in the United States, there has not been enough attention to bringing them together.

This early history of the United States embodies themes that pervade later history as well. Jefferson saw the future of the United States in its past with a concentration of agriculture. This proved accurate for the South up to the Civil War, when the emphasis shifted to settling the outer portions of the Louisiana Purchase. The North, following Hamilton's spirit, was committed to industrialization in the East and transport to the West. The western expansion occupied the North after the Civil War and distracted it from reconstructing the defeated South along more inclusive lines. Workers in both activities were composed of immigrants who were accepted into white society after some delays, while Blacks continued to be held in involuntary servitude.

For example, many Irish came in response to the famine at mid-century. They were grouped initially with Blacks as despised manual workers. The new immigrants joined with abolitionists to oppose slavery out of sympathy with their attempts to free Ireland from English rule. Only when many Irish Americans had abandoned this stance were they considered whites who then joined other whites and adopted their racial views as their own (Temin, 2017, 54).

Bernard Bailyn noted that there were few Blacks in colonial New England, but he asserted that slavery made the New England economy prosper. Profits from the Atlantic trade came from the flow of New

England's products to slave plantations and the sugar and tobacco that slaves produced.

> Without the sugar and tobacco industries, based on slave labor, and without the slave trade, there would not have been markets anywhere nearly sufficient to create the returns that made possible the purchase of European goods, the extended credit, and the leisured life that New Englanders enjoyed. Slavery was the ultimate source of the commercial economy of eighteenth-century New England. Only a few of New England's merchants actually engaged in the slave trade, but all of them profited by it, lived off it. (Bailyn, 2000, 254–55; see also Solow, 1991)

The Declaration of Independence did not come at the start of the Revolutionary War; it was a sequel to the earlier French and Indian War, 1754–63. France and Britain both wanted to control North America at that time. France had Canada, and England held the thirteen colonies east of the Appalachian Mountains. France and Britain came into conflict over access to the Ohio River west of the mountains, and the British won after several years of fighting.

George III of Britain decided after the war that he needed to keep British soldiers in his colonies to protect them from the French. He also decided that the colonists should help pay for the expensive war and the standing army since they were for the colonists' benefit. He instituted the Tea Act and the Stamp Act among other taxes. The Tea Act led to the Boston Tea Party when Bostonians dumped tea into the harbor in late 1773. Tempers flared, and the British marched into Lexington and Concord, Massachusetts, in a fruitless attempt to find American arms in 1775. The Declaration of Independence expressed the colonists' desire to start a new war between Britain and its own colonies.

It is far easier to start wars than is to end them. To end a war, both sides need to stop fighting. This can be arranged in one of two ways. If one side is far stronger, it can fight until the weaker side surrenders without conditions. If the sides are more evenly matched, then they must agree on a peace treaty that binds them both from future violence. The British, with the largest and finest army and navy in the world in the late eighteenth century, thought they were in the first case and that they could easily convince the colonists to abandon their war.

In early December 1776, British commanders believed that they were very close to ending the rebellion, and American leaders feared they might be right. The American rebels had lost every battle throughout the previous five months. George Washington just barely evacuated his army from New York City as the British moved in. But Washington's strategic purposes remained constant: "to win independence by maintaining American resolve to continue the war, by preserving an American army in being, and raising the cost of the war to the enemy" (Fischer, 2004, 372).

On December 25, 1776, George Washington led a ragged army of 2,400 colonials across the Delaware River into New Jersey. There was a terrible storm that night that froze the soldiers and imperiled their voyage, but also kept the British from seeing the colonials coming. The colonials then marched all night and defeated 1,500 Hessians at Trenton. A week later they marched overnight to Princeton and defeated British reinforcements rushing to Trenton. These were small battles – the Battle of Antietam in the Civil War involved one hundred times the number of soldiers – but they were highly significant. The promise of a speedy defeat changed to a continuing struggle (Fischer, 2004, 346–62).

By the spring of 1777, many British officers concluded they could not win the war, and the Americans were confident they would not be defeated. The war continued into 1781 with fighting in the North and the South in what appeared to be a stalemate. The French entered the war to defeat their traditional rivals, the British, in 1778, and broke the stalemate. Washington defeated Cornwallis in Yorktown, Virginia, in 1781 (Ferling, 2007).

While Washington's steadiness was critical in his military success, his views on slavery changed rapidly after 1775, and he began to speak of slavery as a great evil. He wrote of his opposition to slavery in 1777 and emancipated slaves in his will, although his estate was largely his wife's. Washington's views of African immigrants were hardly as well-known as his military victories, but it is intriguing to realize that the South was not universally supportive of American slavery (Fischer, 2004, 15.)

The colonies, now states, signed the Articles of Confederation and Perpetual Union in 1781 and negotiated peace with Britain in 1783. But the Continental Congress needed unanimous consent to impose taxes or raise money in other ways. States therefore failed to honor or repudiated their wartime debts. Delegates to the Continental Congress requested a meeting to propose amendments to the Articles of Confederation. This gave rise to a group in Philadelphia that set out to write a new constitution, which was ratified by all the states in 1788 (Maier, 2010).

The delegates came from all over, and Robert McGuire and others have tried to understand how where they came from affected their choices for the federal government while at the convention. Delegates from large states and coastal areas favored issues that increased the power of the national government over the states. Delegates who represented slave owners were less likely to vote for federal power. The slave owners and their descendants would continue this preference for local rather than national control long after slavery was abolished. Even in the twentieth century, Southern Senators fought for state and local administration of New Deal measures and the GI Bill. These regional patterns from the late eighteenth century lasted for two centuries (McGuire and Ohsfeldt, 1986).

In order to get universal support for the Constitution, the Philadelphia negotiators made compromises with the slave-owning states. They chose not to mention slaves or Blacks by name, but employed euphemisms to make their points, perhaps in response to views like George Washington's. The most important compromise was for allocation of taxes and representatives among the states: "Representatives and direct Taxes shall be apportioned among the several States which may be included within this Union, according to their respective Numbers, which shall be determined by adding to the whole number of free Persons, including those bound to Service for a Term of Years, and excluding Indians not taxed, three fifths of all other Persons (US Constitution, Article I, Section 2)." The final phrase, "three fifths of all other Persons," was eliminated in the Fourteenth Amendment, Section 2.

There were 1.70 million whites and 0.92 million Blacks in the South in 1800. Three-fifths of 0.92 is 0.55. If we add this number to 1.70, it increases it by over 30 percent. There were of course property requirements to vote in various states, but a one-third increase in voting and representation seems about right. This was a huge concession to the slave-owning South, and it ensured their political dominance in the United States for the foreseeable future. All United States presidents for fifty years after the Constitution was ratified were slave owners, with the isolated exceptions of single terms by the revolutionary John Adams and his son, John Quincy Adams (*U. S. Historical Statistics*, 1975, Series A172–194).

To get an idea of how much this concession mattered, consider the effect of mass incarceration today. The Census ruled that prisoners should be counted where they are imprisoned, and most prisons are in rural settings. Since prisoners cannot vote, they are like enslaved persons in the early nineteenth century. They are counted in the representation from rural areas, which helps to explain why there is much discussion of rural voters in the early twenty-first century, despite the exodus of white people from those areas. But while their impact affects policy in rural states, the number of prisoners compared to the total state population is an order of magnitude smaller than the number of slaves. (If I had data for rural populations, the numbers would be closer.)

The Constitution, having allowed this concession to the South, tried to offset its effect by asserting that the slave trade could be abolished after twenty years: "The Migration or Importation of such Persons as any of the States now existing shall think proper to admit, shall not be prohibited by the Congress prior to the Year one thousand eight hundred and eight, but a Tax or duty may be imposed on such Importation, not exceeding ten dollars for each Person" (Article I, Section 9). Again, slaves were not named. Moreover, the offset was limited. Slave imports were allowed for twenty years while the voting aid from slaves took effect immediately. Northern opponents of slavery wanted a compromise, but they lacked the power or perhaps the negotiating skills that delegates from slave-owning states had.

Alexander Hamilton, who had been George Washington's aide during the war, was appointed Secretary of the Treasury in Washington's cabinet. He issued three reports in 1790–91 that were designed to provide an economic foundation for the new country. The first report on public credit urged Congress to assume the wartime debts of the colonies that had not been paid under the Confederation. New excise taxes would provide money for purchasing bonds and paying interest.

This report was violently opposed by James Madison, who followed Jefferson's lead. It was Hamilton's first report, and it would pay all bonds regardless of who owned them after the war. Economic historians have lauded this report as a means to create a good reputation for American debt that would enable the new country to borrow and invest. Madison argued that poor people had sold their bonds to speculators who would gain from Hamilton's plan. He was persuaded to support the report in exchange for moving the nation's capital from Philadelphia to a new portion of Virginia, not by any help to poor people.

The second report recommended that the government propose to charter a national bank for twenty years. Madison again opposed the national bank, saying that the Constitution left that function to the states. I will say more about the national bank when discussing the 1830s.

The third report was on manufacturers. While Hamilton praised agriculture, he argued for manufacturing in addition. Domestically, manufacturers would increase demand for agricultural products and provide employment for varied workers. Internationally, manufacturers would free the United States from having to search out foreign sources and make the United States a good trading partner. Hamilton argued for several programs to encourage manufacturers, from tariffs to raising money for transportation of goods.

The two subjects of Hamilton's reports are connected by what economists call the circular flow model, shown in Figure 1.1. Think of a circle with people on one side and businesses on the other. Money and debts go around clockwise while manufacturers and other goods go around counterclockwise. The two flows are equal and opposite, for people need to work to earn money from farms or businesses, which they spend to buy products, and businesses need to sell their products for money to be able to pay their workers.

Adam Smith explained how this works: "It is not from the benevolence of the butcher, the brewer, or the baker, that we expect our dinner, but from their regard to their own interest." The circular flow model summarizes how buying your dinner fits into the economy as a whole with the interaction of people and businesses. (The model ignores

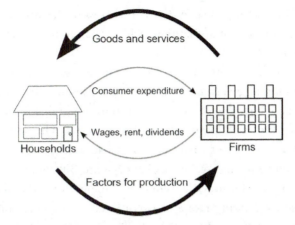

**1.1.** Circular flow model. https://upload.wikimedia.org/wikipedia/commons/b/b8/
Circular_flow_of_goods_income.png

slavery, which was central to the economy Hamilton was improving. I will
show how slavery fits in a little later.)

It is easy to see where the goods come from, but harder to understand where money comes from. Ancient Greece and Rome had coinage and loans by banks, and specialized loans were added as trade
expanded again in the early modern period. The most widespread
loans in the early history of the United States were in bills of exchange.
A bill of exchange was a loan that would be paid back at a later time –
often three or six months – in a different place. The addition of
another place was to simplify loans for trade, as in selling cotton from
the American South to Britain, where customer would be paying off
their loans.

Bills of exchange are confusing because they were most useful when
travel and communication were slow. To clarify this connection, recall
that the Constitution gave the federal government the power to tax,
including taxing imports by tariffs. The Constitution was needed because
the Confederation lacked this power, which is why there were so many
state debts outstanding in the 1780s. Article I, Section 8, states the first
power of the new federal government as follows: "The Congress shall
have Power to lay and collect Taxes Duties, Imposts and Excises." It was
this power to tax that enabled Hamilton in his first report to Congress to

recommend assuming all state debts. Tariffs were the primary tax that funded the government at that time, which Hamilton recommended in his third report.

The new national debt carried an interest rate to compensate investors for investing in government bonds. Banks – led by the national bank Hamilton recommended in his second report – handled the transfer of money from the tariff payments to the investors. This movement of money within and between banks is not visible to most observers, but it is an important function of the banking system. Bills of exchange were like government or business debts in function, but differed in their form. The interest for lending money was collected at the beginning of the loan as a discount from the initial bill. This is why these bills often are listed as "discounts" in bank statements. As David Hume said a century earlier, "It is well known of what advantage it is to a merchant to be able to discount his bills on occasion" (Hume, 2012).

Bills of exchange also were paid in a different place, and this adds another step in pricing them. The discount on the original bill was both an interest charge and an exchange rate for another currency. Economic historians have used this double charge to estimate exchange rates. They assume that the interest charged for a bill of exchange is the same interest rate paid for commercial loans, loans by businesses, which are repaid in the same currency as the loan. Subtracting this from the discount gives an estimate of the exchange rate charged. Today, we assume that investors, lenders, and borrowers knew all of this and competed with each other to create market prices for loans. It is that assumption that enables economic historians to make their calculations by assuming that there is a uniform interest rate for competing loans.

Hamilton's reports contained wise policy, particularly for a new country that needed to recover from a war, pay its debts, and promote expansion. They all were adopted and provided a framework for America's subsequent economic growth and westward expansion. Southerners who wanted a minimal federal government opposed them, although they too were interested in westward expansion. Their descendants appeared again in more recent times, as I will describe in Chapter 7 (Chernow, 2004; Wilentz, 2018).

## 1.2 LOUISIANA PURCHASE, MISSOURI COMPROMISE,
## AND ITS AFTERMATH

President Jefferson bought the Louisiana Purchase from France in 1803. The United States thereby gained land west of the Mississippi River that greatly enlarged the land area of the nascent United States, extending the area Britain had held onto east of the Mississippi River at the end of the French and Indian War thirty years earlier. The war was very expensive, and Britain's efforts to tax the colonists to help pay its debt raised violent protests. The purchase also was expensive, but purchase was a far easier way to extend the United States westward than the French and Indian War. Hamilton's first report to Congress ensured lenders to the new country that their loans to the United States would be paid. Even though Jefferson had opposed Hamilton's reports that restored financial stability to the country after the Revolutionary War, he was happy to utilize the financial tools it gave him.

We think of this transaction as a purchase, but for France it was a sale. France needed the money to fight Britain as it turned away from America to face the threat to Europe under Napoleon's rule. And from the French point of view, the financing of Louisiana was financed by a large and long-lived bill of exchange. France got the money from the sale immediately, although the United States would only pay over time as it settled and incorporated the new land. And while the United States paid in dollars, the French received French francs.

The financial question was who loaned the money in the meantime. This was such a large transaction that it was more like a royal loan than a commercial sale, and it was arranged by Alexander Baring – who went on to help finance many other government loans over time – and other investment bankers. They appealed to the buyers of Hamilton's loans when he paid off the wartime bonds and to other wealthy investors and traders in France and Holland. While the negotiations were difficult and the payments long-lasting, the interest rate on this "bill of exchange" turned out to be only 6 percent (Neal, 2020).

Jefferson also ended the slave trade five years later in 1808, as soon as possible after the Constitution was adopted. These two actions made sure that new slaves would not be brought in to farm the newly purchased lands, but that Blacks already enslaved in the South would be sent west to the new lands. Ira Berlin asserted that there were four large migrations of Blacks in the United States. The Western Passage brought Africans from Africa before 1808 to farm Southern land in the first migration. The Louisiana Purchase stimulated the second migration as new lands were opened for settlement (Berlin, 2010).

Farmers were encouraged to migrate west into territories carved out west of the Allegheny Mountains. Once there, the farmers sought to join the original thirteen states in the United States. Eight additional states were admitted to the union from 1803 to 1819. The Constitutional compromise enabled the new states to acquire influence in the House of Representatives. And each state would also send two senators to Washington. This could easily alter the balance of power between the antislavery North and the proslavery South.

This was a major concern to contemporaries, and they made sure in these early years that the Senate balance would be unchanged. There were two new states admitted before the Louisiana Purchase, on the land gained by the French and Indian War, one above the other on the map, Tennessee was a slave state and Kentucky was free. Six more states were admitted after the purchase, three slave states, Louisiana, Mississippi, and Alabama, and three free states, Ohio, Indiana, and Illinois. So far, so good. The Senate balance held.

Then Missouri, containing a lot of slave-holding landowners, applied for statehood. This set off a furious debate in Congress about the westward spread of slavery. An antislavery position was proclaimed by a Representative from Vermont, starting with the euphemisms used in the Constitution to refer to enslaved people:

> Hitherto, slavery has not been so recognized by the General Government, as to cause our national character to be materially affected by it; for, although there are states in the Union which, from the necessity of the case, may be termed slave-holding States, it cannot, with truth, be alleged that, as a nation, we have permitted slavery. But if, under present circumstances, Congress shall solemnly decide that it cannot restrain the unlimited extension of it, and that a want of power to do so results from an

unqualified recognition of it by the Constitution, our national character will become identified with it; and instead of its being, as heretofore, a local malady, and susceptible of cure, it must henceforth be regarded as affecting the whole system, and past the hope or possibility of a remedy. (Wilentz, 2018, 199–200)

Feelings clearly were running high, and Speaker Henry Clay maneuvered successfully through the conflicts and produced what became known as the Missouri Compromise. There were two parts. Missouri was to be admitted, balanced by the new state of Maine (previously part of Massachusetts). The Senate balance would be unchanged by admitting one slave and one free state. In addition, slavery was not to be allowed elsewhere in the Louisiana Purchase north of 36°30′. This was a well-known latitude, and it continued the line that divided slaves in Tennessee and freedom in Kentucky. Missouri was north of the line, but no other slave states would be permitted north of the line.

Clay's compromise allowed Congress and the country to progress peacefully on, but not without costs. The intensity of the debate had aroused a lot of emotion, and the tension between states was increased. The tension appears to have been intense enough to discourage the western expansion that had been so exuberant. There were eight new states in the first thirty or so years of the United States, but no other states were admitted into the United States for more than fifteen years after Clay's compromise; the wind appears to have gone out of the western sail. In the words of a historian of the compromise: "[T]he Missouri Controversy can perhaps best be understood as a flash of lightning that illuminated the realities of sectional power in the United States and ignited a fire that smoldered for a generation. . . . When this check to slavery's growth was repudiated by the Kansas–Nebraska Act of 1854 and the Dred Scott decision of 1857, the smoldering embers burst into flame" (Forbes, 2007, 5).

While extensive growth was proceeding in the West, intensive growth was prospering in the East. Cotton plants grow bolls containing cottonseeds. The seeds need to be removed if the fibers are to be spun and woven, and wool was easier than cotton to prepare in early modern times. Cotton agriculture and industry got a huge stimulus from the invention of the cotton gin by Eli Whitney in 1793. The cotton gin removed the seeds by combing the cotton fibers into a semblance of linear threads by means of a circular comb that could be turned by hand or other power. The cotton gin lowered the cost of making cotton cloth and started the modern cotton industry. Regional trade grew faster than in the eighteenth century, and international trade grew with clipper ships to China.

Nathan Appleton cooperated with others to introduce the power loom and the manufacture of cotton on a large scale into the United States. He established a water-powered factory at Waltham, Massachusetts in 1814 that employed the first power loom ever used in the United States, copied from the British by a bit of industrial espionage. Appleton sent his foreman to Britain to observe a British cotton factory; the foreman returned with plans for the power loom. Appleton and others purchased the water power at Pawtucket Falls, and he was one of the founders of the Merrimac Manufacturing Company and of the city of Lowell in 1821. Even though the steam engine was a pivotal part of American economic development, water power was key to the rise of the largest antebellum industry.

The growth of the cotton industry, trade related to it, and other production led the nonfarm part of the labor force rise dramatically from 1800 to 1840. Table 1.1 reveals that over one-third of people in Northern states lived in cities by 1860, while less than 10 percent of people in Southern states lived in cities. The North embraced industrialization while the South remained agricultural. The overall growth of the American economy has been roughly estimated from the scarce data, and it looks like per capita GDP grew around 1.3 percent a year on average for the period from the Constitution to the Civil War (David, 1967).

This economic growth was aided by the origin of a Black working class in Southern cities. The cities were small before the Civil War, and Blacks were a minority in them, but Black workers helped urban growth not only as general laborers and household workers, but also as skilled craftsmen and craftswomen. Free Blacks were paid less than slaves and poor whites in the Southern cities, presumably because free Blacks gravitated toward urban living. Women also aided this effort in the cotton industry, which however was only a small part of the Southern economy (Trotter, 2019, Chapter 1).

**Table 1.1** Urban population of the United States in 1860[a]

| Region | Counties with urban populations | Total urban population in the region | Percent of region's population living in urban counties | Region's urban population as percent of US urban population |
|---|---|---|---|---|
| Northeast[b] | 103 | 3,787,337 | 35.75 | 61.66 |
| West[c] | 108 | 1,059,755 | 13.45 | 17.25 |
| Border[d] | 23 | 578,669 | 18.45 | 9.42 |
| South[e] | 51 | 621,757 | 6.83 | 10.12 |
| Far West[f] | 7 | 99,145 | 15.19 | 1.54 |
| Total[g] | 292 | 6,141,914 | 19.77 | 100.00 |

*Notes:*
[a] Urban population means people living in a city or town of at least 2,500.
[b] Includes Connecticut, Maine, Massachusetts, New Hampshire, New Jersey, New York, Pennsylvania, Rhode Island, and Vermont.
[c] Includes Illinois, Indiana, Iowa, Kansas, Minnesota, Nebraska, Ohio, and Wisconsin.
[d] Includes Delaware, Kentucky, Maryland, and Missouri.
[e] Includes Alabama, Arkansas, Florida, Georgia, Louisiana, Mississippi, North Carolina, South Carolina, Tennessee, Texas, and Virginia.
[f] Includes Colorado, California, Dakotas, Nevada, New Mexico, Oregon, Utah, and Washington.
[g] Includes District of Columbia.
*Source:* U.S. Census of Population, 1860.

The Watt steam engine was an important stimulus to this economic growth, which paralleled the growth of the British cotton industry. The Watt engine, like the Newcomen engine that preceded it, was a "low-pressure" engine. That is, it derived its power from the pressure of the atmosphere pushing against a vacuum produced by the condensation of steam. Shortly after 1800 a new type of steam engine, the "high-pressure" engine, was introduced. This engine used steam at higher than atmospheric pressure to push against the atmosphere in the same way that the low-pressure engine used the atmosphere to push against a vacuum. It therefore operated without a condenser. Steam was exhausted into the air at the end of the stroke, and the cumbersome apparatus for condensing it and producing a vacuum was no longer needed.

The possibility of using high-pressure steam was known before 1800, but its use required well-made boilers and accurately machined cylinders and pistons – items that were not within the skills of machinists before the start of the nineteenth century. As a result of many improvements in the years around 1800, some possibly connected with the production of the Watt low-pressure engine, mechanical skill was improved to the point where high-pressure steam could be employed. The high-pressure steam engine with cylindrical boilers was introduced simultaneously in Britain by Richard Trevithick and America by Oliver Evans in 1803–4. This development, which was an application of new mechanical skills to known mechanical principles, came simultaneously in both countries, indicating that there was a community of skills in the two lands, at least among a few adventurous machinists.

A generation later, almost all stationary steam engines in Britain were low-pressure and almost all American steam engines used high pressure. The American engines were built by 250 different builders, and the average builder made less than five engines. Steam engines were built locally except in the South. The New England cotton industry used water power instead of steam in places like Lowell that were on a river's fall line. The ability to build steam engines appears to have been widespread, and high-pressure steam engines were used in the nascent railroads in both countries. But sail was still the preferred means of transport at this time, and international trade grew as the cotton trade and its internal trade prospered (Temin, 1966).

Andrew Jackson became President in 1829 and moved vigorously to deal with problems he saw with arrangements made by the previous generation. The first problem was the desire for land in the South that was occupied by Indians. George Washington sought to integrate Indians into white society as autonomous nations, but Indians did not learn English or adopt Christianity.

In contrast to African immigrants, Indians were treated as autonomous nations and had signed treaties with the United States. Indian society remained strong, while African Americans were isolated from their former comrades and far from their original communities. Despite these differences, native Indians and imported African slaves were not among the European immigrants that formed the basis of the United States. They were not regarded as equal to the descendants of European immigrants.

President Jackson signed the Indian Removal Act in 1830 continuing the voluntary exchange of land west of the Mississippi for eastern lands relinquished by the Indians and did *not* authorize forced eviction. Jackson said to Congress, "This emigration should be voluntary, for it would be as cruel as unjust to compel the aborigines to abandon the graves of their fathers." But he then exceeded his presidential power and ignored previous treaties to force Indians to move. This forceful effort was enforced by a federal bureaucracy that focused on saving money rather than ensuring safety of the movers. They emphasized speed over safety, and the result was that 60,000 Indians were moved west of the Mississippi River and 4,000 of them died along the way or shortly thereafter. The move has been known ever since as the Trail of Tears (Ehle, 1988; Cave, 2003; Davis, 2009–2010).

As noted earlier, the expanding cotton trade required financing, and banks multiplied. The new generation of political leaders was not comfortable with Hamilton's second report to Congress recommending a national bank. Most banks were chartered by states, and the Second Bank of the United States, chartered by President Madison in 1816, stood alone. President Andrew Jackson vetoed the charter renewal for the Second Bank in 1832 for reasons that are incoherent.

President Jackson opened his veto message by labeling the Second Bank a monopoly: "It enjoys an exclusive privilege of banking under the authority of the General Government, a monopoly of its favor and support, and, as a necessary consequence almost a monopoly of the foreign and domestic exchange." The Second Bank was the government's fiscal agent, and it dominated the exchanges, that is, the business of transferring money from place to place. Since the tariff provided about 90 percent of the federal government's revenue, these earnings needed to be transferred from the coast to the interior to be spent on the military, pensions for soldiers, and the public debt (Temin, 1969, 29n3).

The reasons for using a single fiscal agent are simple. The alternative was to use a variety of agents. Instead of a single bank with many branches, there would be many banks in different places. The government would not be able to deal with a single agent that would allocate funds among its branches; it would have to make these administrative decisions itself. The more fiscal agents it had, the greater would be the government's ordinary expenses. Jackson appeared here to be supporting state banks over the Second Bank, even though it would cost the government more.

Jackson also objected to the Second Bank's objective to redeem its notes at par as "a bond of union among the banking establishments of the nation, erecting them into an interest separate from that of the people." Jackson appeared here to be opposed to all banks, not just the Second Bank. Jackson ended his veto message by saying: "We can at least make a stand against all new grants of monopolies and exclusive privileges, against any prostitution of our Government to the advancement of the few at the expense of the many." The relevance of that claim to the Second Bank is unclear, particularly as Jackson turned to his "pet banks" to reallocate the government's tariff revenues (Temin, 1969, Chapter 2).

The economic turmoil of the 1830s often has been blamed on Jackson's incoherence, but it appears more likely that it was the result of events far away that related to United States banks that financed the increasing trade of cotton and other goods. Prices of American goods rose by 59 percent after 1834 and then collapsed in the 1837 banking crisis. The inflation has been blamed on the banks, but it came from an increase in silver imports from Mexico. These imports remained steady at four million dollars a year from 1825 to 1833. They then doubled in 1834–35. Bank reserve ratios barely moved in these years; the quantity of money rose because the banks' silver reserves rose.

Table 1.2 shows the supply of money and its determinants in the 1820s and 1830s. Money at this time was composed of banknotes and silver, and the proportion that was banknotes increased sharply in these decades. Banks issued banknotes, and the banks had to be prepared to honor people holding banknotes who wanted to convert them to silver. In other words, banks held silver as reserves for their banknotes. The reserve ratio is the ratio of silver reserves to the number of banknotes issued. The supply of money rose rapidly until 1837. Their reserves grew also after 1835. The reserve ratio fell from around 30 percent to around 20 percent before 1825, and stayed constant as money rose rapidly in the 1830s.

The cause of these exports was not increased Mexican silver production. It instead was a change in the location of their exports. New England clipper ships were engaged in the China trade. They normally took Mexican silver with them to exchange with British traders for bills of exchange payable in London. The British used the silver to buy tea from the Chinese. The British traders however decided that they would rather

**Table 1.2** The supply of money and its determinants, 1820–39

| Year | Money | Reserves | Reserve ratios |
|------|-------|----------|----------------|
|      | $ millions | $ millions | % |
| 1820 | 85 | 41 | 32 |
| 1825 | 106 | 29 | 19 |
| 1830 | 114 | 32 | 23 |
| 1835 | 246 | 65 | 18 |
| 1836 | 276 | 73 | 16 |
| 1837 | 232 | 88 | 20 |
| 1838 | 240 | 87 | 23 |
| 1839 | 215 | 83 | 20 |

Source: Temin, *Jacksonian Economy* (1969), p. 71.

pay for the Chinese tea with opium from India, using bills of exchange to transmit sales in place of silver. The Chinese government resisted British opium to spare their subjects from addiction. The result was a series of Opium Wars between the Chinese and British.

American traders then were unable to take Mexican silver to China for trade because the wars destroyed the existing trade networks. The silver, not sought elsewhere, ended up in American banks. With constant reserve ratios, the banks loaned more and issued more bank notes. With more money floating around a roughly constant amount of goods, prices rose.

This had to come to an end, which it did spectacularly in the 1837 banking panic. The ultimate cause of the crisis was the Chinese Opium War that disrupted American trade and set the inflation in motion. The panic also was the result of Jackson's veto of the Second Bank, leaving the American banking system without a leader. Three events in 1836 and 1837 precipitated the crisis: The Bank of England refused to discount British loans to the United States, President Jackson forced buyers of public lands use specie instead of banknotes, and he distributed the government surplus that had accumulated after the Revolutionary debt had been paid off. Jackson's first move forced people to withdraw money from banks; his second move moved money westward and hampered trade. In 1837, the price of cotton fell, and Jackson's actions moved bank reserves out of New York (Temin, 1969, Chapter 4; Rousseau, 2002).

The price of cotton fell rapidly after the banking panic, the manufacture of cotton goods fell, and urban employment fell in American cities. States defaulted on their loans in 1839 as plans for canals and railroads were put on hold. Blacks of course suffered as their owners lost income in these hard years. As is often the case, the pain was felt more by the workers than the owners. Lower cotton prices meant less food and other care because slave owners maintained their style of living through thick and thin, while the variations in their incomes were passed down to their slaves.

I noted earlier that Jackson used "pet banks" to distribute government funds around the country. These banks thought that the government deposits were going to be stable and expanded their loaning more than other banks. The crisis started early in 1837 when New York Bank Commissioners uncovered various illegal activities in two large pet banks that led to runs on these banks. These troubles show the effect of corruption in the Jacksonian period, and they probably did more to precipitate the bank crisis than Jackson's actions in 1836–37 did.

As a result of this corruption, the pet banks contracted more than other banks when the 1837 banking crisis came. Few banks failed, but the money supply decreased sharply. As economists calculated recently: "Had the liabilities of the pet banks grown at the same rate as those of other commercial banks after 1833, our calculations indicate that the money stock would have been about 16 percent lower in 1836 and would have declined 30.3 percent less in 1837" (Hilt, 2020).

Jackson may have been a revolutionary, but he was following Jefferson's lead in relying on private banks to distribute the government surplus and allocate taxes. This appeal to state rights and private fiscal agents that anticipated later privatizations had a severe cost. The pet banks expanded rapidly, and the 1837 monetary decline was very large. If Jackson had not relied on his pet banks, the 1837 crash would have been milder. We cannot calculate effects on the rest of the economy as the antebellum economy differed greatly from our modern economy, but it is likely that the hungry 1840s would have been a lot better off.

The difficulties slaves and masterless poor whites had to pay for food with cotton at lower prices would have been far smaller.

Frederick Douglass escaped from slavery in this period. His mistress had taught him to read, which was illegal. She wanted him to be able to read the Bible, and he became aware of the wider world around him. As conditions worsened for him, he escaped from Maryland to the North with the woman who would become his wife. Douglass fell in love with Anna Murray, a free Black woman who lived in Baltimore. Murray encouraged him and supported his efforts to gain his freedom by aid and money. She gave him a sailor's uniform and some money to cover his travel costs, and he carried identification papers and protection papers that he obtained from a free Black seaman. His entire journey to freedom by rail and steamboat took less than 24 hours. Although Douglass emerged as a leading Black author and speaker, his wife never learned to read and write, illustrating how hard it is to make up for an early lack of education (Blight, 2018).

At about the same time, slaves revolted on the coastal ship, *La Amistad*, that was moving them from Cuba to another Caribbean island. The Mende way of fighting, using knives in a surprise attack, carried the day. The Africans wanted to sail back to Africa, but they did not know how. They asked a former owner to guide them, and he sailed slowly west in the day and north at night. They came aground at Montauk, in New York, that recently had abolished slavery in the state. Cinque, the African leader, became a symbol of freedom when a portrait of him in an African setting was painted and publicized.

The Africans were defended by John Quincy Adams in Congress and others in different venues. They were freed by the Supreme Court and helped back to Africa. Their story shows the value of education. We cannot fault newly captured Africans for lacking education, but we should fault American slave owners for attempting to maintain this ignorance forever. A rebellion is only a start to a better place; one needs knowledge to continue on that path (Rediker, 2013).

Blacks were not alone in suffering during the hard years of the 1840s. Poor Southern whites who did not possess more education or skills than slaves also were impoverished. They faced reduced demand for their labor in farming and related activities as the price of cotton fell, and those poor whites who owned land before the 1837 banking crisis lost this land to slave owners in the crisis because they could not pay their bills. We do not know how many poor whites were affected since they were largely illiterate and not in the federal census, but they may have been about as numerous as Southern slaves, doubling the presumed effects of 1837 in the South.

In addition to being landless, these poor whites competed in the labor market with enslaved labor, which led to dramatic declines in their standard of living as their wages fell. This led to large migratory movements of poor whites in search of better labor markets, but migration did not solve the problem as westward movement of slaves matched the movement of poor whites. Even more political and social institutions were being formed in the South to deal with the problem of poor whites, who were frequently jailed for small offenses, forced into unfair labor contracts, and socially ostracized from whites as Southern society became increasingly unequal and favorable to large landowners (Merritt, 2017).

The Specie Circular, whatever its macroeconomic effect, made life more difficult for poor whites who found it impossible to raise the hard cash needed to buy government land. They were frozen out of purchased land and became squatters instead. Plantation owners responded by buying up land around their plantations to keep the squatters out of their neighborhood. The poor whites then were forced into the Appalachian hills or Southern cities to find land they could farm or jobs if they chose urban settings.

Why are poor whites important to the story of racial inequality? They confirm Morgan's division of Southern society into master and pariah classes. The template developed in the antebellum era to police and stigmatize poor whites was applied brutally to Blacks after Emancipation. The political violence and coercion that was used against Blacks had been practiced against poor whites before the Civil War. The restrictive labor policies, which were attempts to depress wages and create a monopsony of planters, had their roots in white bargaining in the antebellum era. Similarly, the role of the carceral state, where punishment for the smallest offenses was imprisonment, and where jury trials were largely shams, fueled the increases in Black incarceration after the Civil War (Merritt, 2017).

As cotton growing moved westward, Maryland shifted into a varied agriculture that reduced the local demand for slaves. Maryland slaves were at risk of being sold to expanding areas, stimulating them to seek freedom in nearby free states. The most famous escape was by Harriet Tubman, born Araminta Ross and known as Minty while she was a slave in the Eastern Shore of Maryland. She was nearly killed as a young teen when an angry overseer threw an iron weight at another slave and hit Minty. She suffered from headaches, seizures, and sleeping spells the rest of her life, diagnosed by biographers as temporal lobe epilepsy. She married a free Black in 1844 and became Harriet Tubman as a result; he was free but their children would be slaves.

Harriet's owner died in 1849 with lots of debts, which left his slaves liable to be sold down south to pay his debts. Tubman had been upset by the sale of her three sisters, and she decided that it was better to choose her own fate than to suffer on the auction block. She tapped into a local underground organization that helped slaves escape. Traveling by night, using the North Star and instructions from Black and white helpers, she arrived in Philadelphia in free Pennsylvania. Her escape was solitary and more arduous and probably more risky than Frederick Douglass's escape a decade earlier.

Tubman returned to the Eastern Shore approximately thirteen times to liberate her family and friends, brought about seventy former slaves to freedom, and gave instructions to an additional fifty more slaves who found their way to freedom. Like Frederick Douglass's wife, she remained illiterate all her life. With two strikes against her – temporal lobe epilepsy, and illiteracy – she still turned out to be a remarkable woman.

Tubman relied heavily on a long-established, intricate, and secretive web of communication among African Americans to accomplish her rescues. Although white Quaker and abolitionist support was vital to Tubman's survival and success, the widespread African-American community provided the protection and sustenance she needed in her continuing fight for freedom. She was often referred to as Moses for the obvious parallel (Larson, 2004).

Increasing escapes from border states increased white support for slavery under tough rules. After the Fugitive Slave Act was signed in

1850, McAllister, the commissioner to adjudicate cases in Harrisburg, Pennsylvania, said: "We do not want to make Pennsylvania a place of refuge for absconding slaves or free negroes; they are a miserable population – a tax and a pest" (Blackett, 2013, 35).

A third escape from slavery in the 1840s was by Linda Brent who described her path to freedom in an 1861 autobiography, reprinted recently. Brent made two important points. First, female slaves suffered even more than male slaves. Enslaved women were treated more harshly than enslaved men, and they frequently were used – often against their will – as sex objects. In Brent's words, "Slavery is terrible for men; but it is far more terrible for women." Second, escape from slavery coulr be unsuccessful or take a long time. Brent's escape took about seven years, many of them endured in hiding and finally ending in legal transactions in the North (Jacobs, 2001).

**1.2.1 TIME ON THE CROSS.** This support for slavery brings up a controversy about the productivity of slavery aroused by an ambitious 1974 book by Robert William Fogel and Stanley L. Engerman, *Time on the Cross*. The authors collected a massive data set on American slavery and argued that slavery was an efficient way of organizing work, harking back to the Handlin's classic statement. Their argument for this point utilized the tools of economics and stimulated continuing discussion of their arguments and their methods.

*Time on the Cross* burst on the academic world to great acclaim. It was featured in popular magazines like *Time* and *Newsweek* and won the Bancroft Prize in American history in 1975. It was reviewed widely in academic journals, and Robert Fogel won the Nobel Prize in economics in 1993, with Douglass North, "for having renewed research in economic history by applying economic theory and quantitative methods in order to explain economic and institutional change" (Nobel Prize, 1993).

*Time on the Cross* presented a paradox. The title declared that slavery was a tragic and awful institution like a crucifixion, while the content of the book argued that twentieth-century African Americans should take pride in the contribution of their enslaved ancestors to the antebellum Southern economy. The presentation of the book made these conflicting claims hard to unify by splitting the book's contents into two volumes.

The first volume presented their argument in great detail, and the second volume provided the numbers and theoretical arguments that underlay the claims in volume one. To understand this complex statement and to evaluate its conclusion, we need to interrupt the narrative history for some economic analysis.

Fogel and Engerman made several assertions to support their conclusions. They claimed that enslaved people consumed more than free people in the South. And they argued enslaved people were *not* exploited under slavery. We need to follow Marc Bloch, the medieval historian who explored the source of his information, "into the kitchen" to explore how the numbers were calculated and evaluate these claims (David and Temin, 1974, 1979 ) .

Fogel and Engerman derived their estimates of slave consumption from large plantations that had over fifty slaves and were at least fifty wagon miles from a city. But less than a quarter of slaves lived on plantations of this size. Given that Fogel and Engerman claimed there were economies of scale in plantation agriculture, this sample overestimated the average consumption of enslaved persons. Their estimates of consumption by free Northern workers came from late nineteenth-century estimates identified by their authors as no more than reasonable guesses on the slenderest basis. In other words, the raw data were misleading, overestimating slave consumption by looking at a biased sample and comparing these data with guesses about free labor a generation later.

The interpretation of these infirm observations raises more questions. The energy required to be field hand in a gang on an antebellum cotton plantation was far higher than the energy required for someone making shoes or constructing houses around 1880. The growth of factories during the Industrial Revolution reduced the calorie needs for more workers as the nineteenth century progressed. Even if enslaved persons on large plantations consumed more than free workers years later, they may have been eating less than they needed to perform their work.

Adult slaves on large plantations were more active and needed more energy than free workers because the labor force participation rates were higher than those of free people. In particular, enslaved women and children worked in the field while free women and children more frequently worked in their houses. Fogel and Engerman claimed in volume one of their book that slaves on large plantations had more pecuniary income per capita than they would have earned if they had been free small farmers. They referred readers to volume two and argued that the labor income of the slave family was 15 percent larger than the labor income of the corresponding free family.

The resolution of this apparent paradox of forced labor is simple. Fogel and Engerman assumed that the women and children of free farm families were putting in the same labor effort as was exacted from their enslaved counterparts. The economists went from men to families too easily, forgetting that family life was far different for free and enslaved people, as seen in Harriet Tubman's experiences. When free Southern farm folk refrained from volunteering for slavery, they were choosing to live their lives the way they wanted rather than being forced to work at the discretion of their owners. Slaves were not more efficient than Northern farmers; they were forced to work more (David and Temin, 1979).

Now consider Fogel and Engerman's description of their finding on the rate of exploitation of American slaves: "Slaves were exploited in the sense that part of the income which they produced was appropriated by their owners. However, the rate of expropriation was much lower than has generally been presumed. Over the course of his lifetime, the typical slave field hand received about 90 percent of the income he produced" (Fogel and Engerman, 1974, I, 5–6).

This is a startling conclusion. It suggests that the Southern attachment to slavery was motivated by a 10 percent charge on the slaves. This is such a small gain that it seems highly unlikely that it could have been the motivation for all of the conflict between the regions of the fledgling United States. There must be something in the measurement that generates such a surprising conclusion.

Fogel and Engerman defined their rate of exploitation as the "expected present value" of a newborn slave. This is the value at the time of the slave's birth of the anticipated future earnings he will produce, less the anticipated future cost of his maintenance. Both of these flows are discounted to the time of the slave's birth. This is a concept from the theory of economic investment that cries for explanation.

Recall the education of Frederick Douglass. His owner's wife taught him the alphabet so he could read the Bible. She clearly was thinking of investing in Frederick's future value, but she had no idea what actually would happen. No one knows when educating a youngster what he or she will do with this education when grown. The first thing about present value is that investors need to make an allowance for the uncertainty of their investment.

The one thing Frederick's owners knew about was that the results of their present activity would emerge years later. A literate slave could do things that an illiterate one could not. He would be more valuable in times to come. How could Frederick's owners have known how much effort they should put into his learning the alphabet? If that seems like a silly question, given how slave owners thought about their slaves, it arises only because Fogel and Engerman used this economic concept in their book. And while his wife thought of religion, the slave owner thought about how much cotton to plant. What he thought his crop would be worth when harvested would affect his investment in planting. He had to plan in the present for his income in the future.

Future costs and earnings are worth less than current costs and earnings. How large is this discount? Fogel and Engerman used the interest rate. They took the concept of discounting the future from investment theory, and they took also the measurement of the discount from this theory. The quantities involved in the comparison are less than the simple totals of the slave revenue and maintenance costs because a dollar of income produced or expended in the future is worth less than that at present. The higher is the rate of interest on any principal invested in the present, and the further removed into the future is the anticipated costs or receipts, the smaller will be its present value. A dollar taken from a slave during his youth must count for more in the present value of all such expropriations than does a dollar taken earned in his life.

For the first decade or so of a slave's life, the costs of caring for him exceeded the value of the revenue he produced. Only thereafter would a slave earn positive net revenue. In reckoning the present value of net revenues anticipated at the time of his birth, each dollar of negative net revenue during his childhood counts more heavily than each dollar of the positive net revenue taken in his adulthood. Using the 10–12 percent exploitation rate referred to in Fogel and Engerman's text, the sum of discounted net revenues is about one half of the simple sum of expected total revenues.

Fogel and Engerman attempted to sidestep these problems by making strong assumptions that allowed them to use different data. They argued that in a competitive market for slaves, the equilibrium price of a newborn slave – labeled the "value of a birthright" – could not be substantially different from the sum of discounted expected net revenues over his lifetime. If we are prepared to grant their unverified assumption that the market for newborn slaves was in competitive equilibrium, then they seemed to have found a way to calculate the net present value of a new slave.

However, the estimated value of a birthright did not derive from market prices at which actual transactions in newborn infant slaves were bought and sold. It was extrapolated from a large body of information about the appraised values placed on older male slaves. These values were found in probate records that did not indicate the geographical or temporal make-up of the sample. They also did not specify the size of estates that were probated, and Fogel and Engerman did not attempt to explain the relationship between appraisal values and market values.

The appraised values were averaged for each age and then fitted to a curve by an informal analysis. This use of averages does not generate accurate statistical estimates of the margin of error surrounding the fitted age profile. In view of the importance that Fogel and Engerman attached to the value at zero age – the intercept of the curve – the absence of a proper estimate of the standard error is a serious omission. Since most price observations were of adult slaves, the value at birth was out of the statistical sample, adding to the error of the estimate.

The yield of a slave is subject to random variation, and only a slave owner who was utterly indifferent to risk would have found the asset worth buying when the present value of its expected yields was close to its purchase price. Most people are risk averse, and the net revenue expected from a slave infant could not be known with certainty. The prevalence of risk aversion of potential slave infant buyers implies that the competitive market price of the infant would be a lower bound estimate of the sum of discounted net revenues. Fogel and Engerman's estimate of the rate of exploitation is a lower bound.

This downward bias is wide for an infant slave. There is a wide distribution of the future physical and intellectual capacities, as of personality traits. Not all slaves were like Frederick Douglass or Harriet Tubman. The variance of the presumed distribution of future net revenues diminished as a male slave passed from infancy to youth and continued to do so as he entered adulthood. Part of the apparent peak of slave prices around age 27 therefore reflects progressively smaller asset-price discounts on account of risk. The high uncertainty about the health, well-being, and future abilities of the infants further depressed the value at birth.

Fogel and Engerman explained their estimate of the rate of exploitation like this: "A substantial part of the income taken from those slaves who survived into the later years was not an act of expropriation, but a payment required to cover the expenses" of rearing children who did not survive (Fogel and Engerman, 1974, I, 155–56).

Free people ordinarily are not required to borrow money for the expenses of their childhood. They are supported by their parents and more generally by their parents' generation. When they become adults, they do not repay their parents with compound interest for the pecuniary cost of their own early years – much less for the upbringing of brothers and sisters prematurely deceased. Instead they support their own children. The way such intergenerational transfers of income are accomplished among the members of free societies does not confront individuals with the costs of raising children and supporting elderly dependents when they themselves are children, but rather allows them to assume these burdens at the same time they earn income in their adulthood. It follows that the undiscounted version of the rate of exploitation is a closer analogue to the proportion of income, which parents devote to the maintenance of children and dependents in a free society. That estimate is around 50 percent, as noted earlier.

This economic analysis has shown that Fogel and Engerman, despite the publicity and honors that greeted their book, failed to prove the points they aspired to use to extol the productive effort of enslaved individuals and the benign nature of American slavery. They overestimated the consumption of slaves leading to the paradoxical question why free farmers did not submit to slavery for themselves. And their estimate of minimal exploitation of slaves was the result of many abstract arguments, including the decision to charge slave children for their own upbringing, which made Southern slavery look like a modern credit union.

In short, Fogel and Engerman wrote mainstream history, viewing slaves as inputs, like steam and water power, to production, instead of considering the views of the enslaved people. Many slaves spoke with their feet and set off for freedom, as typified by our famous – albeit not typical – leaders of the postwar African-American community. The construction of the exploitation index in *Time on the Cross* assumed that families could not preserve themselves as a unit to bring up their children. Each slave was seen as a separate person to finance his or her childhood and training. Harriet Tubman experienced enslaved family disruption. It was the sale of her sisters and her fear of being sold away from what was left of her family that stimulated her to escape from slavery.

That is the view to be presented here. This Black or Northern narrative notes the racial compositions of American slaves and the "closed" nature of American slavery. Free Blacks were tolerated but not allowed full participation in the general white economy. And denying schooling and even literacy to slaves made them unable to compete with whites for good jobs after they were freed. Freed slaves could vote in a few Northern states, but they were not numerous enough to affect the overall pattern.

The South's vast economic stake in its slave labor force was a major factor in the sectional disputes that preceded the Civil War. In the eleven states that eventually became the Confederacy, four out of ten people were slaves in 1860, accounting for more than half the agricultural labor in those states. In the cotton regions slave labor's importance was even greater. There had been one million slaves worth about $300 million in 1805; fifty-five years later there were four million slaves worth close to $3 billion. The capital embodied in slaves roughly equaled the total capital in farmland and farm buildings in the South in 1860. Southern slave owners were optimistic about the economic future of their region as they were experiencing an unparalleled rise in the value of their slave assets. Slave labor was the foundation of a flourishing economic system in the South (Ransom, 2001).

It is not surprising that Southerners – even those who did not own slaves – viewed any attempt by the federal government to limit the rights of slave owners over their property as a potentially mortal threat to their entire economic system. "By itself, the South's economic investment in slavery could easily explain the willingness of Southerners to risk war when faced with what they viewed as a serious threat to their 'peculiar institution' after the electoral victories of the Republican Party and President Abraham Lincoln the fall of 1860" (Gunderson, 1974, 922, Table 1; Ransom, 2001).

Northern states also had a very large economic stake in slavery and the cotton trade. The first half of the nineteenth century saw an enormous increase in the production of short-staple cotton in the South, exported to Massachusetts, Great Britain, and Europe (Bailyn, 2000; Ransom, 2001).

By the mid-1830s, cotton shipments accounted for more than half the value of all exports from the United States. There also was a marked similarity between the trends in the export of cotton and the rising value of the slave population. The prosperity of the American economy clearly rested on its ability to produce cotton more efficiently than any other region or country. Bailyn's description of the colonial North being based on slavery is accurate for the antebellum North as well.

Perhaps the best single indicator of the growth of nonagricultural production and trade in the Northern and Western states is the rise of urban areas in areas where markets became important. About six million people – roughly one out of five persons in the United States – lived in an urban county in 1860, as shown in Table 1.1. This table summarizes the contrast between the backward-looking South and the forward-looking North by depicting the vast difference in urban development in the South compared to the Northern states. "More than two-thirds of all urban counties were in the Northeast and West. Those two regions accounted for nearly 80 percent of the urban population of the country. By contrast, less than 7 percent of people in the 11 Southern states of Table 1.1 lived in urban counties" (Ransom, 2001).

Robert Fogel returned to what he called the slavery debates a quarter century after *Time on the Cross* was published in a series of lectures. He discussed the moral problem of slavery and repeated several points that I have contested earlier. He also added a few that clarify the point of his book. For example, he argued that slavery was immoral because it denied enslaved people of economic opportunity. He of course was discussing American slavery, and he did not mean to condemn all kinds of slavery.

As I said earlier, Roman slavery was far more open than the closed slavery of the Southern states. Manumission was frequent, and Roman freedmen were proud to put their status on their tombstones if they became rich enough to afford them. Education was widespread as it increased the productivity of both slave and master. It is only the severely closed nature of American slavery that appears in Fogel's survey.

Missing in Fogel's summary is an adequate discussion of race. He mentioned racial prejudice in his survey of the literature on American slavery, but he failed to make a connection between the lack of opportunity and the African origin of most American slaves. He appears uninterested in the effects of slavery on freedmen and freedwomen after the Civil War. I will return to this issue several times as the narrative continues (Fogel, 2003).

All people, slave or free, need to have incentives to work. If slaves cannot lay claim to the fruits of their labor, other incentives must be used. These incentives can be classified as positive (rewards for hard or good work), or carrots, and negative (punishment for slacking off or not cooperating), or sticks. Negative incentives dominated the lives of American slaves (David et al., 1976; Patterson, 1982; Fenoaltea, 1984).

Positive incentives were more important than negative ones in motivating Roman slaves. Sticks can get people to work, but generally not to do skilled tasks that require independent work. If it is hard to distinguish poor performance from bad luck when work is complex, carrots are far more effective than sticks in motivating hard work. A manager, for example, would claim that any adverse outcomes were the result of bad luck. Beating or worse punishment would lead to resentment rather than cooperation and possibly more "bad luck." Fogel failed to discuss the nature of control or incentivize American slaves in his discussion of their culture (Fogel, 2003, 46; Temin, 2013, 122).

Fogel and Engerman estimated that slaves were only whipped 0.7 times a year, leaving them ample time to consider other incentives. There are problems with their quantitative estimate, but I want to focus on their conceptualization. Whipping was common on slave plantations, and we need to think about the fear of whipping as much as we think of the frequency. For negative incentives affect behavior through a mental process. And public whipping of some slaves on a plantation undoubtedly made other slaves anticipate punishment if they stepped out of line. We do not know how many whippings a year it took to frighten a large plantation, but we should be aware that incentives operate through the expectations they induce among all the slaves (Fogel and Engerman, 1974, I, 145; Gutman and Sutch, 1976).

We should remember, when discussing the interests of freedmen after the Civil War, that they were not used to the positive rewards that dominate free economies. They only knew negative punishments and were not interested in joining a competitive society. They wanted their independence and to grow food for their families.

Slavery is an abstraction, and Fogel noted variation within the United States between slaves on plantations with different sizes. In his words, "On such matters as the severity of punishment, the supply of clothing, the occupation of the slave, the stability of the family, and the uses of leisure time, the experiences of slaves living on small plantations differed significantly from those living on large plantations" (Fogel, 2003, 41).

How did enslaved people think as they experienced all this? Toni Morrison expressed how American slaves must have felt very succinctly. Words are not data, but they may extend our understanding of the evidence reviewed here:

> White people believed that whatever the manners, under every dark skin was a jungle. Swift unnavigable waters, swinging screaming baboons, sleeping snakes, red gums ready for their sweet white blood. In a way, . . . they were right. The more colored people spent their strength trying to convince them how gentle they were, how clever and loving, how human, the more they used themselves up to persuade whites of something Negroes believed could not be questioned, the deeper and more tangled the jungle grew inside. But it wasn't the jungle Blacks brought with them to this place

from the other (livable) place. It was the jungle white folks planted in them. And it grew. It spread. In, through and after life, it spread until it invaded the whites who had made it. Touched them every one. Changed and altered them. Made them bloody, silly, worse than even they wanted to be, so scared were they of the jungle they had made. The screaming baboon lived under their own white skin; the red gums were their own (Morrison, 1987, 198–99) .

## 1.3 COMPROMISES AND CIVIL WAR

Returning to our narrative, we note that three developments are listed in the literature as setting off the Civil War. The Missouri Compromise of 1820 had set the stage. The three new events were the 1850 compromise about California that further inflamed each side; the Kansas–Nebraska Act in 1854 that set off more local conflicts; and the Supreme Court's 1857 decision in the Dred Scott case that often is seen as the final straw. The first two of these triggers resembled the Missouri Compromise in that they involved the expansion of the United States to the West.

Henry Clay, the architect of the 1820 compromise, is given credit for the 1850 compromise as well. Instead of any single bill, the later compromise was a set of bills that were separately passed. Together, they responded to the Mexican War of the 1840s and included conquered lands into the union. Texas had declared its freedom from Mexico in 1836 and claimed a lot of land in the American territories that it did not actually administer. It was persuaded to give up a lot of this land in return for the federal government's assumption of the Texan state debt.

Throughout this period, Southern officeholders from Secretary of State John C. Calhoun to President James Polk actively pursued the expansion of slavery outside of the United States. While the United States, and later Texas, exported cotton with the aid of slaves, Brazil exported sugar with the aid of slaves, and Cuba exported sugar with the aid of slaves. The United States opposed Great Britain as it sought to end slavery around the world by supporting these states and acquiring more slave-owning land for the United States. This desire to expand slavery within the United States was one of the reasons the country engaged in warfare with Mexico to get control of Texas (Karp, 2016).

The addition of Texas to the United States was both a domestic and foreign policy achievement. The Southerners were pleased to have more slave land good for growing cotton. While Northerners sought a domestic cure to the international aims of the South. California had grown in the gold rush of the late 1840s and also wanted admission into the Union. It was firmly antislavery, even though the line established between slave and free states in 1820 ran through the state. It was admitted as a free state, balancing the slave state of Texas.

Despite Clay's efforts, both Southern Democrats and Northern Whigs opposed his combined bill that dealt with states and other issues of slavery. Clay responded by announcing on the Senate floor the next day that he intended to pass each individual part of the bill. But the seventy-three-year-old Clay was physically exhausted as the tuberculosis that eventually killed him began to take its toll. He left Washington and went to recover in Newport, Rhode Island. Senator Stephen A. Douglas, who was very different from Frederick Douglass, then assumed leadership in attempting to pass Clay's proposals through the Senate.

Senator Douglas was a recent entrant to the Senate who had not grown up with Clay's earlier compromise. He did not regard slavery as a moral issue; it was instead a political issue to be decided by voting. The older senators thought this was nonsense, but Douglas was able to negotiate the Texas northern border to the 36°30′ line from the 1820 compromise. This set the stage for the admission of California and other parts of Clay's compromise (Remini, 2010).

The compromise that most increased the North–South conflict was a new Fugitive Slave Act that extended the original 1793 Fugitive Slave Act. The new version required federal judicial officials in all states and federal territories, including in those states and territories in which slavery was prohibited, to assist with the return of escaped slaves to their masters in the states and territories permitting slavery. A claimant's sworn testimony of ownership was all that was needed to arrest anyone suspected of being a fugitive slave and any federal marshal or other official who did not arrest an alleged runaway slave was liable to a fine of $1,000. Suspected slaves could neither request a jury trial nor testify on their own behalf. Any person providing food or shelter was to be subject to six months' imprisonment and a $1,000 fine. And ordinary citizens of free states could be summoned to join a posse and were required to assist in the capture, custody, and/or transportation of the alleged escaped slave. The law was rigorously proslavery.

The Fugitive Slave Act met Southern demands, but the North objected to the provisions mandating ordinary citizens to aid slave catchers. Many Northerners deeply resented the requirement personally to help slavery. Resentment toward the act heightened tensions between the North and South, which were inflamed further by Harriet Beecher Stowe, who wrote *Uncle Tom's Cabin,* which emphasized the horrors of recapturing escaped slaves and outraged Southerners (Gara, 1964; Remini, 2010; Bordewich, 2012).

The 1850 Compromise may have succeeded in postponing the American Civil War for a decade, which probably contributed to the North's victory as the Midwest was growing wealthier and more populous and was being brought into closer relations with the Northeast.

During that decade, the Whig Party disappeared and was replaced with the new Republican Party in the North and Democrats in the South. Other historians argue that the compromise only laid the groundwork for future conflict. They see the Fugitive Slave Law as helping to polarize the country, as shown in the enormous reaction to *Uncle Tom's Cabin.* The passage of the Fugitive Slave Act aroused feelings of bitterness in the North.

The Compromise of 1850 helped break down the spirit of compromise in the United States before the Civil War. The compromise strained that spirit, and the deaths of influential senators who worked on the compromise, primarily Henry Clay and Daniel Webster, contributed to increasing tension between the North and South. According to one historian,

> The Fugitive Slave Act, the abolition of the slave trade in the District of Columbia, the admission of California as a free state, and even the application of the formula of popular sovereignty to the territories were all less important than the least remembered component of the Compromise of 1850 – the statute by which Texas relinquished its claims to much of New Mexico in return for federal assumption of the debts. (Stegmaier, 1996)

Senator Douglas introduced a bill to organize the territory of Nebraska in order to bring the area under civil control and help promote a railroad from Illinois to Nebraska. Southern senators opposed it. The region lay north of latitude 36°30′ and would become a free state under the terms of the 1820 Missouri Compromise. Douglas responded by proposing to create two territories in the area, Kansas and Nebraska, and repeal of the Missouri Compromise line. Whether the territories would be slave or free was left to the settlers under Douglas's principle of popular sovereignty. Presumably, the Northern territory would oppose slavery while the Southern one would permit it.

The Kansas–Nebraska Act that resulted was an 1854 bill that mandated popular sovereignty, allowing settlers of a territory to decide whether slavery would be allowed within a new state's borders. The conflicts between the proslavery and antislavery settlers that arose in the aftermath of the act's passage led to the period of violence known as Bleeding Kansas, and helped paved the way for the Civil War. By the time Kansas became a state in 1861, however, Southern states had begun to secede from the Union. Douglas's railroad was eventually built, but not along the route he wanted and with funds voted by a Republican Congress during the Civil War. Railroads were the largest companies in the 1850s, and they did not want the South to impede their expansion (Foner and Garraty, 1991; Ferguson, 1995, 65).

*Dred Scott v. Sandford*, 60 U.S. (19 How.) 393 (1857), was a landmark decision of the US Supreme Court that ruled that the US Constitution was not meant to include American citizenship for Black people, whether they were enslaved or free. The rights and privileges that the Constitution conferred upon American citizens therefore could not apply to them. The euphemisms invented by the authors of the Constitution ended up as a substantive distinction in this decision.

The decision was made in the case of Dred Scott, an enslaved Black man whose owners had taken him from Missouri, which was a slaveholding state, into the Missouri Territory, most of which had been designated "free" territory by the Missouri Compromise of 1820. Back in Missouri, Scott sued in court for his freedom, claiming that because he had been taken into "free" territory, he automatically had been freed and was legally no longer a slave. Scott lost first in Missouri state court, and then in federal court, which ruled against him by deciding that it had to apply Missouri law to the case. He appealed to the US Supreme Court.

The Court ruled in an opinion written by Chief Justice Roger Taney that Black people "are not included, and were not intended to be included, under the word 'citizens' in the Constitution, and can therefore claim none of the rights and privileges which that instrument provides for and secures to citizens of the United States." Taney went further and struck down the entire Missouri Compromise as a limitation on slavery that exceeded the US Congress's powers under the Constitution.

Chief Justice Taney and several of the other justices hoped that the ruling would permanently settle the slavery controversy, but it had almost the complete opposite effect. Taney's opinion "was greeted with unmitigated wrath from every segment of the United States except the slave holding states," and the decision was a contributing factor in the outbreak of the American Civil War four years later in 1861 (Ehrlich, 1968; Finkelman, 2007).

The geographic shape of the United States changed greatly in the first half century or so of its existence, but the opposition found between Jefferson and Hamilton still endured on the eve of the Civil War. Slave owners had prospered as the industrial production of cotton expanded, but the organization of society and production remained starkly divergent in the North and the South. Slave owners looked backward to preserve their position in their society, while people in free states seemed entranced by future possibilities. The 1849 California gold rush showed that these forward-looking people did not have clairvoyance. The Civil War was in part fought over a general view of the economy – not simply slavery.

For example, cotton growers wanted free trade in order to sell their cotton and buy British manufactures. The cotton industry wanted tariffs to protect their infant industries and help it grow. The iron industry in the North shared the view of the cotton industry, and tariff debates were as regionally determined as slavery debates. President Lincoln did not focus on slavery at the start of his administration, but rather on holding this complex mix of economic issues together in a single country.

Most Republicans opposed slavery in principle, but their opposition was limited to battling its extension into the West. Few Republicans sought to end slavery immediately. These Republicans supported an economic policy to secure Northern domination of western lands as the initial step in a broad plan to end slavery eventually. Preceding disagreements had led to compromises, but the economic argument gained strength in the 1850s and led moderates to become extremists (Egnal, 2010, Introduction).

As interregional antagonism rose to fever pitch, the new Republican Party elected Abraham Lincoln as president in 1860. The new party was a successor of the old Whigs, supported by the railroads that wanted freedom in their westward expansion. In direct response to Lincoln's election as president, seven Southern states seceded from the Union rather than continue to negotiate and compromise over the issue of slavery, which had been the norm for so many decades. Lincoln wanted to preserve the unions' integrity, and he only gradually saw ending slavery immediately as the war dragged on as a tool to win the war.

Lincoln tried to resupply Fort Sumter, outside Charleston, South Carolina – the first state to secede – but was rebuffed by the rebels. A brief siege that led to the surrender of Fort Sumter and started the Civil War that lasted four years and killed over 600,000 Americans. The song, *The Star Spangled Banner,* now helps us remember Fort Sumter, but it dates from the 1812 war with England and an attack on a different fort.

Three key events in 1863 show the role of the war in an inclusive economic history: General Grant's initiation of the Freedman's Bureau, the siege of Vicksburg, and the Battle of Gettysburg. But the economics of the Civil War became apparent in 1861. As in the 1830s, the interruption of foreign trade led to inflation. While silver accumulated in the United States in the 1830s, gold became scarce in the 1860s.

The California gold discoveries in 1849 not only set off a gold rush; they also shifted the dollar from a silver to a gold currency. Then war broke out between the states, and the cotton trade that had been central to interregional and international trade was disrupted. Without American cotton, the British cotton industry experienced a "cotton famine" and was forced to look around for alternate supplies. In the

North, the lack of cotton cloth exports led to a scarcity of gold revenue. The price of gold in American banknotes rose.

The United States could not preserve the link between its currency – greenbacks – and gold, and it abandoned the gold standard soon after it had joined it. The value of greenbacks in gold fell, and gold rose to a premium. But while banks only stayed off silver for months in 1837, the United States stayed off gold from 1861 to 1879.

Economic distress followed the abandonment of the gold standard. The United States needed to pay soldiers and buy wartime supplies, and the gold value of greenbacks continued to fall. History follows the progress of the war, but people – Black and white, Northern and Southern – suffered from a lack of imports and work far more than after the Bank panic of 1837. Part of the growing alienation of the North from the war and from the idea of slavery abolition must have come from the economic hardship of the war.

General Grant recalled that the idea of the Freedman's Bureau came to him in late 1862 as he pressed into the South. As planters fled before the Union army, cotton agriculture was disrupted and thousands of Negroes appealed to the army for help. Grant explained in his memoir that, "orders of the government prohibited the expulsion of the negroes from the protection of the army, when they came in voluntarily. Humanity forbade allowing them to starve. ... There was no special authority for feeding them unless they were employed as teamsters, cooks and pioneers with the army." Grant appointed John Eaton, later to become Secretary of Education, to create and administer what would become the Freedman's Bureau that employed the fugitives to harvest the abandoned cotton crops (Grant, 1885, I, 424–26).

Grant described to Eaton a range of useful tasks that the "contrabands" could perform; the men could help with construction of various sorts while the women could work in kitchens and hospitals. Eaton quoted Grant's thinking at this point:

> He then went on to say that when it had been made clear that the Negro, as an independent laborer ... could do these things well, it would be very easy to put a musket in his hands and make a soldier of him, and if he fought well, eventually to put the ballot in his hands and make him a

citizen. .... Never before in those early and bewildering days had I heard the problem of the future of the Negro attacked with such humanity combined with practical good sense. (Chernow, 2017, 228–30)

Over the next few years, many slaves escaped from their masters to Union army camps, forcing the issue of emancipation on Lincoln's administration to help him on his intellectual and political journey. Union officers, then Congress, and finally Lincoln decided to confiscate this human property belonging to the enemy and put it to work for the Union in the form of servants, teamsters, laborers, and eventually soldiers. The resulting additions to the Union force – 200,000 Black soldiers and sailors and added Black army laborers – may well have tipped the balance in favor of a Union victory (McPherson, 1995).

Grant's efforts grew into the Freedmen's Bureau, formally established on March 3, 1865, and intended to last for a year after the end of the Civil War. The Bureau was an important agency of early Reconstruction, assisting freedmen in the South. The bureau ran schools for freedmen during the war, but they had little impact because the schools were urban while the freedmen were rural. As Chernow explained, "This man who so recently balked at abolitionism now made a startling leap into America's future" (Chernow, 2017, 229).

Around the same time, Grant was trying to conquer Vicksburg, which occupied the first high ground on the Mississippi River below Memphis. Railroads went east to all points in the Confederacy and west to Louisiana. It was the only connection between the eastern and western parts of the Confederacy. But because Vicksburg occupied the high ground, conquering it was a difficult problem. Grant sent General Sherman to the south via a loop west of the Mississippi River, enabling him to find crossing points far south of Vicksburg for Grant to use. Grant went far from the river to conquer Jackson, the Mississippi state capital. He then faced Vicksburg from the landward side and besieged it in May 1863.

The siege of Vicksburg was the result of a long campaign with many shifts of plans as Grant took advantage of smaller breakthroughs. While the plan looks logical in retrospect, it seemed endless and roundabout to contemporaries. General Grant ordered his troops around with an objective clearer in his mind than in any of his subordinates. Grant considered how to get his troops across the river south of Vicksburg over the winter of 1862; only as the waters receded in the spring of 1863 could he see a practical way to approach his objective. As he said in April, "When this was effected I felt a degree of relief scarcely ever equaled since. Vicksburg was not yet taken, it is true, nor were its defenders demoralized by any of our previous moves. ... but I was now on dry ground on the same side of the river with the enemy" (Grant, 1885, I, 480).

It took another month of battles and reverses for Grant to approach Vicksburg. The Confederate defenders hoped for reinforcements to come from other parts of their army, but they never arrived. The Confederates finally capitulated to Grant on July 4, 1863, one day after Lee's defeat at Gettysburg. The two Union victories turned the war from a defense of the North to the defeat of the South. Grant's victory split the Confederacy in two, and he sent Sherman on his march to the sea to disrupt the eastern part.

Lee's approach to Gettysburg was straightforward, contrasting with Grant's circuitous approach to Vicksburg. Lee hoped for a traditional clash of armies typical of past wars. He got his wish and fought with the Union army for three days, finally accepting defeat and retreating back to Virginia. Gettysburg was the costliest of Civil War battles, with around 50,000 casualties on both sides. Lee's defeat and Grant's victory in July 1863 ultimately led to the Union victory two years later. Gettysburg now is remembered primarily for the memorial address Lincoln gave there in November during the dedication of the Union cemetery.

Lincoln famously began, "Four score and seven years ago our fathers brought forth on this continent, a new nation, conceived in Liberty, and dedicated to the proposition that all men are created equal." This is a refrain from the Declaration of Independence, but the meaning of "all men" had been changed by Lincoln's Emancipation Proclamation at the beginning of 1863. This reframing would be embodied in the Thirteenth Amendment soon after the war ended, albeit after a close vote in the House of Representatives. Lincoln concluded his short address, "We here highly resolve that this nation, under God, shall have a new birth of freedom – and that government of the people, by the people, for the people, shall not perish from the earth." He expanded the aims of the war from restoring the union to promoting equality to all men, whatever their color (Wills, 1992; Donald, 1995, 466).

Lincoln was assassinated shortly after the Civil War ended. One hundred and fifty years later, Harvard University President Drew Faust wrote about the human cost of the Civil War, ending with:

> The nation was a survivor, too, transformed by its encounter with death, obligated by the sacrifices of the dead. The war's staggering human cost demanded a new sense of national destiny, one designed to ensure that lives had been sacrificed for appropriately lofty ends. So much suffering had to have transcendent purpose, a 'sacred significance' as Frederick Douglass had insisted in the middle of the war. For him, such purpose was freedom, but this would prove an unrealized ideal in a nation unwilling to guarantee the equal citizenship on which true liberty must rest. Slavery had divided the nation, but assumptions of racial hierarchy would unite whites North and South in a century-long abandonment of the emancipationist legacy. (Faust, 2008, 268)

# CHAPTER 2

# Reconstruction

## 2.1 A TROUBLED BEGINNING

The Civil War ended on April 9, 1865, when General Robert E. Lee surrendered to General Ulysses S. Grant at Appomattox. The two generals reminisced about their previous service in the US Army before agreeing on the following terms: "The officers [are] to give their individual paroles not to take up arms against the Government of the United States until properly exchanged, and each company or regimental commander [will] sign a like parole for the men of their commands. ... This will not embrace the side-arms of the officers nor their private horses or baggage." This was an agreement between equals that left the class structure of each side intact, totally different from the unconditional surrender of World War II. In other words, the political, social, and economic organization of the South was not altered as Lee agreed to this surrender, rather continuing the constitutional struggle between the forward-looking North and the backward-looking South (Grant, 1885, Chapter 67).

This was a cessation of hostilities, but it was not a change in politics or economics in the South. The structure of the Southern army mirrored the structure of the Southern society – and landownership – and was untouched in the formal surrender. General Grant was implementing Lincoln's aim to rejoin the states of the union, not fundamentally to reorganize them. The impact of ending slavery was not anticipated in the surrender, although it would determine the progress of Reconstruction. Grant had shown his sympathy with freedmen and women by organizing the forerunner of the Freedman's Bureau, and he would show it again when he was elected president.

Even before the American Civil War ended in May of 1865, politicians and Union officials had thought about how they would rebuild the nation and incorporate the eleven states that had succeeded from the Union between December of 1860 and June of 1861. Lincoln had several different thoughts on Reconstruction, but it does not appear that he had a fully articulated strategy for the process. He would have allowed Congress to rule on the legality of Southern elections and choose whether or not to seat elected Southern Congressmen, giving some federal role and Congressional oversight to the process. It was not clear how much of a role Congress was to play beyond the decision to seat representatives (Dunning, 1901; Franklin, 1961; DuBois, 1992; Foner, 2014).

Lincoln implemented his so-called 10-Percent Plan in late 1863. It allowed for recognition by the federal government of any Southern state in which 10 percent of the white population swore allegiance to the United States. Specifically, if 10 percent of 1860 voters from each Southern state pledged allegiance to the Union, abolished slavery, and prohibited Confederate leaders and military officers from voting and holding office, they would be readmitted to the Union.

Lincoln's plan stemmed in part from a belief that Secession was null and void. Since Blacks (free or slave) could not vote in 1860, the requirement of 10 percent of voters was a de facto continuation of the white votes policy of 1863. In his last public address, Lincoln stated that he would like to see the franchise extended to at least the educated class of Blacks and Black Union soldiers in Louisiana, which was relatively far progressed in its reconstruction in early 1865. Beyond that, his exact goals for Black political participation were unclear.

Lincoln's plans for freedmen after the war were not spelled out because he had other concerns during the war. The year 1863 was framed by Lincoln's actions, starting with the Emancipation Proclamation and ending with the Gettysburg Address. Those influential statements addressed Lincoln's aims as they developed during the Civil War. Enslaved persons should be freed, and they should be included in society as equals. But instead of elaborating on these aims, Lincoln had to manage the war and run for reelection in 1864.

A group of Confederate emissaries in Canada tried to negotiate peace with Lincoln in the summer of 1864. Lincoln, suspecting that this was an attempt to influence his reelection, drafted a letter in response, saying, "Any proposition which embraces the restoration of peace, the integrity of the whole Union, and the abandonment of slavery . . . will be received and considered by the United States." This reiteration of the Emancipation Proclamation did not advance the negotiation, but it stated clearly that the abandonment of slavery was an essential aim of the federal government.

This statement, although consistent with Lincoln's past positions, angered Democrats who had supported Lincoln's efforts to preserve the Union. Lincoln tried to respond to them in a letter that said he was willing to discuss terms widely. Frederick Douglass, the escaped slave who already was a prominent spokesperson for African Americans, urged Lincoln not to send the letter, saying it appeared to abandon the antislavery position that Lincoln had advanced. Lincoln did not send the letter, and he lost the support of northern Democrats in the forthcoming presidential election (Donald, 1995, 520–23).

Republicans in Congress and prominent abolitionists argued that Lincoln's plans were unsatisfactory for several reasons. First, requiring only 10 percent of support from Southern states represented a tenuous basis for the new Southern governments. Second, the policy on Confederate amnesty was relatively lenient. Third, states did not have to guarantee freed slaves nor free Blacks any civil or political rights beyond abolition. Congressional Republicans submitted their own outline for Reconstruction, which required a majority of male white voters to take the loyalty oath before a state was readmitted and with more stringent amnesty requirements for former Confederates. At the time, this was only a proposal as the president retained authority over the Reconstruction process.

Lincoln continued to thread his way through appeals on both his right and left in what everyone expected would be a close election. But it was not close, and Lincoln's leadership was reaffirmed; he was the first president to be reelected since Andrew Jackson. He tried to proceed from the Emancipation Proclamations, which might not last beyond the war, to the Thirteenth Amendment, guaranteeing slavery's abolition, but he could not get Congress to go along with him when he proposed in his

State of the Union address. It finally was adopted at the end of 1865 (Donald, 1995, 396–98).

Lincoln's views on freedmen were summarized by one of his biographers as follows:

> Lincoln had not given much thought to the role that the freedmen would play in the reorganization of the South. The stalwart service rendered by nearly 200,000 African-Americans in the military had eroded his earlier doubts about their courage and intelligence. . . . He believed that the more intelligent Blacks, especially those who served in the army, were entitled to the suffrage. Hence he encouraged the education of the freedman, and he supported the Freedman's Bureau to protect them from exploitation by their former masters. But beyond this he was not prepared to go. (Donald, 1995, 583)

Lincoln's assassination one month into his second term created an extreme hurdle for freedmen, since all the preliminary plans that he had made were abandoned. He was replaced by his vice president, Andrew Johnson, who had been selected from a border state to help Lincoln's campaign and who brought a Southern attitude to the problem. This sudden and dramatic political reversal added a political shift that vastly altered postwar options to a modern historian considering the economic problem of replacing slavery.

President Johnson implemented a relatively lenient Reconstruction policy and prepared to admit former Confederate states to the union with little regard for Black civil rights or political participation after Lincoln's assassination. Similar to Lincoln, Johnson believed that states had not left the Union, and therefore that states should resume normalized relations in the Union quickly. To stipulate extensive conditions on their readmission would be unnecessary as they had always remained states in the union.

Before describing the progress of Reconstruction under President Johnson, it should be noted that there are two descriptions of the Reconstruction, which I call the White or Southern and Black or Northern versions. The difference is that Blacks, enslaved persons, and freedmen, are considered in the white version to be a pariah class, as Edmund Morgan termed it. Their point of view is not worth considering, and they are treated like a factor of production, land, or a beast of burden in this version. This was the view taken in *Time on the Cross*, which I discussed in Chapter 1 (Foner, 2013).

The white version of Reconstruction portrayed it as the lowest point in the history of the United States. In this story, President Lincoln wanted to bring the Confederate states back into the Union quickly and easily. President Johnson attempted to continue this policy, but was thwarted by the villainous Radical Republicans in a vindictive hatred toward the South. They wanted to impose their form of capitalism on the South and retain their political power.

As championed by William A. Dunning, a Columbia University professor around 1900, President Johnson established loyal white governments in the South, but Radical Republicans instituted Black male suffrage and imposed Black governments on the South. Since Blacks were incapable of exercising the rights of political democracy in this white story, corruption and mismanagement ensued. The freedmen needed and were helped by Northern carpetbaggers, who became the operative leaders of Reconstruction. African Americans, carpetbaggers, and Southerners who abandoned their racial identity and cooperated with Blacks despoiled the South. Eventually patriotic members of the Ku Klux Clan restored white supremacy and home rule to the South. Dunning argued that the Black codes of early Reconstruction "corresponded very closely to the actual facts of the situation [in 1865]. The freedmen were not, and in the nature of the case could not for generations be, on the same social, moral, and intellectual plane with the whites; and this fact was recognized by constituting them a separate class in the civil order" (Dunning, 1897, 58).

This view of Reconstruction dominated discussion for a century and was only replaced after World War II. It was replaced by a history, based on closer observations of freedmen and with the aid of quantitative data on Reconstruction, into a story that includes respect for enslaved persons and freedmen. I call this story Black or Northern history, which is now the standard history of Reconstruction.

Even with the new tools of economic history, the description of *Time on the Cross* in Chapter 1 reveals how distorted interpretations of data are still used to support the Southern version of Reconstruction. This is due partly to the complexity of the transformation of the Southern economy that resulted from the Civil War. For it was unclear what kind of labor relations would replace slavery as the Civil War ended. As noted in Chapter 1, the United States had an extremely closed form of slavery. The founders knew a lot of Roman history, but they did not realize that Roman slavery was vastly different from American slavery. Freedmen fit easily into the general Roman economy in way that was closed to American freedmen.

It was difficult for Northerners to understand the resistance of white Southerners to altering the social relations that had developed under slavery. And the economics of labor relations were undeveloped and offered little assistance in constructing new institutions. It is hard even today, after all the history and economics that have developed, to construct a coherent narrative to get from a closed system of slavery to free labor markets. I describe Reconstruction in two stages to start the Black narrative: Presidential Reconstruction and Congressional Reconstruction.

Republicans originally confused Johnson's antipathy for the Southern planter aristocracy with a progressive outlook on Reconstruction. Charles Sumner, a noted Radical Republican senator, considered himself and the president to be on the same page in advocating for Black suffrage, which had become the defining issue for Radicals in the spring of 1865. This was based on private conversations with Johnson along with an oft-quoted speech of Johnson's from October 1864 in which he promised to "be their Moses" to a group of African Americans in Nashville, Tennessee.

When President Johnson assumed office, four Confederate states, Louisiana, Arkansas, Virginia, and Tennessee, had functioning local civil governments due to wartime reconstruction measures implemented by Lincoln. In May 1865, Johnson extended Lincoln's amnesty provisions, with allowances for high-ranking Confederate officers and those with wealth exceeding $20,000. The next month, Johnson allowed for the state conventions to amend their constitutions to meet his three conditions for acceptance back into the Union: the abolishing of slavery, the repudiation of Confederate debt, and the repealing of ordinances of secession. Beyond the restrictions on Confederate officers and wealthy Southerners (who were able to apply for individual presidential pardons), each state was left to decide for itself who was eligible to vote and hold office in elections.

Radical Republicans – as they proudly identified themselves – were surprised at Johnson's policy and outraged at the lack of provisions for Black voting rights, which were not a stipulation for readmission under Presidential Reconstruction. The President nominally argued that Black voting rights could be given after Southern states had been readmitted rather than as a condition for readmittance, but by October of the same year he was openly speaking against Black suffrage and claiming it would lead to extensive racial strife.

In February 1866, only nine months after Johnson had issued his amnesty provision, 14,000 leading Confederates had received pardons from the President, making them eligible to hold office. Before Congress had resumed its session, Mississippi, Alabama, South Carolina, North Carolina, Georgia, and Florida all had held elections for delegates to constitutional conventions with few restrictions on either former Confederate voting or office holding and none with significant voting rights for Blacks.

The governments that these conventions produced, along with subsequent elections held by the newly constituted states, maintained a strong pro-Confederate character. For example, these states elected to the US Congress the vice president of the Confederacy, four Confederate generals, five Confederate colonels, six Confederate cabinet members, and fifty-eight members of the Confederate Congress. These results were mirrored and even amplified at the state and local levels in the South, and some elected officials continued to wear their Confederate uniforms while in office. Presidential Reconstruction offered little room for Black political concerns to be addressed, much to the Blacks' distress.

While the states abolished slavery as directed, the reconstituted states worked to implement a postbellum racial policy referred to as Black codes. While some of these laws allowed Blacks to own property and initiate litigation, their chief design was to legally reinforce and resystematize labor control in the absence of chattel slavery. The codes differed from state to state, but common provisions included requirements for Black laborers to have verification of employment every year, prohibitive taxes on Black landownership, apprenticeship laws that allowed white employers to take over custody of Black children if their parents were deemed unfit, bans on Blacks owning firearms, and making intermarriage between a Black citizen and white citizen a felony for the Black individual.

Mississippi led the way before the 1865 Congress met. Freedmen generally were referred to as persons of color, defined as having one-eighth or more Negro blood. Mississippi ruled that freedmen could not own land, while Louisiana said each person of color had to be in the service of a white person and South Carolina restricted persons of color to husbandry and farm or domestic service unless they had a license for another activity. The measures varied between Southern states, but they all relegated freedmen to second-class citizenship.

These codes were enforced upon both newly freed slaves and formerly free Blacks with no distinction between the two. They ironically encouraged the development of a unified Black polity in the South, which might not have formed otherwise. Johnson rejected and suppressed reports of the enforcement of Black codes and appeared to do little to stop widespread racial violence occurring in Southern states. Many Republicans disagreed with the policies but were reluctant to oppose them for fear of a split within the party (Dunning, 1897, Chapter 4; Dunning, 1901; Franklin, 1961, Chapter 3; Foner, 2014).

The rapid removal of federal troops from the South was disconcerting to Republicans as well, as this was a Johnson policy that Republicans felt left the South vulnerable to Confederate interests. By June 1866, hardly a year after the war had ended, there remained only 3,000 troops in North and South Carolina combined. This growing discontent culminated in the political maneuvering by Radicals before the December 1865 session of Congress, which persuaded the Clerk of the House of Representatives to refuse to include members from the former rebel states on the roll call, effectively denying these states' representation and readmittance to the Union. Congress denied to seat representatives from the Tennessee government, which had been reconstructed under Lincoln's wartime program in September 1865. It was unclear what the next stage for readmission would be since neither Lincoln nor Johnson had a policy if Congress refused to seat representatives.

The Radical Republicans, fresh from the war, were fearful that the Southern states would revert to their antebellum state. True, the slaves would be free, but as future developments made clear, Black Americans could be constrained in other ways that were equally distasteful – and will be described in future chapters. For the moment, the Republicans needed to make Congress responsive to the new conditions produced by the war and the Emancipation Proclamation rather than the antebellum legislature.

Accordingly, Congress established the Joint Committee of Fifteen in 1865 to investigate the current conditions in former rebel states after refusing to seat the elected Southern representatives. Among the Committee's principal findings were its assertions of the continuing need for a significant federal military presence in the Southern states and the necessity of the Freedmen's Bureau. Following the advice of the Joint Committee, the Senate passed a bill that expanded the Bureau's lifespan indefinitely. This also validated land deeds given through the Bureau or Military Field Orders such as Sherman's Field Order 15, which had reserved a strip of land running down the Charleston to Jacksonville coastline for freedmen homesteads.

Johnson vetoed the Bureau bill, calling it unconstitutional as it gave judicial power to the Bureau and terming its cost prohibitive. While Congress could not unify to defeat the presidential veto, only a few months later Johnson again surprised nearly everyone when he vetoed a Civil Rights Bill for Freedmen. Johnson's obstinacy disturbed even Congressional moderates and his veto was quickly overturned, one of the first overturns in American history.

Black political equality quickly became a defining issue for Presidential Reconstruction. In April 1866, the Joint Committee of Fifteen proposed a set of resolutions that would become the Fourteenth Amendment to the US Constitution. The resolutions included a definition of citizenship, and they disallowed states who abridged or violated these civil rights. One clause reduced the representation in Congress of any states proportional to the number of male residents it denied the franchise to, and excluded from Congress, the Electoral Congress, and other federal offices of people who had left federal government and held oath-sworn positions to aid the rebellion. Southern states' readmission was to be contingent on the ratification of the Fourteenth Amendment.

The necessity of more stringent policy was reinforced by widespread Southern violence in the summer of 1866. Most notable of these murderous instances was the bloody New Orleans Riot in June where forty-four Blacks and four whites were killed attempting to attend a constitutional convention and the massacre in Memphis of forty-five Blacks and two whites over two days in May. Johnson went on an ill-conceived press junket in the fall of 1866 to campaign for his Reconstruction policies while denouncing the Civil Rights Bill and the Fourteenth Amendment. By the end of 1866, seven Southern states had rejected the Fourteenth Amendment,

The results of the 1866 elections gave significant strength to Radical Republicans. They now had the necessary two-thirds majority to override a presidential veto, assuring the implementation of a more radical program and more rigorous conditions for readmission, which would include Black suffrage. A new, wholesale Reconstruction program that prioritized Black suffrage was passed and vetoed by Johnson. Congress quickly overrode the President's veto. Congressional Reconstruction began in early 1867 (Foner, 2014, Chapter 6).

Unhappily for freedmen, the chaos following their freedom had been resolved in a series of changes for their employment that preceded the 1866 election. The South had been devastated by the Civil War, and recovery was going to take a while. The Shenandoah Valley – the Virginia breadbasket – looked like a desert, buildings burned and equipment destroyed. Labor was scarce to effect this recovery, both from the high mortality during the war and the newly acquired freedom of freedmen and freedwomen.

Any paternalistic attitudes of former slave owners were replaced with transactions mediated by an abstract market. As a Southern editor wrote in 1865, "The Law which freed the negro at the same time freed the master; all obligations springing out of the relations of master and slave, except those of kindness, cease mutually to exist." And kindness was not very much in evidence as well. Planters resolved never to rent or sell land to freedmen (Foner, 2014, 59–60).

Freedwomen dropped out of the labor force at the same time. Not being forced to work in the fields, Negro women sought the home life that characterized free families. This reduced the labor force substantially after the war. This change should have enhanced freed-men's bargaining power, but the chaos of the postwar South decreased it. Bad weather and bad equipment and seeds led to a succession of poor cotton harvests. Southern whites interpreted the Black response as a sign of Negro indolence and frivolity. Not having experienced slavery them-selves, they could not understand that suddenly becoming free might set off a celebration of the change. Freedwomen wanted to devote their time to the family, and freedmen – as they earned a bit of money – experi-enced their freedom by varying their diet and even buying some jewelry for their wives (Ransom and Sutch, 1977, 46).

The Freedmen's Bureau tried its best to help freedmen in this com-plex setting. The director of the Bureau in South Carolina, Georgia, and Florida in mid-1865 was an abolitionist, who thought that Black land-ownership would provide a cure for this mayhem. He settled thousands of Blacks on lands open to them by Sherman's Field Order 15, issued at the conclusion of his march to the coast at the beginning of 1865. As ordered by Sherman, the freedmen were settled in forty-acre plots. But President Johnson forced the head of the Freedmen's Bureau to rescind this order and issue Circular 15 restoring all land owned to their previous owners.

The general in charge of the Bureau asked the freedmen to appoint a committee to come up with a fair way to restore lands to the prior owners. They replied: "General, we want Homesteads, we were prom-ised Homesteads by the government. If it does not carry out the prom-ises its agents made to us, if the government having concluded to befriend its late enemies and to neglect to observe the principles of common faith between itself and us its allies in the war you said was over, now takes away from them all right to the soil they stand upon . . . you will see this is not the condition of really freemen" (Foner, 2014, 73).

Early in 1866, Johnson ordered the director who had implemented Sherman's order be fired. The idea that the Bureau could help redistrib-ute land to freedmen died. Congress only reinforced this decision. Nothing came of a Congressional effort to redistribute Southern land to give freedmen an economic path to inclusion. There was no enthusi-asm in Congress to expand General Sherman's plan of giving freedmen forty acres and a mule to a national policy. Congress thought that transferring land from Southern landowners to freedmen was a denial of property rights that the Constitution guaranteed. There was also fear that redistributing land would exacerbate violence since emancipation took place without any compensation. While this fear severely limited the extent of Reconstruction, Congress in 1867 was not ready to go further than the uncompensated freedom of slaves. The freedmen were to become like the poor whites of the antebellum period (Ransom and Sutch, 1977; Foner, 2014, 308–11; Merritt, 2017).

The Republicans were not very radical. They could have given land to freedmen by punishing slave owners for starting the Civil War or by compensating landowners as the Russian did when they freed their serfs in 1861. African Americans consequently started out on their path to citizenship with very little education or land, that is, very little human or physical capital. It would be their fate to continue in that state, having great trouble getting a decent education and accumulating wealth. Some Blacks obtained various kinds of human capital, such as Frederick Douglass and Harriet Tubman, and become leaders in society, but most African Americans remained poor and lacking in wealth into the twenty-first century.

The Bureau's supervision of labor relations peaked in 1866–87 and then fell as federal authorities withdrew from local labor markets. The head of the Bureau said that labor contracts were designed to be among free parties, but how fair could be labor contracts signed by freedmen who were denied access to land, coerced by troops and Bureau agents if they refused to sign, and fired and even imprisoned if they went on strike? Blacks' desire for greater autonomy in their daily work started a trend toward sharecropping. They would sign a contract for a piece of land and farm on their own, dividing their crops between them and the landowner (Foner, 2014, Chapter 4).

There were a lot of experiments with sharecropping arrangements, but they quickly settled down to a fifty-fifty division. The details were described by Ransom and Sutch:

> The sharecropping contracts that had become standard by the early 1870s
> required the landlord to provide the land, housing, fuel, working stock,

feed for the stock, farming implements, and seed. The freedman and his family provided the labor and fed and clothed themselves. If fertilizer was to be used, the landlord would choose the brand and amount and its cost was to be deducted from the final output before the crop was divided. (Ransom and Sutch, 1977, 90)

Sharecropping was an improvement over slavery, but it was not a full step toward inclusion in the broader economy. Agriculture requires a sharecropper to plant in one season and harvest later when the crop is gathered. The sharecropper and his family need to eat in the meantime. Without preexiting capital, they need to borrow to survive until the harvest. Adam Smith noted that people who worry about where the next meal will come from do not plan for savings or the future. And the only place to borrow was the local merchant's company store. Advances were given by the merchant to the freedmen, since the freedmen had to borrow to get started, and the store had a lien on the crop. Freedman started to go to cities in the later nineteenth century, slowly beginning the migration that would become interregional in the twentieth century (Boustan, 2017, 15–20).

The merchants could not have established this system on their own. It had been started soon after the 1837 banking crisis by a mercantile agency, which organized a network of correspondents who collected information about small businesses. This network was taken over by Dun just before the Civil War, who established criteria for credit rationing that applied to the local stores in the rural South. Northern manufacturers used this information to loan money to the rural stores, extend credit to them, and ship Northern products to them. Since the freedmen were poor, cornmeal, salt pork or "bacon," flour, lard, coffee, and molasses were the bulk of the food, and shoes and calico cloth were for wearing. Green vegetables were exceedingly rare. Some modern economists see this as paternalism, whereby landowners helped share-croppers with equipment and supplies as part of their pay, but not everyone is convinced (Ransom and Sutch, 1977, Chapter 6; Alston and Ferrie, 1999).

Congress passed the Congressional Reconstruction Act in the spring of 1867 that divided the eleven former Confederate states, except

Tennessee, into five military districts: (1) Virginia, (2) North Carolina and South Carolina, (3) Georgia, Alabama, and Florida, (4) Mississippi and Arkansas, and (5) Louisiana and Texas. The Act placed the former rebel states under martial law as the army commander in charge of each district was allowed to use military commissions rather than civilian courts to enforce laws. The program also specified the more stringent requirements for readmission into the Union: (1) the ratification of the Fourteenth Amendment, (2) new state constitutions, which allowed for manhood suffrage irrespective of race, color, or religion, (3) approval of these new constitutions by a majority of a state's eligible voters, and (4) the establishment of governments under the new constitutions to replace the governments established under Presidential Reconstruction.

Subsequent Reconstruction acts were passed strengthening the original legislation. In March 1867, voters were required to take a loyalty oath. In July, federal voting registrars were authorized to disenfranchise those thought to be taking the oath dishonestly. A fourth act passed in March 1868 changed the requirement for passage of state constitutions from a majority of a state's registered voters to a majority of the voters who voted in the election, as many white Southerners had registered and then did not vote in hopes of preventing the ratification of the new constitutions.

Excluding Confederates from the franchise was one step; including freedmen in the franchise was a much bigger step. Not only was Lincoln unsure how to include freedmen, but William Lloyd Garrison, leader of the Northern abolitionists, said in 1864:

> When was it ever known that liberation from bondage was accompanied by a recognition of political equality? Chattels personal may be instantly translated from the auction-block into freedmen, but when were they ever taken at the same time to the ballet-box, and invested with all political rights and immunities? According to the laws of development and progress, it is not practical. (Woodward, 1968, 89–90)

Only five Northern states, all with very few Black residents, included Negro franchise. Wisconsin, Minnesota, and Connecticut defeated the proposal to authorize Negroes to vote in 1865; Nebraska's 1866 constitution confined suffrage to whites. Michigan, New Jersey, Ohio, and

Pennsylvania turned down proposals for Negro suffrage in 1867 and 1868. Various contemporary pundits affirmed that Negroes could only vote if they were educated. They followed Lincoln and Johnson in this position in the face of antebellum laws that forbade the education of slaves (Woodward, 1968, Chapter 5).

Linking suffrage to education recalls the distinction between open and closed types of slavery made in Chapter 1. The United States had a very closed kind of slavery, which precluded education for slaves. Although the politicians of the mid-nineteenth century knew Roman history, they were not conscious of the difference between ancient and modern American slavery. They ignored their own history and speculated – falsely as it turned out – that immediate Negro franchise would bring chaos and disaster.

The passage of the Reconstruction Act enfranchised more than one million Southern Black males. It stimulated Black political activity in the South, and the potential of Blacks to be active in politics was one the largest areas of conflict during Reconstruction. Republicans in Congress wanted to look forward, while Southerners wanted to return to be antebellum Democrats. Black institutions and leaders, particularly churches and ministers, quickly became politicized channels of Republican organization in the South. The Union League, previously a Northern upper-class organization, became a conduit of Black political activity in the South through political education initiatives and the building of churches and schools, aimed primarily at Freedmen (Hahn, 2005; Foner, 2014).

While Black support for the Republican Party was extensive to the point of being unanimous, in only three Southern states (South Carolina, Mississippi, and Louisiana) did Blacks hold an outright majority, and even with this influx of newly eligible voters there was extensive local political competition. This meant that attracting the support of whites living in the South would be critical in establishing a foundation for the Republican Party in the region. Republicans originally hoped to attract former Whigs to the party, since the Democrats had a firm base among the Southern elite. They hoped to unite Northern and Southern whites to keep down poor Southern whites as well as Blacks. In many areas of the South, Black turnout for constitutional ratification and subsequent elections exceeded 90 percent, even under the consistent threat of losing employment or physical violence in retaliation for voting (DuBois, 1992; Foner, 2014).

Disenfranchisement of former Confederates varied, as some states disenfranchised only those barred from office by the Fourteenth Amendment, while others had more far-reaching proscriptive measures. The resulting constitutions drafted and passed by these Southern state conventions were notable for their progressiveness. Public responsibilities were greatly increased as provisions were made for the establishing of public-school systems, orphan asylums, and homes for the mentally ill. The constitutions also abolished the extremely high poll taxes, which existed in most Southern states and rewrote the antebellum tax codes so that tax revenues now came from assessed land values as opposed to high poll and licensing fees.

Along with the progressive nature of the newly adopted state constitutions, the Reconstruction-era Southern governments also boasted many noteworthy accomplishments. One of the first actions of these governments was to repeal the Black codes implemented under Presidential Reconstruction. With these discriminatory laws gone, freedmen finally were able to move somewhat freely throughout the South and engage in labor contracts that were much more equitable than before. Many white planters responded by suggesting that landowners collude to set low wages, while others argued that such strategies were against free labor ideals (Higgs, 1977; Litwack, 1979; Foner 2014).

In addition, the institutional infrastructure to provide a higher level of public goods was established. With expanded civil rights, Blacks began to assert themselves more fully by seeking legal redress for disputes. It is important to note the social shock whites experienced by having even the possibility of facing Blacks in court, particularly on juries, which was not allowed in the antebellum era. The expanded social responsibilities of government as well as the accompanying costs are best demonstrated in South Carolina. In the six years between 1870 and 1876, the enrollment in the state's public schools increased from 30,000 to 123,000, while the state budget more than doubled between 1860 and the end of Reconstruction. The period of Congressional Reconstruction represents a dramatic change in the political and social organization of the American South.

Black politicians during Reconstruction did not bring chaos; they instead promoted social spending to increase the services to all citizens. They increased taxes significantly, although not greatly, and they improved Black land tenancy and education. These effects however were undone by their successors after the Black officials left office (Logan, 2020).

## 2.2 JOHNSON'S IMPEACHMENT AND INCREASED VIOLENCE

Two political events of 1868 grew out of the tensions just described. Republicans in the House of Representatives impeached President Johnson in the spring of 1868, and General Grant defeated the Democrats' bid for another term in the presidential election in the fall.

The ostensible reason for Johnson's impeachment was his firing of Secretary of War Edwin Stanton, who had been appointed by Lincoln. The real reasons for impeachment were Johnson's political outlook, his poor administration of the Reconstruction Acts, and his general incompetence. Opposing impeachment were Democrats who argued that since there was no vice president, the presidency would go to Ben Wade, president of the Senate and a Radical Republican. Wade also favored high tariffs, while Northern supporters of Johnson wanted free trade to support economic growth. When the Senate trial came to a vote, conviction failed by one vote. While this discussion has focused on the South, Johnson's acquittal was produced by an attorney for the New York Astor family and the New York Central Railroad to protect free trade and Southern railroads (Foner, 1988, 333–36; Ferguson, 1995, 69).

In the early 1870s, Southern whites began mobilizing to roll back the process of Reconstruction. They wanted to reduce the level of Black political involvement and reestablish antebellum social relations in what they called "Redemption." The eventual establishment of Jim Crow and Black disenfranchisement after Reconstruction were not automatic; they required Southern states to overturn Congressional Reconstruction policies.

Former Confederate soldiers formed the Ku Klux Klan (KKK) in 1866 to oppose Congress and recreate antebellum social structures. Its first and only Grand Wizard was Nathan Forrest, a famous former general in the Confederate army. His title came from the war, when he was known as the Wizard of the Saddle. The cavalry was in turn representative of the planter class, who supplied the horses they rode and had the most to lose; after the war the Klan was relatively restrained in its actions in the August 1867 state elections. White Americans who made up the KKK hoped to persuade Black voters that a return to their prewar state of bondage was in their best interest. Forrest assisted in maintaining order. It was after these efforts failed that Klan violence and intimidation escalated and became widespread (Wills, 1993, 338; Parsons, 2015, 30).

Redemption was a project to return to antebellum political institutions, and the post-Redemption constitutional conventions that undid the Reconstruction-era policies featured an inordinate number of representatives from Johnson's Presidential Reconstruction constitutional conventions. White Southern populists were sharply opposed to Black political power and enfranchisement in the Redemption. Political arguments about "excessive" taxation were associated with rising KKK activity and overt acts of racial intimidation, including many that targeted Black voters and officeholders (Woodward, 1971; Fitzgerald, 2007; Lemann, 2007; Rable, 2007; Ager, 2013; Acharya, Blackwell, and Sen, 2016; Logan, 2020).

Violence was so rampant in the Reconstruction era that President Grant and his administration acted on violence and voter intimidation through the Enforcement Acts, which were passed in 1870 and 1871. The acts made it a federal crime to prevent or obstruct voting and to bar those constitutionally excluded from holding office from serving, and gave the federal government authority to prosecute cases. In situations where violence was acute, such as race riots, the acts specifically suspended habeas corpus. Additional sections of the acts were direct responses to the strategies employed by the KKK, and gave federal authorities power to prosecute violent acts as well as conspiracies to intimidate voters or fix elections. The acts were effective in leading to prosecution of the KKK, the establishment of Black voting, and the creation of a class of Black officeholders in the early years of Reconstruction.

The Congressional gains were short-lived. One-third of all of the race riots in 1873 occurred the week before a local election. Rifle clubs and other civic-named organizations sprang up throughout the South to intimidate voters and threaten local officials over policy. While contemporary news reports concentrated on corruption, historians now conclude that one of the chief goals of violence was to oust Republican leaders and lower taxes, particularly those earmarked for education. Democrats routinely signaled education expenditures, which were controlled by local officials, as an area rife with corruption because they helped Blacks.

Resistance to Black enfranchisement and Reconstruction was particularly violent at the local level. The backlash against these policy changes was nestled in an antebellum past, which featured racial violence and a political regime where taxes were low and public goods relatively few. It would be simplistic to connect all racial crime to politics or racism during this time. At the same time, the politics of Reconstruction gave rise to a class of Black leaders whose very presence violated the racist belief that Blacks were inferior. Attacks on Black voters, Black officials, and Republican sympathizers were common (Logan, 2018).

The strategy of violence for political aims lasted throughout the Gilded Age in the South following the 1874 "Alabama Plan." Democrats in Alabama labeled themselves a "white man's party" while publicly issuing a call to end violence as a means to attract moderate white support. White newspapers carried stories of Blacks being trained to take up arms, with little evidence that this actually happened. In the Alabama Black belt, the tactics ranged from preventing Republicans from assembling, murder of locally prominent politicians, intimidation of Black voters in the form of forcing them to vote for Democrats or lose their jobs, forcing Blacks to leave polling stations without voting, encouraging whites to from neighboring states to come over and cast ballots, and preventing Republicans who won their elections from raising their bonds thus securing losing Democrats those offices by default. "The general strategy was not to incite total violence, which would increase the prospects of Congressional or military intervention, but to intimidate Black voters to alter election outcomes. ... [T]he Attorney General in Alabama publicly stated that anyone could murder a Republican for political intimidation without fear of punishment" (Logan, 2018).

This activity was illegal under the Enforcement Acts at the time, but by the mid-1870s Congressional will to root out voter intimidation and racial violence had ebbed. Congressional investigations of the 1874 elections in Alabama concluded that "Democrats had used force to overturn the state's Republican majority," but took no action on the issue. The state of Alabama itself did nothing to investigate this accusation nor act on the results of the Congressional investigation (Rable, 2007, 118).

The political strategy of Redemption then had a successful template. The plan was adopted in Mississippi in 1875 when terroristic attacks by Redshirts, a paramilitary arm of the Democratic Party, directed their actions to decrease Black voter turnout. This widespread voter intimidation produced a significant majority for Democrats, and elected high-profile Black individuals were targeted to serve as a warning for others of the dangers of being politically active. The use of violence and intimidation was a de facto policy throughout the South by the time of the *United States v. Cruikshank* ruling in 1876. The 1876 elections featured rampant "fraud, intimidation, and terrorism in the South that returned the region to conservative control and restored Blacks to a condition more resembling serfdom than freedom" (Rable, 2007, 185).

Despite the continued use of military occupation and martial law in the South, attempts to have federal authorities intervene were not well organized. When anti-Black violence erupted in Mississippi in 1875, for example, President Grant agreed to send troops only if Mississippi could raise its own militia. This exacerbated the problem of violence because the white mobs and rifle clubs were typically well armed, and Black militias often lacked basic ammunition. Even more, the violence went undeterred. In South Carolina, armed whites, who brought their own cannon, attacked the predominantly Black town of Hamburg in July of 1876, killing five men and pillaging the town. The mayor, following an investigation, issued arrest warrants for eighty-seven men believed to be responsible for the violence. One of the indicted, Matthew Butler, was made a state senator that same year. Another, Benjamin Tillman, would become governor of South Carolina a short time later.

Though states' rights were central to it, Redemption featured strong federalism in public finance when it limited Black political prerogatives. This is consistent with the political ideology that led to succession, which was more related to hostility to Blacks than political concerns (Dew, 2002; Jones, 2012).

The contested issue of public-school financing reflected the divide over public schools generally, which split traditional Redemption Democrats and Independents in the 1870s. Black literacy declined precipitously from 1880 to 1900 as overall funding declined and Black–white disparities in funding grew. In Mississippi and Alabama, state taxes for education were ended, placing the burden of school financing at the local level after Blacks had been removed from office. Mississippi Democrats called for the abolition of the entire public education system. Strong Democrat opposition to tax policy and Black policy makers toward fiscal policy were turned into arguments about Black political officials being corrupt. Southern poor whites suffered from poor schools along with Blacks – as incarcerated poor whites suffer today (Williamson, 1965; Holt, 1977; Bellesiles, 2010; Foner, 2014).

Local white resistance to Reconstruction-era public finance was common during Redemption, and withholding of taxes became a means to overthrow local Black political leaders. The Charleston Chamber of Commerce even passed a resolution in 1871 to encourage local businesses to stop paying all taxes. There were general restrictions on local public finance during Redemption, and whites systematically removed Black politicians from offices, which controlled public finance during Redemption – including the abolition of several state boards of education during Redemption. White legislators justified Black disenfranchisement by arguing that it was not "incumbent" upon them to educate Blacks and then, as uneducated citizens, they should not vote (Williamson, 1965; DuBois, 1992; Logan, 2020).

In 1875 landowners put a tax limit for public schools into the Alabama state constitution. In Vicksburg, opposition to taxes became a justification for racial violence. Many conservatives also hoped that the Supreme Court would invalidate the provisions of the Civil Rights Bills mandating equal access to public education. In Texas, Governor Roberts vetoed appropriations for public schools out of fiscal conservatism (Bond 1938; Woodward, 1971; Gillette, 1982; Rabinowitz, 1982; Duncan, 1986; Current, 1988; Bellesiles, 2010; Foner, 2014).

Some white officials sought to reduce all education expenditures after Redemption drastically, though because public schools were also popular among whites, they did not cut expenditures for whites as much. When white Democrats complained to Congress about the rise in tax rates, South Carolina's Governor responded by directing State Treasurer Francis Cardozo to issue an itemized response that mentioned state and normal school expenditures as two of the largest reasons for increasing expenditures. This made cuts more difficult politically. Still, school term lengths declined by 20 percent while spending per pupil fell by 60 percent between 1871 and 1880. In Virginia, the governor promised planters that the property tax funding public schools would not be enforced (Williamson, 1965; Woodward, 1971; McPherson; 1995; Sterling, 1999; Valelly, 2004; Fitzgerald, 2007; Logan, 2020).

Black policymakers acted consistently to defend public education, in contrast to other public expenditures such as infrastructure. In Mississippi, Black officials in the state legislature united to defeat a measure advanced by white Democrats, which would have reduced the tax base for public schools. In Louisiana Blacks petitioned to have local taxes as a source to continue funding public schools after the tax that funded local education expenditures was suspended by state government. The State Superintendent of Education in Louisiana further investigated the wholesale disappearance of funds intended for public schools after white Democrats returned to power. Black/white school funding ratios changed drastically under Redemption. And school enrollment decreased from 1874 to 1876 when Democrats seized control of the Arkansas legislature. Political disenfranchisement was linked to education.

The narrative history of events after Reconstruction give some important clues as to effects of the end of Black political leadership. Although narrative histories focus on voting and intimidation, public finance was also very important. The tax policies of the Redemption provide additional telling evidence of the differences in priorities between Black and white officeholders in the South after the Civil War. At the end of

Reconstruction, Blacks were placed firmly in second-class status with limited access to public goods and seriously curtailed access to schools and the ballot box.

## 2.3 CONGRESS' WESTERN EXPANSION
## AND GRANT'S SCANDALS

The Homestead Act of 1862 was one of the most revolutionary concepts for distributing public land in American history. Signed into law by President Lincoln during the Civil War, the act eventually led to the transfer of 270 million acres of public lands – or 10 percent of the area of the United States – to private individuals. It enlisted individual farmers in the settlement of the West.

An applicant needed "only to be the head of a household, at least 21 years of age and certify that he or she had never taken up arms against the United States to claim a 160-acre parcel of land. Settlers from all walks of life including newly arrived immigrants, farmers without land of their own from the East, single women and former slaves came to meet the challenge of 'proving up' and keeping this 'free land.' Each home-steader had to live on the land, build a home, make improvements and farm for five years before they were eligible to 'prove up.' A total filing fee of $18 was the only money required, but sacrifice and hard work exacted a different price from the hopeful settlers" (National Park Service, 2019).

Once people put their intentions on record at the closest Land Office, there followed a quick check for any earlier ownership claims, payment of another $10 dollar filing fee, and a $2 commission to the land agent before a temporary claim was awarded. The homesteader then "began the process of building a home and farming the land, both requirements for taking ownership at the end of five years. When all requirements had been completed and the homesteader was ready to take legal possession, the homesteader had to find two neighbors or friends willing to vouch for the truth of his or her statements about the land's improvements and sign a document as proof of the improvements. After successful completion of this final form and payment of a $6 fee, the homesteader received the patent for the land, signed with the name of the current President of the United States. This paper was often proudly displayed on a cabin wall and represented the culmination of hard work and determination" (National Park Service, 2019).

Homesteading clearly was very different from the forty acres offered, albeit only temporarily, to freedmen in the South. Geography determined part of this contrast since most homesteading took place on the plains where farms were larger than along the Atlantic Coast. But the more relevant difference is that Congress allowed freed slaves to claim homesteads before the Emancipation Proclamation, and these words had a different meaning than after the Thirteenth Amendment was passed. Congress could not bring itself to apply the Homesteading Act to freedmen in the South after the war to support giving land to freedmen, albeit in the west.

Hinton Helper, in his thought-provoking book of 1857, argued that slavery had given all the prosperity to Southern plantations. He argued that the land should be taxed and the revenues used to purchase land for freedmen. Of course, he was not listened to (Helper, 1857; Merritt, 2017, 1–2).

The Morrill Act, also passed in 1862, provided land grants to states to establish agricultural and related universities. This Act showed that Congress thought it wise to accompany the free land with some education. Alas, they did not provide either land or education to freedmen. On the other hand, Massachusetts started MIT where I taught for close to half a century.

After promoting land settlement and education, Congress turned to the urgent need for banking reform to enable the North to fight the war. Ever since Andrew Jackson vetoed the renewal of the Bank of the United States in 1832, the control of banking regimes devolved to the states. The states adopted a variety of policies including a total ban on banking (Wisconsin), a single state-chartered bank (Indiana and Illinois), limited chartering of banks (Ohio), and free entry (New York). Though all banknotes were uniformly denominated in dollars, notes would often circulate at a steep discount in states beyond their issue.

The first effort to issue a national currency came when Congress approved the Legal Tender Act of 1862 in the early days of the Civil

War, allowing the issue of $150 million in national notes known as greenbacks and mandating that paper money be accepted in lieu of gold and silver coins. The bills were backed by the national government's promise to redeem them. Their value consequentially was dependent on public confidence in the government and the ability of the government to give out specie in exchange for the bills in the future. Many people thought this promise was about as good as the green ink printed on one side, hence the name "greenbacks."

The National Bank Act was passed in 1863 and was supplemented a year later by the National Banking Act of 1864. The goals of these acts were to create a single national currency to raise money for the Union war effort by creating a system of chartered nationalized banks. The national banks could issue notes, which were printed by the government and backed by the US Treasury. But the quantity of notes that a bank was allowed to issue was proportional to the bank's level of capital deposited with the Comptroller of the Currency at the Treasury. To further control the currency, the Act taxed notes issued by state and local banks, essentially pushing nonfederally issued paper out of circulation (Grossman, 2010).

The Freedmen's Savings Bank was chartered in March 1865. The bank was formed to provide a place for freedmen to hold their earnings from the work they did for the Union during the war. The bank, however, was more like a piggy bank than a commercial bank as the freedmen could not borrow from it. Therefore, the bank did not help freedmen buy land in the immediate aftermath of the war. It was administered by whites who invested it first in government securities and then in railroad securities. It failed in June 1874, shortly after the failure of the Northern Pacific and the resulting financial crisis (Baradaran, 2017, 23–30).

Also, arrangements for transcontinental railroads began to unify the east and west coasts of the United States during the Civil War. The first transcontinental railroad was made possible by the American government under the Pacific Railroad Acts of 1862, 1864, and 1867 and built by the Union Pacific Railroads. The new transcontinental railroad linked the San Francisco Bay in California with the nation's existing eastern railroad network when it opened in 1869.

As expressed early in *The Robber Barons,*

> The whole symbolism of this era attached itself to the construction of the transcontinental or Pacific Railroads more than to any other multifarious activities. By spanning the continent between the two oceans, the nation was to be physically unified, its natural resources thoroughly absorbed, its Manifest Destiny achieved. Hence "the winning of the West," by means of the transcontinental railroads, represented the heart and soul of the national industrial plan which engaged the whole people between 1865 and 1873 [while Reconstruction was waxing and waning in the South]. (Josephson, 1934, 76)

The 1862 Act granted each railroad company contiguous rights of way for their rail lines as well as all public lands within 100 feet on either side of the track. It also granted an additional 10 square miles of public land for every mile of grade save where railroads crossed rivers or ran through cities. The method for apportioning these other land grants was in the form of "five alternate sections per mile on each side of said railroad, on the line thereof, and within the limits of ten miles on each side," which thus provided the companies with a total of 10 square miles for each mile of their railroad. The nongranted areas remained public lands under the custody and control of the US General Land Office.

The companies were authorized to issue US Government Pacific Railroad Bonds at the rate of $16,000 per mile of tracked grade completed west of the Sierra Nevada mountains and east of the Rocky Mountains. The Act provided that the issuance of bonds "shall be treble the number per mile" (or $48,000) for tracked grade completed over and within the two mountain ranges, though with a limit of 300 miles at this rate, and doubled (or $32,000) per mile of completed grade laid between the two mountain ranges (US Congress, 1862).

The US government backed the 30-year US government bonds authorized by the act, which provided capital to the railroad companies upon completion of sections of the railroads in exchange for a lien on that section. The liens covered the railroads and their fixtures, and all loans were repaid in full (and with interest) by the companies as and when they became due. The subsequent railroad acts amended and clarified this initial legislation in several ways (Fogel, 1960).

These acts, in addition to defining an era, also created problems with the financing of the railroads that immediately were controversial. The root of the problem was that transcontinental railroads had joint sponsors. The government passed the acts and provided land and money. Private investors used these assets to build and operate railroads. There were many opportunities for these private investors to enrich themselves along the way, particularly in the railroad's unregulated construction companies.

Congress in early 1869 was warned about gigantic schemes of public plunder, chiefly through the construction company, Crédit Mobilier, that was formed to build the Union Pacific Railroad. The investigation continued for several years and concluded in 1872 that the promoters had earned profits of at least $23 million on personal investments of less than $4 million. As a result, the railroad was saddled with enormous debts that revenues could not pay.

Modern economists have claimed that the contemporary arguments failed to take account of the risks involved in building a transcontinental railroad. As the contemporary discussion showed, the railroad was to open up the West; it was not servicing an already settled and prosperous economy in the regions it traversed. Revenues were not immediately forthcoming. They had to wait until the existence of the railroad convinced farmers to settle the Great Plains, investors to mine iron and copper north of the farmers, and provided linkages between California after the Gold Rush to the rest of the country.

Fogel, whose work on slavery was discussed in Chapter 1, argued that most of the Union Pacific' debt was used for actual construction. Even without allowing for the risk incurred by the Crédit Mobilier, the interest charges on the railroad's debt would have exceeded the net income of the railroad in 1872. The problem, as Fogel saw it, was Congress wanted the *social* returns of the railroad – Manifest Destiny – while investors gained from the *private* returns. Most of the controversy over the Crédit Mobilier over the years is due to this distinction, which was only introduced a century after the Union Pacific Railroad was built (Fogel, 1960, Chapter 3, 51–90).

Since Congress wanted private investors to build the railroad, they flocked to the railroads. They invested in the new transcontinental railroads and competed for control of more local railroads like the Erie Railroad in the Northeast. Vanderbilt, Gould, and Fisk bought and sold railroad bonds to make money off of these diverse railroads. They got rich, partly at the expense of investors whose losses have not been remembered, as they focused on finance more than railroad construction. President Grant was naïve in financial matters, and he got involved with some of Gould and Fisk's financial operations after his reelection in 1872 (Josephson, 1934, Chapter 3, 75–99).

All the railroad construction was enabled by the second of two revolutions in the iron and steel industry that produced cheap good steel for railroad tracks. The first revolution was the adoption of coal instead of charcoal to make pig iron that happened around the time of Andrew Jackson's presidency. The expanded supply of pig iron was made into wrought iron and used in the construction of New England railroads that aided the North in the Civil War. During the war, the Bessemer process for making steel from pig iron was introduced, which made steel rails as cheap as wrought iron ones and lasted ten times as long as the wrought iron rails.

This was the start of the American steel industry that started from rails and bridges and went into all kinds of construction. Andrew Carnegie was attracted to the new technology and opened his first steel mill in 1875. The introduction of cheap and durable steel represented a large step forward in the industrialization of the North, and it would change the industrial basis of economic growth for many years. As noted earlier, this innovation did not have much impact in the South, which had not invested much in canals or other transportation improvements (Temin, 1964).

The steel industry grew over time, but Congress had to deal with the inflation during the Civil War soon after the war ended. Before the Civil War, the United States was on a gold standard. Bank notes were legal tender issued by state banks, which could be exchanged for gold at any bank. The United States passed the First Legal Tender Act to help finance the Civil War early in 1862, shifting the economy to a fiat currency called the United States Notes or greenbacks. Greenbacks were issued as an immediate relief for the country's growing wartime demand for currency. Unlike bank notes, greenbacks were not backed by any metallic standard and functioned as a loan without interest.

There was strong inflation during the Civil War. The price level almost doubled between 1861 and 1865, making British pounds more expensive. After the war ended, the price level and exchange rate began to fall. Congress mandated a severe monetary contraction to lower the price level so that they could reinstate the gold standard at the old level. Congress passed the Public Credit Act of 1869 that moved toward reinstating a gold standard by stating that the government would pay off its loans in gold. Deflation continued during the 1870s, and the United States did not return to the gold standard until 1879.

This was the context in which Ulysses Grant was elected president in 1868. (Even the Democrats had not dared to nominate Andrew Johnson.) The tension between Congress and the President evaporated while the advancement of Reconstruction interacted with railroad expansion in the West. Chernow, in his magisterial biography of Grant, summarized the complexity of Grant's context clearly:

> Fueled by war contracts, the northern economy had burgeoned into mighty, productive engine that exploded with entrepreneurial energy, eclipsing the small-scale, largely agricultural antebellum economy and catapulting the country into the front ranks of world powers. As the flush of wartime idealism faded, the Grant presidency ushered in the Gilded Age, marked by a mad scramble to money and producing colossal new fortunes. ... New technologies, especially the railroad and telegraph, made the economy continental in scope, bringing forth modern industries and flooding the country with a cornucopia of consumer goods. (Chernow, 2017, 644)

In his first year in office, Grant signed the Public Credit Act and conferred equal rights on Blacks in Washington. He also revived the Freedmen's Bureau under Eaton who had helped him during the war. But he became an unwilling part of Fisk and Gould's abortive plan to corner the gold market at the same time. The corner worked briefly, and Gould discovered Grant's effort to destroy his corner and made a lot of money. Grant's actions plunged the financial world into chaos and became a public relations tragedy. "Grant's dealings with Gould, Fisk, and Corbin show that even as president, he [Grant] was still the same trusting rube who had been hoodwinked by business sharpers before the war. ... The Gold Corner set the pattern for future Grant scandals" (Chernow, 2017, 678).

It also gave rise to all sorts of financial machinations that Charles Francis Adams and Henry Adams, the sons of John Quincy Adams, chronicled in *Chapters of Erie* in 1871. Charles Francis Adams kept the British from supporting the South in the Civil War, but he and Henry were not fond of President Grant. They were not masters of finance, but they understood people very well.

President Grant was simultaneously dealing with events in the South and in the West. To impose order on the narrative, it seems best to focus on Grant's actions in the South first and on his actions for the West later. This separation does violence to the complexity of Grant's presidency, but it allows us to appreciate different aspects of Grant's administration more clearly. As we will see, Grant's ability to preserve the mission of Reconstruction in the South decreased over time as Northern enthusiasm for Negro suffrage declined, and Democrats and railroad and steel Republicans replaced Radical Republicans in Congress.

The Fifteenth Amendment was ratified on February 3, 1870; it was far simpler than the Fourteenth. It said, "The right of citizens of the United States to vote shall not be denied or abridged by the United States or by any State on account of race, color, or previous condition of servitude. Congress shall have the power to enforce this article by appropriate legislation." Freedmen, it was stated, are citizens of the United States. And all citizens have the right to vote. Grant said, "[It] is indeed a measure of grander importance than any other one act of the kind from the foundation of our government to the present day." Its acceptance was required for every Southern state readmitted to the Union, and Grant urged Congress to promote education for all citizens to enable them to vote wisely (Chernow, 2017, 685).

Congress created the Department of Justice in mid-1870 to enforce the Civil War amendments, which had produced a flood of litigations. The primary job of the new department was to stop the KKK and its offshoots that were trying to keep freedmen from voting by an epidemic of violence. As the Governor of North Carolina said, "Bands of these armed men ride at night through various neighborhoods, whipping and maltreating peaceable citizens, hanging some, burning churches and breaking up schools which have been established for the colored people." The Governor continued that witnesses to these violent activities were so terrified by the Klan that they would not testify in court and juries would not convict them. Witnesses who tried to testify often were murdered. Grant offered help in the form of more federal troops, but the Justice Department faced a great challenge in enforcing the law (Chernow, 2017, 700–2).

Violence rose as the 1870 election approached. Many observers thought that the Southerners were acting as if it was a decade earlier and the Civil War had not taken place. The election was a great setback for the Grant administration, as midterm elections often are. Democrats gained in the North, sharply reducing the Republican majority. On the other hand, six Black congressmen were elected in the South. Their election spurred more backlash with a surge of Democrats elected to Southern state governments.

Grant signed several enforcement acts to reduce white violence against Blacks in the South as local governments appeared unable to address the resulting chaos. He called the new Congress into session early and tried to use all his powers to stem the violence. His opponents complained that Grant was trespassing on state's rights in his attempts to stop the KKK. Congress debated these issues at length with Democrats trying to reframe the opposition to freedmen in the South as some kind of Republican fraud. Grant signed the third of the enforcement acts, known as the Ku Klux Klan Act, in April 1871.

While enthusiasm for full citizenship of freedmen decreased in the North, Grant's faithfulness to the aims of Black citizenship continued. The new Department of Justice continued to prosecute violence in the South during the early 1870s even as the Attorney General was being solicited by the rapidly expanding railroads to grant favors to them.

President Grant easily won reelection in 1872. He was inaugurated in March 1873, and made a speech supporting the freedmen's struggle, saying they were "not possessed of the civil rights that citizenship should carry with it. This is wrong and should be corrected." He also looked forward to restoration of the gold standard.

An extreme example of the conflict over full citizenship can be found in the Colfax Massacre of 1873, which eventually provided legal cover to white voter intimidation. The struggle in Louisiana began with the gubernatorial election in 1872. The Republican candidate supported by Grant won, but the Democrats refused to concede. Grant refused to send troops or take sides other than to reiterate his support for the Republican candidate. Violence increased, and a businessman informed Grant that he was being persecuted for voting the Republican ticket. Masked men surrounded his warehouse and fired many shots into it, saying they would burn it down if the owner did not move away. A court ruled in favor of the Republican governor in early 1873, but the violence continued.

In addition to the governor's election, a Black Republican and a white Democrat vied for office in Grant Parish, Louisiana, in a con-tested election. The Republican, fearing violence, fortified the court-house in Colfax. On Easter Sunday, April 13, 1873, a white mob attacked the courthouse. Even after the Blacks in the courthouse raised a white flag to surrender, whites continued cannon and rifle fire. The courthouse was burned with Blacks still inside after it was seized by whites, and survivors were led off to be shot dead. The death toll is believed to be above 100 dead in this massacre. There were heaps of Black bodies left around the courthouse, but not a single white body (Logan, 2018).

Federal troops finally came to Colfax, arrested eight of the attacking whites, and counted over seventy Black victims. Others claimed there were hundreds of victims. Invoking the 1870 Enforcement Act, a federal grand jury handed down seventy-two indictments. Only three men were convicted. Litigation followed, and the trail went up to the Supreme Court, which ruled in *The United States v. Cruikshank*, 92 U.S. 542 (1876), that federal prosecution of conspiracy charges under the Enforcement Acts was illegal. The Supreme Court overturned the con-victions of the defendants, holding that the plaintiffs had to rely on state courts for protection. The court also ruled that neither the First Amendment nor the Second Amendment applied to the actions of state governments or to individuals. The decision left African Americans at the mercy of increasingly hostile Southern state governments dominated by white Democratic legislatures. And it allowed groups such as the KKK to continue to use paramilitary forces to suppress Black voting.

The decision left gangs of armed whites immune from prosecution, and it emboldened whites in Southern states to re-double their efforts to intimidate Black voters. Black murders were so common in Louisiana that Grant sent a commander to Louisiana in early 1874 who estimated that there were over 2,000 Blacks killed by whites since the Civil War and another 2,000 injured (Chernow, 2017, 759–63).

The die was cast in Louisiana even before the Supreme Court decision; whites seized control of counties and forced Black officials to resign from their elected offices. Some opposition to taxes was rooted in the belief that high tax rates were keeping capital investment out of the South, even though Southern tax rates were relatively low. Redemption often came with state policies that limited the ability of local bodies (such as school boards and boards of equalization) to levy taxes and even created systems where board members were selected by the governor as opposed to the local electorate (Hesseltine, Hesseltine1935; Williamson 1965; Woodward, 1971; Ayers, 1992; Foner 2014; Logan, 2020).

The Louisiana troubles in 1873 gave way to similar troubles in Mississippi elections in 1874. The Mississippi state legislator reflected the Black majority in the state. Blacks held 55 of 115 seats in the House of Representatives and 9 out of 37 seats in the Senate. White agitators were out to purge the voting rolls, and armed white thugs opened fire on a Black celebration of Grant's victory at Vicksburg eleven years earlier. The first Black Vicksburg sheriff pleaded with the state government to ask the federal government send soldiers to contain the violence against freedmen. Grant – deviating from his Louisiana pattern – refused. The August election passed peacefully, but Blacks lost all their legislative seats.

Armed members of a KKK offshoot forced the Black sheriff to flee and chased the board of supervisors out as well in December. Black and white militias faced each other just outside Vicksburg. When the Blacks began to retreat, the whites opened fire and killed several of them. More firing led to twenty deaths on the same spot where the confederate commander of Vicksburg surrendered to Grant in 1863. The governor appealed to Grant, who responded by putting federal troops in Jackson on alert and ordering "disorderly and turbulent persons to retire peacefully within five days."

There also was a resumption of hostilities in Louisiana that winter as whites contested the legislative election of 1874. Grant sent Phillip Sheridan to investigate these various uprisings, and Sheridan spoke up in opposition to white vigilantes. Grant was upset at Democrats forcing out Blacks from state governments, while Northerners expressed reluctance to resend federal soldiers to the South. Instead of sending soldiers, Congress passed the Civil Rights Act of 1875, outlawing racial segregation in public accommodations, schools, transportation, and juries. The act was ruled unconstitutional by the Supreme Court in 1883 and only revived in 1957.

## 2.4 GRANT'S WOES AND RECONSTRUCTION'S END

Railroad construction went into a boom after the Civil War, laying 33,000 miles of new track across the country between 1868 and 1873. Much of the mania for railroad investment was driven by land grants and other government subsidies to the railroads. The railroad industry was the nation's largest nonagricultural employer, and it involved large amounts of money and risk. Speculators financed abnormal growth in the industry as well as overbuilding docks, factories, and ancillary facilities. A period of post-Civil War economic overexpansion arose from the Northern railroad boom.

These then ensued a series of economic setbacks: the Black Friday panic of 1869, the Chicago fire of 1871, the outbreak of equine influenza in 1872, and the demonetization of silver in 1873. The Coinage Act that moved the United States onto the gold standard depressed silver prices. This hurt Western mining interests, who called the Act "The Crime of '73." The development of new silver deposits at Virginia City, Nevada, led to some new investment in mining activity. But the coinage law reduced the domestic money supply, raising interest rates and hurting farmers and anyone else who normally carried a lot of debt. The ensuing outcry raised serious questions about how long the new policy would last. This apparent instability in United States monetary policy caused investors to shy away from long-term obligations, particularly long-term railroad bonds.

In September 1873, Jay Cooke & Company, a pillar of the US banking establishment, found itself unable to market several million dollars of Northern Pacific Railway bonds. With investment banks anxious for more capital for their enterprises, President Grant's policy of contracting the money supply made matters worse for those in debt. As businesses tried to expand, the money they needed to finance that growth became scarcer. Cooke's firm declared bankruptcy on September 18, 1873.

The announcement of the bankruptcy touched off a panic on Wall Street, plunging the country into a prolonged depression. Americans interpreted this economic crisis in the light of the financial debates of the Civil War – the question of what is money chief among them. The consequences transformed American politics. Political parties split along sectional lines. Sharply divided over President Grant's veto of the 1874 Inflation Bill, the Republican Party decisively lost the 1874 congressional elections. The new Democratic majority in the House spelled the doom of Reconstruction, and the ongoing divisions of both parties on economic issues triggered a political realignment (White, 2012).

In September the New York Stock Exchange closed for ten days and some 55 railroads had failed by November, 1873. By the first anniversary of the crisis, another sixty were bankrupt. Construction of new rail lines plummeted. Almost 20,000 businesses failed between 1873 and 1875. Unemployment peaked in 1878 at 8.25 percent. Building construction halted, wages were cut, real estate values fell, and corporate profits vanished (Kindleberger, 2005; Mixon, 2008).

Poor economic conditions led voters to turn against the Republican Party, and the Democrats assumed control of the House in the 1874 congressional elections. The Grant administration found it difficult to develop a coherent policy regarding the Southern states as the North began to steer away from Reconstruction. Railroad building programs crashed across the South in the depression, leaving most states deep in debt and burdened with heavy taxes. One by one, Southern states fell to the Democrats, and the Republicans lost power.

President Grant was drowning in scandals as the economic trouble mounted. His biographer stated, "Hardly had the Louisiana furor died down than Grant found his administration descending into a scandal that would eclipse all previous scandals, which had soiled individual cabinet members but had not touched the president himself. This new one would widen, surround Grant, and threaten him directly" (Chernow, 2017, 796).

During the Civil War, the federal government had imposed a stiff excise tax on whiskey to help pay the wartime bills. A shady organization orchestrated evasion of the tax, paying off some of the Grant administration appointees along the way. As the story developed throughout 1874–75, Grant relied on his long-standing aide, Orville Babcock, to stay abreast of the developing prosecution of the Whiskey Ring. When Babcock was accused of being part of the ring in early 1876, Grant supported him, saying that he had long been a member of his team.

Then Grant discovered that Babcock had colluded with Gould and Fisk as they attempted to corner gold in 1869. As Chernow summarized, "Grant had received a sudden and terrible education in misplaced loyalty. ... The scales had fallen much too late from the president's eyes. ... Grant had succumbed to the curse of second-term presidents: spreading scandal" (2017, 807–8).

The Whiskey Ring was followed by the Indian Ring, where scandal and corruption out of the Secretary of the Interior's office led to profiteering at the expense of American Indians. Orvil Grant, the president's son, was implicated in the Indian corruption through his ownership of Indian trading posts. The Secretary of War was implicated as well and resigned. And Orvil's corruption then led to bribes and kickbacks in the president's household. All these scandals were well publicized to become the hallmark of Grant's presidential tenures.

The public followed these stories avidly, and Grant's presidency is known far more widely for this and other scandals than for his support of freedmen in the South. The loss of the Republican control of Congress in the 1874 midterm elections, although affected strongly by the financial crisis of 1873, must also have been affected by Grant's loyalty to his assistants in the Whiskey Ring.

The 1876 presidential election was marked by the violence that had become endemic in the South. There were many examples of vote suppression and doubtful outcomes from several states. The result was a close vote that bothered Grant acutely. He was unable to act as he had done earlier due to a lack of Congressional support, but he did not want the presidency to go to a Democrat. A bargain that allowed the Pennsylvania Railroad to reach California was reached only weeks before Grant's successor was to be inaugurated. The Republicans would end Reconstruction by removing all federal troops, and the Democrats would treat Blacks fairly – whatever that meant at that time. Reconstruction officially ended. Republican Rutherford B. Hayes was declared the winner in the South Carolina election by a special commission, and he gained a 185 to 184 victory in the Electoral College. The end of the economic crisis coincided with the beginning of the great wave of immigration into the United States, which lasted until the early 1920s (Chernow, 2017, 848–49).

# CHAPTER 3

# The Gilded Age and Jim Crow Laws

## 3.1 INDUSTRY AND INEQUALITY GREW

Election Day in 1876 featured a number of firsts in the United States. It featured the highest white participation rate in the South at that time or since. In South Carolina, more white votes were cast than white adult males in the state, and more than 150 Blacks were murdered during the campaign. When Rutherford Hayes emerged as the President after the disputed election, the withdrawal of all federal forces from the South was met with a promise to protect Black civil rights. But Hayes simply noted that there was "atrocious" violence throughout the South in 1878. Southern states repudiated the debt incurred under Republican leadership and curtailed the ability of local bodies to levy taxes. Black political participation was already stymied – none of the three Republicans elected from the South that year served in majority Black districts (Holt, 2008, 167, 255; Logan and Temin, 2020).

Mainstream history sees the end of Reconstruction in 1876 as the return of democracy to the United States. This is expressed clearly in a recent political-science analysis of the future of American democracy in the twenty-first century:

> The disenfranchisement of African Americans preserved white supremacy and Democratic Party dominance in the South, which helped maintain the Democrats' national viability. With racial equality off the agenda, southern Democrats' fears subsided. Only then did partisan hostility begin to soften. Paradoxically, then, the norms that would later serve as a

foundation for American democracy emerged out of a profoundly undemocratic arrangement: racial exclusion and the consolidation of single-party rule in the South. (Levitsky and Ziblatt, 2018, 124–25)

This political alignment is important in several ways. The Republican Party abandoned the Reconstruction efforts that had been its primary interest, leading to a sharp decline in the relevance of race and the legacy of American slavery in the national discussion. The national story obscures the reality for most of African Americans, who remained in the South until the early twentieth century. The national priority to leave Southern issues to themselves left the political hegemony in the South to have serious implications for African-American welfare at the time of the expansion of the federal government. In spite of the nondiscrimination written into policy, the actual practice exacerbated racial disparities. Racial violence was rampant during this period, and much of it had political goals. All of this was situated in a period where nationalization merged with xenophobic policies toward Native Americans, southern and eastern European immigrants, and Asians (both native and immigrants).

White economic history largely ignores the new political alignment and focuses on the fall in price discrepancies due to better transport. Price convergence is seen as key to the Great Divergence, when America and Western Europe grew faster and richer than countries elsewhere. In addition to rising inequality between nations, there was also increasing inequality within nations, leading to Gilded Ages in the progressive nations. I will describe the Gilded Age and illustrate its implications for Black history with a fuller account of racial violence.

The economic fortunes of the American South and West diverged at this point. The cotton industry and associated cotton agriculture were replaced as centers of economic growth by growing wheat exports, manufacturing, and mining. Tobacco, a staple crop of the Atlantic coast, continued to prosper. Southern violence that had grown during Reconstruction increased after its end, and Blacks were trapped in a stagnant agricultural setting without education or votes to alleviate their lot. Their conditions deteriorated as the South stagnated while the North leapt ahead with the settlement of the West.

Freedmen became sharecroppers since Congress did not adopt the Republican initiative to give each Freedman forty acres and a mule. Without land or education, freedmen had little choice. The landowners provided food and loans to the share croppers in a company store, increasing their power over the freedmen for the remainder of the nineteenth century. Economic growth slowed in the South, due to both a lower growth of demand for cotton and the withdrawal of many freed-women from the labor force (Temin, 1976).

The ownership of land did not change much between 1860 and 1870, and owners who leased two to four tenants accounted for 30 percent of Southern tenant farms in 1900. The remaining tenant farms were spread out among larger owners; the largest owners who had twenty or more tenants accounted for only 15 percent of the sharecropper holdings. Sharecroppers were about as efficient as renters, according to tests with scant data. But annual sharecropping contracts discouraged improvements in farming practices and discouraged investments in agricultural equipment. With the slow growth of cotton demand, these incentives condemned most freedmen to continue at low incomes (Ransom and Sutch, 1977; Wright, 1978).

The banking system that supported the export of cotton before the Civil War fell apart in the Civil War. The National Banking Acts of the 1860s made it hard to start new southern banks. Some succeeded, but they were mostly urban, and the few rural worked with large landowners. Smaller landlords and sharecroppers needed cash, and they turned to their country stores for help. The older stores had failed in the war, and new stores typically were owned by Northerners who were trying to revive cotton agriculture. In many cases, the stores were unlicensed financial intermediaries – that is, not banks – who funneled Northern capital to the rural South.

Sharecroppers did not have capital to support themselves through the growing season. They could not pay cash for food to eat while they planted, grew, and harvested cotton. They therefore borrowed money by buying their food on credit. This did not create a new loan. Instead merchants had cash and credit prices for their goods, and the loan was implicit in the different price. It was like a rural copy of the bank discounts for commercial bills described in Chapter 1 that were loans offered by paying the interest upfront with a lower price for the bills.

How would Northern storeowners know which sharecroppers and smaller landlords would succeed to repay any loans? The key was Dun's Mercantile Agency that provided credit evaluations for the stores. The rural merchant maintained his monopoly by his control of credit more than by the extent of his store. The credit price was about 50 percent higher than the cash price. This large difference implies that the interest rate for sharecroppers was an average of about 60 percent through the decade of the 1880s. This rate of profit is higher than the costs of lending locally, given the credit supervision at one end and the knowledge of the locals at the other. It must have been a monopoly return (Ransom and Sutch, 1977).

There was a lot of turnover in these stores, suggesting that there were unseen costs that may have justified part of the high profits. But the successful store owners spent their profits in buying land. Landowners and storekeepers became a single group oppressing sharecroppers. They earned good money and encourage sharecroppers to specialize in growing cotton. The sharecroppers became dependent on the stores for their consumption. This loss of diversity in production reduced the self-sufficiency of sharecroppers and increased their reliance on rural merchants. That in turn reduced the mobility of sharecroppers, who were forced into relations reminiscent of slavery. This worked well for the white overlords for the 1880s, but cotton crops were attacked by the boll weevil around 1890. The boll weevil led to poverty among the sharecroppers and bad times for their storekeepers (Ransom and Sutch, 1977).

In fact, one can speak of the postwar situation of the freedmen as being in a plantation economy. That is an economy organized to have the freedmen do the work, partly by contract as sharecroppers or a variant, and partly because they had nowhere else to go. A few of them left to the cities, but they had little training for good jobs and did not encourage others to follow. The plantation owners had some paternalistic attitudes toward the freedmen and their families, but nowhere near as extensive as under slavery. The plantation economy survived until World War II, although various parts of the plantation economy were under pressure from law and freedmen activities (Mandle, 1978).

**Table 3.1** Distribution of Georgia agricultural
workers, 1910 (percent)

| Status | Blacks | Whites |
|---|---|---|
| Owners | 6.9 | 40.8 |
| Cash tenants | 20.3 | 14.2 |
| Share tenants | 8.4 | 12.5 |
| Sharecroppers | 14.6 | 15.2 |
| Wage workers | 49.9 | 17.3 |

*Source:* Alston and Kauffman, 2001. There were more than
200,000 observations for both Blacks and whites.

The kinds of contracts that freedmen had just before World War I can
be seen in Table 3.1. The data come from Georgia in 1910 and show how
the whites and Blacks differed at that time. Forty percent of whites owned
the land they farmed, as opposed to seven percent of Blacks. At the other
extreme, half the Blacks were wage earners, while less than 20 percent of
whites were. In the middle, there were several kinds of contracts that
both freedmen and poor whites had to farm cotton.

Twenty years later, in 1930, about 13 percent of North Carolina
sharecroppers finished the year in debt, averaging over $100 per family.
Interest payments accounted for more than 10 percent of tenant
income. The landowners borrowed money at 6.5 percent and loaned
it to their tenants at 21 percent. The legacy of the plantation economy
was that freedmen did not acquire property even if they worked hard.
In addition, they were last in line for desirable employment (Mandle,
1978, 49, 99).

Conditions were very different in the North and West. The West
expanded and eventually allied with Southern Democrats. The North
expanded its wheat production and opened up a new export to industri-
alizing Europe. The United States made a big advance on the world stage
at the same time it regressed on race relations within the country.
I discuss this apparent contradiction between American progress and
regression, starting with the West.

The gold rush to California and transcontinental railroads led to
dramatic political and economic changes. The political tensions led to
the inclusion of many Western states, filling in Jefferson's Louisiana
Purchase between California and the expanded thirteen states. The access

to Western areas gave rise to a Western economy that differed from the East in two ways: The land that was opened up was more suited to cattle ranching than cropping, and the mountains that became accessible contained deposits of gold, iron, copper, and other minerals that gave rise to a massive mining interest.

These two activities had similar economies of scale. They were most efficiently run as centralized management and large numbers of workers. The landowners needed cowboys, who were memorialized as universally white, but which were composed of Blacks, Mexicans, and whites. The mines needed miners who were composed of these groups plus Chinese immigrants who had been imported to help build the continental railroads. In other words, the economy of the new West was more like the old South than it was to the new North.

Given our history, we should not be surprised that similar economic structures gave rise to similar racial prejudices. The new workers were not slaves, but they also – like the freedmen of the time – were not full citizens. Western politics idolized whiteness and vilified Black, yellow, and brown people. The new Western states adopted laws that were highly similar to the Jim Crow laws that the North would enact at the end of the century. This convergent racial view led the new Western states to join the Democratic Party in the old Confederate states, opposing the Republican desire to make freedmen into full citizens.

Frederick Turner glorified white cowboys and the settlement of the West in 1893 in a fashion that echoed *Time on the Cross* by providing a narrative that did not consider how the workers thought. This influential contribution to mainstream history largely ignored the underpaid cowboys and miners that were building the West. He analyzed the psychological effect of the closing of the Western frontier on white consciousness helped transform racial prejudice into class divisions. Teddy Roosevelt's Rough Riders in Cuba at the turn of the twentieth century were a symbol of the new Western hierarchy. Roosevelt will appear again as we discuss the North, but his racial views may well have come from a long visit to his Western ranch after his wife and daughter died (Richardson, 2020).

Economic conditions were very different in the Midwest, which was closely tied to the North. Wheat exports from those areas of America increased as American wheat farming expanded and transport costs fell. European countries adopted diverse policies to deal with American wheat, setting the stage for armed conflicts to come. Britain was largely industrialized by the late nineteenth century, and it allowed American wheat to benefit its urban consumers without generating much opposition. France and Germany, which still retained large agrarian sectors, blocked the import of American wheat by imposing high tariffs. These divergent responses set up divisions within Europe that would affect their fortunes in the twentieth century.

The steel industry expanded to provide rails for the transcontinental train routes and ships for exports. Growth in the North continued, although farmers suffered from the deflation. These diverse trends came together again in the presidential campaign of 1896 at the trough of the deflation started in 1868. The Republican candidate won (as in 1876), new gold discoveries led to inflation, and great power conflicts intensified, eventually leading to international war.

Economic growth rose in the North due to both Western expansion and industrialization. As described earlier, the first transcontinental railroad was completed in 1869, and it opened up the West. The railroad increased the demand for iron and steel, lowered costs for wheat exports, and added to economic instability. The increased demand for iron and steel from the railroad construction promoted industrialization. Earlier railroads had been constructed from imported iron, but the discovery of Bessemer steel allowed American steelmakers and other industrial firms to flourish. Inequality that had been high before industrialization remained high as industry expanded. The attempt to construct a second intercontinental railroad, the Northern Pacific Railway, failed in 1873, setting off a deep depression for the rest of the decade (Temin, 1964; Williamson and Lindert, 1980).

The limited tax records suggest that there was a plateau of high-income inequality from the Civil War to the onset of the Great Depression. In other words, we had a Gilded Age. Williamson and Lindert summarized their findings as follows: "Although America drifted along at high inequality levels up to the 1890s, this period of quiescence ended around the turn of the century. . . . Trending inequality seems to have been more an urban phenomenon, since the nonfarm inequality indicators exhibit a much more pronounced inequality after 1900 than do the economy-wide indicators" (1980, 77).

American exports rose by a factor of ten from the 1850s to the 1890s. The falling price of transport, due to the transcontinental railroads and new steamships, led to a massive change in the volume of wheat being exported from the United States. Wheat prices did not change very much in Chicago, but they fell by almost half in Liverpool during the last half of the nineteenth century.

The changing price relationships, the fall of wheat prices in consuming regions, and their rise in distant potential producing areas led to an enormous growth in long-distance trade and increased specialization. The long-distance trade in wheat exports from the Black Sea, North America, India, Australia, and Argentina-grew from around 5 million imperial quarters (of 8 bushels or about 480 pounds each) to over 75 million quarters between the early 1850s and the years prior to the outbreak of the war. That is a growth rate of about 4.5 percent annually. In contrast world population grew less than .75 percent annually and wheat production grew about 1.7 percent annually between 1875 and the war (Harley, 1980).

European countries reacted differently to these massive wheat exports. Britain, which was the most industrialized, let the wheat in, preserving their standing for free trade and gaining the benefits of trade. France and Germany imposed tariffs to help their farmers, a choice that had different implications for these two countries. While Germany industrialized in this period, France continued to remain largely agricultural. Germany benefited in the recovery from World War II because its tariffs had preserved an agricultural labor force for industrialization after the war (O'Rourke, 1997).

The so-called crossing the courses came in 1893 when German steel exports first exceeded British exports. Germany and the United States overtook Britain largely by shifting resources out of agriculture and by improving comparative labor productivity in services rather than by improving comparative labor productivity in manufacturing (Broadberry, 1998).

Anglo-American labor-productivity gaps remained much smaller in agriculture and services than in industry. While British labor-productivity performance looks better in services than in industry in terms of levels, the deterioration of Britain's productivity performance over the long run was heavily concentrated in services. The high labor productivity of British agriculture reflected both the composition of output and the degree of capital intensity. The composition effect arose from the mid-nineteenth-century shift of the product mix away from grain toward pastoral products with the growth of grain imports from the New World, while the high capital intensity reflected the moves toward modernized efficient farming in response to the increased competition.

The growth of the American steel industry was almost as dramatic. Stimulated by the growth of railroads, the new steel industry blossomed. Andrew Carnegie invested in the industry early and expanded his plants and holdings over time. He opened a Bessemer steel plant near Pittsburgh, Pennsylvania, in 1872 and improved and expanded over the next thirty years. He was helped to dominance in the American steel industry by his skill in hiring great subordinates. He was guided in the technological development of his plants by Captain Bill Jones, who was key to the increasing productivity of the steel mill. He was so valuable that Carnegie offered him a position in his partnership where Jones could share in the growing profits. Jones, in the wild world of Gilded Age finance, famously said he would rather have a good salary, like that of the president of the United States. The price of steel rails for railroads fell steadily from $70 a ton to $20. Jones died in an industrial accident in 1889 (Temin, 1969).

Carnegie integrated his steel plants with the coke plants of Henry Clay Frick in 1883 to provide vertical integration of the steel production process. He is remembered now often by his role in the Homestead Strike of 1892. Carnegie installed the open-hearth system at the Homestead plant in 1886, which improved the Bessemer process and produced steel suitable for structural beams and armor plate for the US Navy. They were premium products that sold for higher prices.

In addition, the plant moved increasingly toward a continuous system of production that sped up the process of steelmaking, and enabled the production of larger quantities of the product. The labor force grew rapidly, particularly among unskilled workers. However, while Carnegie

Steel progressed, workers at Homestead saw their wages drop as the national deflation continued.

The 1892 Homestead strike was an inauguration of the type of strike that marked modern labor relations in the United States because it was organized and purposeful. Carnegie placed Frick in charge of his company's operations in 1881, and Frick resolved to destroy the union: "The mills have never been able to turn out the product they should, owing to being held back by the Amalgamated men," he complained in a letter to Carnegie (Harvey, 2002, 177).

In public, Carnegie professed to be in favor of labor unions. He publicly condemned the use of strikebreakers and told associates that no steel mill was worth a single drop of blood. But Carnegie shared Frick's desire to break the union in 1892 and to "reorganize the whole affair, and . . . exact good reasons for employing every man. Far too many men required by Amalgamated rules. Carnegie ordered the Homestead plant to manufacture large amounts of inventory so the plant could weather a strike" (Bridge, 1992, 206).

Frick, after announcing that wages would be cut, locked workers out of the mill on June 29, 1982. A high fence Topped with barbed wire was completed and the plant was sealed to the workers. Various aspects of the plant were protected or shielded, and Frick planned to open the works with nonunion men on July 6. With the mill surrounded by striking workers, the agents needed to access the plant from the river. Three hundred Pinkerton detective agents assembled on the Ohio River about five miles below Pittsburgh on the night of July 5, armed with rifles, and were placed on two specially equipped barges that were towed upriver. The Pinkerton agents attempted to disembark, and some shots were fired.

After a day of armed struggle, the Pinkertons wished to surrender, and they raised a white flag. The strike leaders guaranteed them safe passage out of town. The strike committee also dispatched a telegram to Pennsylvania Governor Pattison on July 7 seeking to convince him that order had been restored in the town. Pattison replied that he had heard differently, and he was unconvinced by the strikers' arguments. He had won election with the backing of a Carnegie-supported political machine, and he now moved to protect Carnegie's interests. Pattison felt a need to act, and Pennsylvania state militia arrived at the Homestead mill on July 12 and surrounded the plant. Their commander made it clear to local officials that he sided with the owners. Within 20 minutes they displaced the picketers, and company officials were back in their offices an hour later (Foner, 1955, Chapter 14).

Though the AFL picketed some places where Frick recruited, Frick readily recruited replacements to work in the factory. The company erected new accommodations for them along with new dining facilities. Many of the new employees were Black. They were not, however, allowed to join the white unions in the steel mills after the furnaces were restarted. They were employed by the Pullman Sleeping Car Company, as will be described shortly, but in an antebellum framework. Black workers, eager to find jobs in the new economy, found that only as strikebreakers could they get jobs.

One question that emerges from this description of the Homestead strike: Why didn't Carnegie and Frick continue with their racially integrated strikebreakers? If they had, the idea of Black workers integrated into Northern manufacturing might have prepared the way for the Great Migration that would start about twenty years later. The answer probably is that they did not think about it at all. Robber barons had and still have very little contact with Blacks, which allows them to project all sorts of hateful actions on them. Carnegie tried to regain his reputation by donating money to construct Carnegie Libraries around the country as the Great Migration continued. In the age of Jim Crow, Blacks were not educated, and these libraries clearly supplied books to the white population.

National attention focused on Homestead when a New York anarchist with no connection to steel or to organized labor plotted to assassinate Frick. He came from New York, gained entrance to Frick's office, and shot, and stabbed the executive. Frick survived and continued his role; his attacker was sentenced to twenty-two years in prison. The attempt on Frick's life undermined public support for the union and prompted the final collapse of the strike. The Secretary of the Carnegie Steel Company concluded, "This outbreak settles one matter forever, and that is that the Homestead mill hereafter will be run by non-union and the Carnegie company will never again recognize the Amalgamated Associates or any other labor organization." Unions disappeared throughout the steel industry (Foner, 1955, Chapter 14; Krause, 1992, Chapter 6; Trotter, 2019, Chapter 3).

Matthew Josephson argued that Rockefeller was faced with more problems in monopolizing the oil business than Carnegie faced in the steel industry. There were economies of scale in steel mills, but not in kerosene production. "Hence the tactics of Rockefeller, the bold architecture of the industrial edifice he reared, have always the liveliest interest" (Josephson, 1934, 265).

Rockefeller proposed that cooperation was more profitable than competition and proposed the Pittsburgh Plan in the 1870s. He brought fifteen of the largest oil firms into cooperation in that decade, comprising about four-fifths of the refining capacity of the country. He then set about purchasing other refineries by various means. He had secret deals with the railroads to get kickbacks for his oil, and this made other firms poorer. He also made particular deals and threats that were tailored to specific firms, like cutting off the supply of oil to a producer of lubricating oils. When Rockefeller's arrangements with the railroads were threatened by a new pipeline, Rockefeller followed the lead of the railroad speculators and built a parallel pipeline to compete with – and eventually purchase – the pipeline in 1879.

As railroads expanded in the North and West, speculation in railroad securities increased. Josephson chronicled the railroad wars and saw them as the center of robin baron activities. The contest for control of the Erie Railroad in the Northeast was emblematic and was written up at the time by Charles Francis and Henry Adams. The scale can be seen with a few examples. Commodore Vanderbilt died in 1879, worth $94 million. Two decades later, Andrew Carnegie sold his steel company worth $942 million, of which he took home $300 million. When US Steel was formed, it was part of a great consolidation around 1900 that subordinated corporations to trusts (Adams and Adams, 1871; Josephson, 1934, 183, 425).

The gains of the robber barons were made mostly in the 1880s, after the United States went back on gold. The 1890s had economic problems, both internally with financial crises and externally with the resumed gold standard. The 1893 depression was one of the deepest in American history with unemployment exceeding 10 percent for half a decade.

The recession of 1893 had deep roots: a slowdown in railroad expansion, a decline in building construction, and a foreign depression that reduced investment opportunities. Agricultural prices fell after a brief upturn as a result of the bumper wheat crop of 1891, as did exports and commerce in general. Amid successive contractions of credit, many essentially sound firms failed. The financial crisis of 1893 accelerated the recession into a major contraction that spread throughout the economy. Investment, commerce, prices, employment, and wages were depressed for several years. Changing expectations, and a persistent federal deficit, subjected the treasury gold reserve to intense pressure and generated sharp counterflows of gold. The Democratic nomination of William Jennings Bryan for the presidency on a free silver platform the following year amid an upsurge of silver support contributed to a second downturn (Whitten, 2001).

The 1893 depression stimulated a great merger movement at the end of the century. The annual number of company consolidations was well under ten before 1898. It jumped to sixteen the next year and eighty-three in 1899. It fell below ten again by 1903. More than half of the merged companies controlled more than half of their industries, and nearly a third absorbed more than 70 percent. These consolidations were stimulated by the effect of the 1893 depression on the recent growth of mass production and capital-intensive firms. After trying simpler methods to reverse falling prices, capital-intensive firms turned to mergers.

The new capital-intensive firms had large fixed costs, and they suffered losses as prices fell after 1893. One result of the industrial growth of the 1880s was that many new and undercapitalized firms were in trouble. They chose integration. Without the depression, older firms like those in the steel rail business could have developed informal ties that led large firms to behave as oligopolists. Without the 1893 depression, the United States might have followed that path over time. The economic consequences might have been similar, but the political influence of the richest robber barons and lesser industrialists might have been lower at the end of the nineteenth century (Lamoreaux, 1985).

The growing importance of extractives fueled the machine age. Raw materials fed a lengthening list of consumer goods and produced and

fueled locomotives, industrial machinery and equipment, farm implements, and electrical equipment for commerce and industry. The rapid
expansion and diversification of manufacturing allowed a growing independence from European imports and supported the allocation of new
goods to American exports. The value of American manufactures grew to
over half the value of European manufactures and twice that of Britain at
the start of the twentieth century.

These problems had effects on both the very rich as they tried to deal
with their competition through mergers into giant trusts and on the very
poor as the economic frustrations of the 1890s led to the growth of Jim
Crow repression in the South. These connections often get lost in
monographs on different parts of this story, but the parts are intercon-
nected. Josephson focused on the very rich, while Woodward lectured
(in the 1950s) on the fate of poor freedmen. They both described the
change between the decades, marked symbolically by the formation of
the Interstate Commerce Commission in 1887 that began to restore
order to competing railroads and passage of the Sherman Antitrust
Act in 1890 – which are featured in other specialized monographs
(Josephson, 1934, Chapter 12; Kolko, 1965, Chapter 2; Woodward,
2002, Chapter 3).

The interaction between the North and South can be seen in the role
of Pullman porters. As railroads expanded for freight, they also became
the focus of personal travel. George Pullman championed the elegant
sleeping car during the Civil War and drove plainer sleeping cars out of
business as the growing class of white merchants, investors, industrialists,
speculators, and their wives craved comfort while traveling.

Coming on line after the war ended, Pullman faced the question of
service. Who would clean the sleeping cars? Who would help customers
on the way? Who would help people with tasks they had as they traveled?
Pullman knew that being treated like royalty is something his customers
would remember even after they had been accommodated well in his
Pullman railroad cars. This showed Pullman's ability to market his products, a skill that would stand him well in the Gilded Age.

But who could he hire to do all the services that his customers would
expect from a fine hotel? Suddenly, after the war and the Thirteenth
Amendment, there was an abundance of Black workers looking for a new

life. Most found their way into sharecropping, which was not that different from their previous servitude, but some also aspired to find a better
occupation and moved to cities (Boustan, 2017, 15–20).

Pullman needed to hire people who would focus on giving service. He
baptized them Pullman porters. They came to define the vocation of
railroad attendants and, for most Americans, made porter synonymous
with Negro. For Pullman decided to hire only Blacks to be Pullman
porters. He wanted service from a mythical servant who was distinct from
the passengers themselves. Passengers going to sleep might behave in all
sorts of antisocial behavior, and they did not want to be helped by people
who might gossip with their friends.

Negroes fit the bill. Negroes had been employed at railroads from the
very beginning. They were fireman, brakemen, switchmen, and they did
a variety of physically demanding jobs. They served as strikebreakers
when white employees tried to improve their lot. And they were used
to working long days from their enslaved histories. Whites did not need
to see them as individuals, but rather as porters or "boy" or "George"
(after Pullman's first name). They were part of the furniture – as they
had been in plantation houses for centuries. Pullman wanted dark
porters, to look uniform and to emphasize their distance from the white
passengers. And he wanted lots of them as his business grew.

Pullman was the first Northern business to hire a lot of freedmen. He
hired thousands of them who were glad not to be farming and excited
about riding around the country in these ornate railroad cars. They
could talk about their experiences among their friends and families
without any worry that these tales would get back to the passengers.
They were known as Uncle Toms and often addressed as Tom (Tye,
2004, 231).

Pullman was making two changes to the lives of freedmen at the same
time. He offered an outlet for many freedmen from the stagnating
agricultural life in the South. This was like education, promising a
brighter future for the Negro community after freedom was assured.
But at the same time, Pullman was dividing the American people into
two separate parts. Whites were the favored people who were prosperous
enough to enjoy the new technology of railroad travel. Blacks were the
undifferentiated servants who helped them without calling for individual

recognition. The freedmen, no longer slaves, were incorporated into the continued vitality of the Southern antebellum society of superior whites and inferior Blacks. We will see that as the railroads declined as luxury travel in the twentieth century, this ambiguous gain led in unusual directions.

## 3.2 THE SUPREME COURT ACTED

As Pullman's business expanded in the acceleration of American settlement and industrialization in the last quarter of the nineteenth century, white people decided that American democracy was only possible if African Americans were excluded from it. The Thirteenth, Fourteenth, and Fifteenth Amendments destroyed democracy, and the end of Reconstruction could start the reconstruction of American democracy. The late nineteenth century witnessed rapid industrial and geographic growth of the white economy with the denial of the Civil War's victory and Reconstruction.

The Pullman porters symbolize the continuation of the slavery relations, while the mainstream economy surged ahead with expansion to the West and productive new technologies. The United States became the manufacturing capital of the world and is compared favorably with European countries. But Blacks were largely stuck in the stagnant agricultural economy in the South. They were absent in the growing manufacturing, although they were employed in Western ranches and mines. But they were mostly stuck in the South and excluded from new travel and production during the late nineteenth-century economic expansion.

The exclusion can be seen in Supreme Court opinions in 1883, only seven years after federal troops were removed from the South, signaling the end of Reconstruction. I described the decision in *United States v. Cruikshank* in 1876 in Chapter 2. The Supreme Court used this decision as a precedent as it began to deal with cases from the previous decade. It was cited in *United States v. Harris*, 106 US 629 (1883), a case that considered the actions of twenty white men in Tennessee who dragged four Black men out of jail where they were awaiting trial and beat them so severely that one of them died. The white men were tried under the Enforcement Act of 1871, also known as the Ku Klux Klan Act, and the unanimous decision included also judgment on the Fourteenth Amendment. The Court argued in *The Civil Rights Cases,* 109 U.S. 3 (1883) that the first section of the amendment placed a restraint on the states, not individuals.

This was an originalist interpretation of the Constitution, which did not allow for federal actions on or by individuals, even though the first section of the Fourteenth Amendment mentions persons several times. The Court clearly did not credit the Civil War and Reconstruction to have changed the meaning of the Constitution. Freedmen were not entitled to equal protection, and were excluded from postbellum progress. Neither side to this case seems to have noticed the second clause of the Fourteenth Amendment, which says that a state should lose seats in Congress if it excludes citizens from voting (Goldstone, 2011, 121–23).

More details of the Supreme Court, in its 8–1 decision in *The Civil Rights Cases,* 109 U.S. 3 (1883) makes the court's reasoning clear. The opinion by Justice Joseph P. Bradley held that the language of the Fourteenth Amendment prohibited denial of equal protection by a state and did not give Congress power to regulate private acts. The court claimed that it was private conduct by private individuals, not state law or action, that caused Black people to suffer. Section five of the amendment empowered Congress only to enforce the prohibition on state action. The Fourteenth Amendment did not authorize legislation by Congress on subjects that are within the domain of the state. Private acts of racial discrimination were treated as private wrongs that the national government was powerless to correct.

Bradley said the Constitution did "not authorize Congress to create a code of municipal law for the regulation of private rights," separate from "state" laws. Only state bodies were sufficiently "public" so as to be subject to regulation: "... individual invasion of individual rights is not the subject-matter of the [Fourteenth] Amendment. It has a deeper and broader scope. It nullifies and makes void all state legislation, and state action of every kind, which impairs the privileges and immunities of citizens of the United States, or which injures them in life, liberty or property without due process of law, or which denies to any of them the equal protection of the laws."

It does not invest Congress with power to legislate upon subjects which are within the domain of state legislation; but to provide modes of relief against state legislation, or state action, of the kind referred to. It does not authorize Congress to create a code of municipal law for the regulation of private rights; but to provide modes of redress against the operation of state laws, and the action of state officers, executive or judicial, when these are subversive of the fundamental rights specified in the amendment. Positive rights and privileges are undoubtedly secured by the Fourteenth Amendment; but they are secured by way of prohibition against state laws and state proceedings affecting those rights and privileges, and by power given to congress to legislate for the purpose of carrying such prohibition into effect; and such legislation must necessarily be predicated upon such supposed state laws or state proceedings, and be directed to the correction of their operation and effect. A quite full discussion of this aspect of the amendment may be found in *U.S. v. Cruikshank*, 92 U.S. 542; *Virginia v. Rives*, 100 U.S. 313, and *Ex parte Virginia*, Id. 339.

[...]

When a man has emerged from slavery, and by the aid of beneficent legislation has shaken off the inseparable concomitants of that state, there must be some stage in the progress of his elevation when he takes the rank of a mere citizen, and ceases to be the special favorite of the laws, and when his rights as a citizen, or a man, are to be protected in the ordinary modes by which other men's rights are protected. There were thousands of free colored people in this country before the abolition of slavery, enjoying all the essential rights of life, liberty, and property the same as white citizens; yet no one, at that time, thought that it was any invasion of their personal status as freemen because they were not admitted to all the privileges enjoyed by white citizens, or because they were subjected to discriminations in the enjoyment of accommodations in inns, public conveyances, and places of amusement. Mere discriminations on account of race or color were not regarded as badges of slavery (*Civil Rights Cases*, 109 U.S. 3 (1883)).

Justice Harlan dissented from the court's narrow interpretation of the Thirteenth and Fourteenth Amendments for all five cases. He argued that Congress had attempted to overturn states' refusals to protect rights for African Americans that white citizens took as a matter of course. He noted that private railroads were legally public highways and that a function of government was to protect and maintain highways for the use of the public. He observed that innkeepers have long been held to be "a sort of public servants" who did not have a right to deny anyone "conducting himself in a proper manner" admission to their establishments; and that public amusements operated under licenses coming from the State.

Harlan's views are important because they reveal contemporary opposition to Jim Crow laws. He was the only dissident on the court, and he did not convince anyone else to join him. But while the majority decision is long forgotten, Harlan's dissent anticipated views that have kept their force over time. His judgment included the following paragraphs:

> The opinion in these cases proceeds, as it seems to me, upon grounds entirely too narrow and artificial. The substance and spirit of the recent amendments of the Constitution have been sacrificed by a subtle and ingenious verbal criticism. "It is not the words of the law but the internal sense of it that makes the law. The letter of the law is the body; the sense and reason of the law is the soul." Constitutional provisions, adopted in the interest of liberty, and for the purpose of securing, through national legislation, if need be, rights inhering in a state of freedom, and belonging to American citizenship, have been so construed as to defeat the ends the people desired to accomplish, which they attempted to accomplish, and which they supposed they had accomplished by changes in their fundamental law. By this I do not mean that the determination of these cases should have been materially controlled by considerations of mere expediency or policy. I mean only, in this form, to express an earnest conviction that the court has departed from the familiar rule requiring, in the interpretation of Constitutional provisions, that full effect be given to the intent with which they were adopted.
>
> [...]
>
> I do not contend that the Thirteenth Amendment invests congress with authority, by legislation, to regulate the entire body of the civil rights

which citizens enjoy, or may enjoy, in the several states. But I do hold that since slavery, as the court has repeatedly declared, was the moving or principal cause of the adoption of that amendment, and since that institution rested wholly upon the inferiority, as a race, of those held in bondage, their freedom necessarily involved immunity from, and protection against, all discrimination against them, because of their race, in respect of such civil rights as belong to freemen of other races. Congress, therefore, under its express power to enforce that amendment, by appropriate legislation, may enact laws to protect that people against the deprivation, on account of their race, of any civil rights enjoyed by other freemen in the same state; and such legislation may be of a direct and primary character, operating upon states, their officers and agents, and also upon, at least, such individuals and corporations as exercise public functions and wield power and authority under the state.

[...]

Such being the relations these corporations hold to the public, it would seem that the right of a colored person to use an improved public highway, upon the terms accorded to freemen of other races, is as fundamental in the state of freedom, established in this country, as are any of the rights which my brethren concede to be so far fundamental as to be deemed the essence of civil freedom. "Personal liberty consists," says *Blackstone*, "in the power of locomotion, of changing situation, or removing one's person to whatever place one's own inclination may direct, without restraint, unless by due course of law." But of what value is this right of locomotion, if it may be clogged by such burdens as congress intended by the act of 1875 to remove? They are burdens which lay at the very foundation of the institution of slavery as it once existed.

They are not to be sustained, except upon the assumption that there is still, in this land of universal liberty, a class which may yet be discriminated against, even in respect of rights of a character so essential and so supreme, that, deprived of their enjoyment, in common with others, a freeman is not only branded as one inferior and infected, but, in the competitions of life, is robbed of some of the most necessary means of existence; and all this solely because they belong to a particular race which the nation has liberated. The Thirteenth Amendment alone obliterated the race line, so far as all rights fundamental in a state of freedom are concerned.

[. . .]

The supreme law of the land has decreed that no authority shall be exercised in this country upon the basis of discrimination, in respect of civil rights, against freemen and citizens because of their race, color, or previous condition of servitude. To that decree – for the due enforcement of which, by appropriate legislation, congress has been invested with express power – everyone must bow, whatever may have been, or whatever now are, his individual views as to the wisdom or policy, either of the recent changes in the fundamental law, or of the legislation which has been enacted to give them effect. For the reasons stated I feel constrained to withhold my assent to the opinion of the court. (Civil Rights Cases, 109 U.S. 3 (1883))

Justice Harlan was eloquent, but he was not persuasive; the Supreme Court was moving in the opposite direction. Not content with negating the first section of the Fourteenth Amendment as it related to freedmen, the Supreme Court reinterpreted this part of the amendment to provide more power to corporations. It is almost as if the Supreme Court asked: If the Fourteenth Amendment was not designed to help Negroes, who was it to favor? The answer: emerging robber barons.

The answer, however, was not given in a decision like *The Civil Rights Cases* (1883); it was a process that started at the same time as the decision on this case, a process that lasted to 1886. There was no decision with opinions and possibly minority opinions, but there apparently was a revolution of thought that evolved over time in mysterious ways until it appeared in official documents as a done deal. There is a legal history literature that attempts to reconstruct this momentous change in jurisprudence (Winkler, 2018; Foner, 1955).

Roscoe Conkling initiated this process in testifying before the Supreme Court in *San Mateo County v. Southern Pacific R.R.*, 116 U.S. 138 (1885). Conkling was a skilled politician who served in both the House and Senate. He was a firm supporter of the Radical Republicans during the Civil War. He was nominated to the Supreme Court twice, and he is the only person to turn down the nomination to lead the court after he had been confirmed. He was known as a great orator.

Conkling was representing the Southern Pacific Railroad in 1882, having resigned from the Senate. Charles Crocker was head of the railroad at that time, succeeded by Leland Stanford in 1885. Conkling had helped write the Fourteenth Amendment when he was in the Senate, and he referred to this process before the Supreme Court. He said that an early version of the amendment used the word "citizen" in place of "people" as appears in the amendment. He said this substitution was made and approved by the subcommittee with a unanimous vote. This change was made, according to Conkling, because the committee had received many complaints from businesses about discriminatory laws. His oral argument was written and is preserved in a volume on that decision in the Stanford University library and in an appendix to Graham's book. It contains memories of the drafting process and description of addressing businesses as people, but they are not connected or interactive (Graham, 1968).

According to Graham, Conkling's argument was an admission of a conspiracy of constitutional dimensions. The drafters of the Fourteenth Amendment wanted to protect corporations under the guise of protecting freedmen. The Congressional committee replaced "citizens" with "persons" with that goal in mind but did not tell anyone of their purpose or of the effect of their word choice. The constitutional rights of corporations were not mentioned in any of the ratification debates of the amendment.

This account is fanciful. Scholars who have gone over the Congressional records have failed to find evidence of this conspiracy to sneak new protections for corporations into the Constitution. Instead there was cooperation and perhaps an implicit conspiracy in the 1880s to alter the interpretation of the amendment. In addition to Conkling and his ties to the Southern Pacific Railroad, Justice Field was a personal friend of Leland Stanford, and the railroad itself was actively involved. The Fourteenth Amendment was converted from a shield for the rights of racial minorities – who received little actual protection from the Supreme Court – into a weapon that corporations could use against state laws regulating their activities (Collins, 1912; Graham, 1968; Winkler, 2018, Chapter 4).

It is unclear what happened between the 1882 arguments in *San Mateo County v. Southern Pacific R.R.*, 116 U.S. 138 (1885), and *San Clara County v. Southern Pacific R.R.*, 118 U.S. 394 (1886), but a headnote to the opinion in the latter case said: "One of the points made and discussed at length in the brief of counsel for defendants in error was that 'corporations are persons within the meaning of the Fourteenth Amendment to the Constitution of the United States.'" Chief Justice Waite stated: "The court does not wish to hear argument on the question whether the provision in the Fourteenth Amendment to the Constitution, which forbids a State to deny to any person within its jurisdiction the equal protection of the laws, applies to these corporations. We are all of the opinion that it does" (Winkler, 2018, 147).

Head notes are written by the court reporter and have little official meaning. The court reporter wrote to Chief Justice Waite to verify the content of the message: "Dear Chief Justice, I have a memorandum in the California Cases *Santa Clara County v. Southern Pacific &c* as follows. In opening the Court stated that it did not wish to hear argument on the question whether the Fourteenth Amendment applies to such corporations as are parties in these suits. All the Judges were of the opinion that it does." Chief Justice Waite responded: "I think your memo in the California Railroad Tax cases expresses with sufficient accuracy what was said before the argument began. I leave it with you to determine whether anything need be said about it in the report inasmuch as we avoided meeting the constitutional question in the decision" (Winkler, 2018, 151–53).

This redirection of the Fourteenth Amendment's people from Blacks to corporation was held to be obvious in future Supreme Court decisions without any actual Supreme Court decision. The process by which this was possible is even more problematical than the reconstruction of earlier bargaining by Roscoe Conkling. The Supreme Court heard 604 cases between 1868 and 1912. Fewer than 5 percent of them (28) involved African Americans, and the Blacks lost almost all of them. More than half of them involved corporations, which succeeded in striking down numerous state laws regarding their business. This redirection of the Fourteenth Amendment led to *Plessy v. Ferguson,* 163 U.S. 537 (1896) that approved segregation in education and other activities. According to the 1912 legal analysis that generated the data on cases, "The operation of the Fourteenth Amendment is an economic waste" (Collins, 1912, 160, 183).

The most recent and comprehensive legal history of Santa Clara summarized its conclusions after analyzing some effects of personifying corporations: "The Framers did not explicitly provide corporations with any rights in the text of the Constitution, and the document was *never formally amended* to extend rights to corporations, the way it was for women and racial minorities. Yet corporations had nonetheless secured nearly all the same rights as individuals through a two-centuries-long effort concentrated on the Supreme Court" (Winkler, 2018, 376, emphasis added).

### 3.3 JIM CROW LAWS

The 1877 compromise and the 1883 Supreme Court decision enabled Jim Crow laws to proliferate in states. Freed of federal interventions, Southern states were free to impose segregation and exclude freedman from voting. Woodward summarized this development eloquently:

> The South's adoption of extreme racism was due not so much to a conversion as it was to a relaxation of the opposition. All the elements of fear, jealousy, proscription, hatred, and fanaticism had long been present, as they are present in various degrees of intensity in any society. What enabled them to rise to dominance was not so much cleverness or ingenuity as it was a general weakening and discrediting of the numerous forces that had hitherto kept them in check. ... What happened toward the end of the century was an almost simultaneous – and sometimes not unrelated – decline in the effectiveness of restraint that had been exercised by all three forces: Northern liberalism, Southern conservatism, and Southern radicalism. (Woodward, 2002, 69)

The first step in the Jim Crow pattern of excluding Blacks from a dominant white society was to disenfranchise them. Various mechanisms were introduced. Property requirements and literacy tests were effective. Loopholes were introduced to allow poor whites to vote, as this was a racist rather than a class operation. Poll taxes also were introduced to exclude Negroes in several states. The results are shown in Table 3.2, which includes voting percentages of the relevant populations in the South from 1872 to 1916. About two-thirds of the populations voted

**Table 3.2** Percent voting in
presidential elections, 1872–1916

| Year | Percent voting |
|------|----------------|
| 1872 | 67.2 |
| 1876 | 75.1 |
| 1880 | 65.2 |
| 1884 | 64.3 |
| 1888 | 64.0 |
| 1892 | 59.4 |
| 1896 | 57.7 |
| 1900 | 43.5 |
| 1904 | 29.0 |
| 1908 | 30.8 |
| 1912 | 27.9 |
| 1916 | 31.6 |

*Source:* Burnham, 2010.

regularly in presidential elections through 1888. Then the voting proportion fell off sharply, coming to rest around one-third voting by 1904.
Despite the lack of Black voters, eleven Black members of Congress were
elected from the South from 1877 to 1901 and Blacks also sat in many
Sothern state legislatures (Aptheker, 1971, 103–3).

It is instructive to see an adaptation from the circular flow model
shown in Figure 1.1, as it applies to race and politics. The model in
Figure 1.1 clarified economics; this adaptation in Figure 3.1 conceptual-
izes political views after the Civil War. There are two opposite poles in the
model: education and voting, on the left and right. There are two circles
with each of these on one side of the figure. At the top of the circle,
I separate the circles into opposite "flows." The Black view is that freedmen should have the vote, as they had briefly in Reconstruction, in order
to establish and fund public schools. That is a counterclockwise trip
around the circle. It can be seen clearly in Frederick Douglass speeches.
For example, "I say to these gentlemen, I would not make illiteracy a bar
to the ballot, but would make the ballot a bar to illiteracy. Take the ballot
from the negro and you take from him the means and motive that make
for education. ... I would not make suffrage more exclusive, but more
inclusive. I would not have it embrace merely the elite, but would include

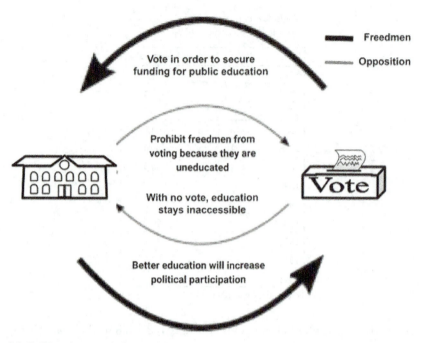

**3.1.** Politics of race and class model

the lowly. I would not only include the men, I would gladly include the women, and make our government in reality as in name a government of the whole people" (Douglass, 1894, "Lessons of the Hour").

The white view, represented in *Birth of a Nation*, is that freedmen should not be educated, as slaves before them were denied education, and their lack of education then can be used as an argument against allowing these ignoramuses to vote. This is exactly what happened under the Jim Crow laws at the end of the nineteenth century.

Slaves were not educated before the Civil War. In fact, it typically was against the law to educate slaves. Enslaved persons therefore were restricted to unskilled work on plantations and other farms. During the Civil War, the Freedmen's Bureau ran schools for freedmen. But they had little effect because both they were largely urban, while most freedmen were rural, and the Freedmen's Bureau did not last very long. In 1880, almost 80 percent of Southern Blacks were illiterate, compared to 20 percent of whites. These proportions fell over time, but the illiteracy rates were still 50 and 10 percent for Blacks and whites in 1900 (Margo, 1990).

States began to spend more on education after 1900, but only for whites. Louisiana, for example, had a sharply rising educational budget for whites after 1900 but no rise at all in the budget for Black education. Blacks continued to suffer from low school budgets, large classes, and badly paid teachers before World War I.

Blacks who got an education somehow were barred by racial prejudice from using their education to get a good job. Blacks could not get jobs as farm managers. They could not lease land on better terms. And other, more urban, jobs were also closed; a white artisan could not hire a Black assistant and sell his goods to other whites. As other Blacks saw that you could not get a better job from education, they lost interest in gaining more education. Jim Crow laws and public policies carried over later when Blacks moved North in the Great Migration and had trouble finding work (Kousser, 1974; Ransom and Sutch, 1977; Margo, 1990).

Violence ranged from threats of death to murder all through this period. "For example, George Barber of South Carolina fled his home in Fairfield County, South Carolina, over Ku Klux Klan death threats in 1871. James Alston and his family were threatened by the Ku Klux Klan in 1869 and wounded by them two years later. Theophilus Steward of Georgia received death threats after he asserted that juries should involve both Black and white citizens. Charles Caldwell of Mississippi was murdered in 1875, months after he escaped an armed mob by fleeing to Jackson, Mississippi. Simon Corker of South Carolina was killed in 1876 by Democrats in the Ellerton riot as he was kneeling in prayer after being captured" (Logan, 2018).

The Florida Secretary of State Jonathan Gibbs estimated that more than 50,000 Blacks had been murdered in the South by 1887. Official testimony and many local news accounts highlight the ubiquity of racial violence in the South, with much of it overtly political. From the late 1860s to the 1880s, voting turnout by Blacks fell by more than 20 percent. By the 1890s, funding for Black schools was greatly diminished; taxes were lower, and the range of services and public goods offered in the South was much less than in other parts of the country (Margo, 1990; Logan and Temin, 2020).

The period from the end of the Civil War to the end of the nineteenth century continued a range of racialized violence throughout the

United States. The Indian Wars, violence against the Chinese in the West, and attacks along the Mexican–American border all featured dimensions of racial conflict. Southern white conservatives employed terrorism to restore the old racial order that had defined the South before the Civil War. Their campaign rallied support not only for the policy, but for broad efforts to roll back the gains Blacks had made after the War. These included Black enfranchisement, Black political leadership, expanded federal authority, and an altered public finance structure.

The best data we have on lynching begins in the Gilded Age and extends through the early twentieth century. The Historical American Lynching (HAL) Project covers the time period from 1882 to 1930. This is the best existing dataset publicly available, which has the most extensively verified and publicly available set of lynchings in the literature. "The lynchings in the database conform to the NAACP definition of lynching which requires a murder to meet the following criteria to be counted as a lynching: (1) there must be evidence that someone was killed, (2) the killings must have occurred illegally, (3) three or more persons must have taken part in the killing, and (4) the killers must have claimed to be serving justice or tradition" (Cook 2012).

"The HAL database contains detailed information on 2,805 lynchings including name, race and gender of the victim, the race of the mob, the stated reason for the lynching, the date of the lynching and the county in which the lynching took place. These observations include the vast majority of the recorded lynchings. 88 percent of victims were Black, while only six percent of the mobs were Black. Only four of the 155 Black lynch mobs targeted white victims. Most of the lynching victims were Black victims of interracial violence. The white lynching victims were almost entirely victims of intra-racial conflicts" (Historical American Lynching (HAL) Data Collection Project, nd; Cook, Logan, and Parman, 2018).

The distribution of lynching over time is given in Figure 3.2. The HAL data reveal that lynching reached a peak in the middle of the 1890s with over 100 lynchings per year. And lynching continued each year through 1930, the end of the period covered by the data. The geographical distribution of lynching across the Southern states is also shown in Figure 3.2. The number of lynchings across counties in the state varied

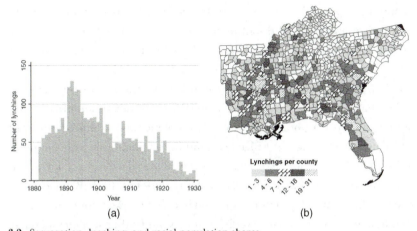

(a)                                                           (b)

**3.2.** Segregation, lynching, and racial population shares.
*Source:* Cook, Logan, and Parman, 2018; Historical American Lynching (HAL) Data Collection Project. Note that Virginia is not included in the lynching data. (a) Number of lynchings by year, 1882–1930; (b) lynchings per county, 1882–1930. A black-and-white version of this figure will appear in some formats. For the color version, refer to the plate section.

widely, and they were not concentrated in urban areas. They were a predominantly rural phenomenon (Cook, 2012).

Slavery's geographic spread and constraints on free Blacks' mobility had led to resulted heavy concentrations of the Black population in the cotton-growing regions of the South at the time of emancipation, an area that corresponds closely to the areas in Figure 3.2 with high Black population shares today.

In 1880, 90 percent of the Black population still lived in the South and 87 percent of the Black population lived in a rural area. In contrast, only 24 percent of the white population lived in the South. This meant that Black individuals were disproportionately affected by constraints on economic opportunity in the rural South. Over the second half of the nineteenth century, Southern and Northern incomes diverged significantly, with average income in the South only half of the national average by 1900. The destruction of the Civil War and the emergence of Northern manufacturing while the Southern economy remained predominantly agricultural contributed to these trends (Kim and Margo, 2004; Logan and Temin, 2020).

The Black population therefore found itself in a region with far less economic opportunity than the rest of the nation. More importantly, economic opportunity was further restricted by individual and institutionalized racism and political disenfranchisement. Discrimination in hiring by employers and intimidation of Black workers through violence placed Black workers at a direct disadvantage in the labor market. Mob violence against Southern Blacks was higher when the price of cotton was declining and inflationary pressures were rising, making the economic conditions of white agricultural workers more precarious. This violence also extended to attacks on economically successful Black communities, infamously with the political coup in Wilmington, North Carolina, in 1898 and the destruction of the Greenwood community during the Tulsa race riot in 1921. Beyond labor markets, Blacks also faced discrimination in credit markets, for example the discrimination in merchant credit, hospitals, and other facilities (Tolnay and Beck, 1992; Olney, 1998; Dymski, 2006; Logan and Temin, 2020).

Black individuals living in the same cities and towns as white individuals had access to far fewer resource schools as a result of discriminatory restrictions on the right to vote. Despite large Black populations in the South at the start of the twentieth century, Blacks had no political power due to disenfranchisement and voter intimidation. Without the power of the ballot box, Black Southerners remained subjected to overtly racist policies constraining their economic opportunities (Margo, 1982; Carruthers and Wanamaker, 2013; Baker, 2015; Logan and Temin, 2020).

The Populist attempt to introduce a third party into American politics started early in the 1890s. This predominantly was a white movement, but Blacks also were interested in having a voice. The problem was that Populists were interested in economics, while Blacks were interested in finding a way to acquire some political voice in a racist society. Perhaps the best summary is that Populism came from the white West, while Blacks were still in the racist South. The Colored Farmers National Alliance and Cooperative Union came into being around 1890, but the white Populists and corporations both wanted to distance themselves from the "race problem" that was the focus of the Colored Farmers Alliance. As historian Lawrence Goodwyn stated, "Before the Black man could worry about injustice, he had to worry about survival" (1978, 121).

The 1896 presidential contest between William Jennings Bryan and William McKinley, supporting silver and gold respectively, showed a new form of political contest based on corporate politics. Massive amounts of money were raised and spent in a coordinated Republican campaign of political salesmanship. A press bureau coordinated newspaper defenses of the gold standard, and churches stressed the morality of sound money. The Chicago office spent a million dollars, and the New York office spent $1.6 million. Standard Oil and J. P. Morgan each contributed a half million dollars. Mark Hanna and railroad executives raised more from similar corporate sources. The Republican majority in the 1896 presidential election was to prove one of the most enduring majorities in American political history. With only a temporary split in 1912, the Republican dominance persisted until the Great Depression of the 1930s. Blacks were excluded from this white consensus, but the Republicans reached out to other minorities in consolidating their political dominance (Goodwyn, 1978, 279–85).

The onset of corporate money vanquished the free silver movement and consolidated the Compromise of 1877. White supremacy took charge, and Blacks were confirmed in their subordinate status. Blacks were no longer slaves, but they lacked any way to make their desires heard politically. They could protest individually, but violence and lynching contained or eliminated individual acts. Jim Crow laws translated the presidential victory into state laws, and Blacks were reduced to a condition that resembled slavery more than the full citizenship embodied in the Civil War Constitutional amendments.

There were several other turning points in 1896 as well. Gold was discovered in western Canada, and the resulting inflation satisfied the Populists desire for an end to the long deflation. Prices rose after 1896, and Southern agriculture was profitable. Blacks continued to be share-croppers and cash tenants, although the plantation economy was being replaced by more paying jobs. Only a few poor whites went to the cities to work in the new cotton factories. The industry was successful, but it remained small. The South did not gain much from the southward migration of the cotton industry because it did not make the machinery or develop any new ancillary technology. And the labor skills acquired in the cotton industry did not help workers expand into other urban activities (Hofstadter, 1956, 109; Mandle, 1978; Wright, 1986, 125).

In addition, the Supreme Court weighed in again to enforce segregation of the races. The court ruled in *Plessy V. Ferguson,* 163 U.S. 537

(1896) that segregation was legal. The opinion stated that, "The object of the [Fourteenth] Amendment was undoubtedly to enforce the absolute equality of the two races before the law, but in the nature of things, it could not have been intended to abolish distinctions based upon color, or to enforce social, as distinguished from political equality, or a commingling of the two races upon terms unsatisfactory to either." And Justice Harlan objected again:

> But in view of the constitution, in the eye of the law, there is in this country no superior, dominant, ruling class of citizens. There is no caste here. Our constitution is color-blind, and neither knows nor tolerates classes among citizens. In respect of civil rights, all citizens are equal before the law. The humblest is the peer of the most powerful. The law regards man as man, and takes no account of his surroundings or of his color when his civil rights as guaranteed by the supreme law of the land are involved. . . . In my opinion, the judgment this day rendered will, in time, prove to be quite as pernicious as the decision made by this tribunal in the *Dred Scott* case (*Plessy, 163 U.S. at 543–44, 559*).

*Plessy v. Ferguson* dominated Southern life for half a century. It allowed the states to generalize their segregation to all kinds of activities and keep voting by Blacks to miniscule numbers. Only the shocks from two world wars would arouse the rest of the country to attempt to limit the damage to the citizens freed by the Thirteenth Amendment to assume full citizenship rights. See Part II of this book.

The 1896 election giving Republicans control of national policy lasted for many years. The solid Democratic South confined its interests to regional issue like Jim Crow laws. McKinley was assassinated in 1901 and Theodore Roosevelt succeeded him. Roosevelt was a Progressive president, and he converted rural Populists to his urban Progressivism, although the two movements overlapped. The movement's most important success was to break up Standard Oil in 1911, although most of the parts have recombined recently into ExxonMobil (*Standard Oil Co. of New Jersey v. United States*, 221 U.S. 1 (1911)).

Theodore Roosevelt often is remembered as a reformer but his reforms typically assumed that the community's welfare could be served by satisfying the concrete needs of business. Roosevelt liked informal agreements between businesses and the federal government. In addition, he supported regulation and administrative commissions to supervise the economy. It was no accident that the results of Progressivism were what major business interest desired (Kolko, 1963).

This did not mean a cessation of racial prejudice, but rather a codification of Jim Crow laws that excluded freedmen from voting. American racism was stimulated by a wave of imperialistic adventures. People defending their countries in the Caribbean and the Pacific were demonized as inferior races. As public opinion supported late nineteenth-century imperialism, it lumped freedmen with people the United States said could not govern themselves. Anglo-Saxon superiority around the world flooded public and academic discussion. If Americans thought it proper to deprive inferior people of self-government, why wasn't it proper to do the same in South Carolina and Mississippi?

American imperialism and the jingo press that accompanied conquests in Cuba and the Philippines encouraged Jim Crow attitudes and laws. The prejudice against dark-skinned people was general among the population, and Jim Crow laws were in concert with the general tenor of public discourse at the end of the nineteenth century (Aptheker, 1971, 107).

The first step was the total disenfranchisement of Black people. Southerners accepted this disfranchisement as a reform without a second thought. The standard forms of disfranchisement were invented by Mississippi and adopted with varying additions by other states. The plan set up barriers to voting such as property or literacy, and added loopholes in the barriers like residence requirements that only some white men could use to vote. The Mississippi law was adopted by South Carolina in 1895, Louisiana in 1898, North Carolina in 1900, Alabama in 1901, Virginia in 1902, Georgia in 1908, and Oklahoma in 1910. In addition to these rules, these states as well as other formerly Confederate states adopted poll taxes. Jury duty was linked to voting rights.

To raise the barrier higher, Southern Democrats inaugurated white primaries to select candidates. The primary rules often excluded minority participation, and they became white man's clubs. Democrats adopted statewide primaries in South Carolina in 1896, Arkansas in 1897, Georgia in 1898, Florida and Tennessee in 1901, Alabama and Mississippi in 1902, Kentucky and Texas in 1903, Louisiana in 1906, Oklahoma in 1907,

Virginia in 1913, and North Carolina in 1915. Racial violence accompanied these reforms as shown in Figure 3.2. Lynching was only one form of anti-Black harassment and attack that spread widely and became the norm rather than an exception in the Gilded Age (Woodward, 2002, Chapter 3).

These state actions were amplified at local levels in ways that set examples for African Americans seeking more integration into the white power structure. A dominant example is the massacre of Blacks in Wilmington, North Carolina, in 1898 that overturned a democratically elected biracial urban government and murdered hundreds of Blacks.

Wilmington was North Carolina's largest city and had a majority Black population, including numerous Black professionals and businessmen, and a rising middle class. By the early 1890s, more than 30 percent of the city's skilled craftsmen were Black. But property ownership among them was rare, and per capita wealth for Wilmington Blacks in the county was less than 10 percent of the wealth of whites. This experience shows the gains and problems that freedmen faced when they moved to the city. They could succeed by using their skills in the city, but the contrast between the extent of white and Black property ownership was as severe in urban North Carolina as in rural Georgia, which is shown in Table 3.1.

Table 3.1 shows that while half of rural Blacks were laborers were workers, less than 20 percent of whites were ordinary workers in 1910. And while 40 percent of whites owned property, only about 7 percent of Blacks owned property. In between these extremes, various kinds of tenancy were common for both races.

The Wilmington Republican Party was biracial in membership. Black people in Wilmington were elected to local office on a fusion ticket, and gained prominent positions in the community in 1892. Three of the city's aldermen and one of the five members on the constituent board of audit and finance were Black. And Black people also were justices of the peace, deputy clerks of court, street superintendents, coroners, policemen, mail clerks, and mail carriers.

The Wilmington "riot" or coup of 1898 took place in Wilmington, North Carolina, on Thursday, November 10. White Southern Democrats organized a mob of 2,000 Democrats to remove the city's elected, fusionist government. The mob expelled opposition Black and white political leaders from the city, destroyed the property and businesses of Black citizens built up since the Civil War, including the only Black newspaper in the city, and killed about 300 people. The coup affirmed that whiteness eclipsed legal citizenship, individual rights, and equal protection under the law that Blacks were guaranteed under the Fourteenth Amendment, and it anticipated the Tulsa massacre of 1921 (Cecelsky and Tyson, 1998; Prather, 1998; Staples, 2006).

A detailed narrative by a Pulitzer Prize–winning author concluded that Wilmington whites overthrew a legally elected government by force. The whites murdered Black men with impunity and robbed Black citizens of their right to vote and hold public office. They forcibly removed elected officials from office and banished them forever. They drove hundreds of Black citizens from their jobs and homes, turning a Black-majority city into a white citadel. "The killings and coup in Wilmington inspired white supremacists across the South. No one had ever seen anything like it" (Zucchino, 2020, 329).

A book on the populist revolt that climaxed in the 1896 election was published at the same time as Woodward's *Strange Career of Jim Crow*. It revealed how far the Northern and Western regions had diverged from the static South. And it barely mentioned Negroes as an occasional distraction to the revolt. Hofstadter's *Age of Reform* stands as a monument to white history. It is interesting to read his exposition as an example of white history.

Hofstadter opened his survey of Populism by saying it assumed harmony between the land and people. The United States was full of good land and all people should be prosperous as a result. The prosperity should encourage a natural harmony among people. While there are corrupt people in all groups, the overall view should be of harmony between groups. The Republican view of opposition between workers and farmers and between workers and employers was misplaced.

The way to get to these harmonious states was to oppose all injustice by opposing the power of the rich. Hofstadter quoted a populist writer as saying, "With the destruction of the money power, the death knell of gambling in grain and other commodities will be sounded; for the business of the worst men on earth will have been broken up, and the mainstay of the gamblers removed. It will be an easy matter, after that greater spoilsmen have been shorn of their power, to clip the wings of the little ones" (Hofstadter, 1956, Chapter 2).

The Populists were more afraid of Jewish entrepreneurs than Black freedmen. The fear of Wall Street is an old one. The Populists, hurt by the deflation started after the Civil War that was harming them, supported monetizing silver as an inflationary antidote. They had not adopted this position as they formulated their ideas, but they adopted the silver program in 1896 as an election issue. They adopted the program of William Jennings Bryan, "You shall not crucify mankind upon a cross of gold" (Bryan, 1896).

### 3.3.1 BIRTH OF A NATION.

A revised view of Reconstruction was formed to accompany the Jim Crow laws of the Gilded Age. The Dunning School at Columbia University presented this view in historical settings and a very popular film by D. W. Griffith, *The Birth of a Nation*, disseminated it for other audiences at the start of World War I. The "Dunningite" analysis of Reconstruction was the primary stimulus of the movie. Griffin said that his film was a vehicle "to tell the truth about the War between the States. . . . It hasn't been told accurately in history books. Only the winning side in the war ever gets to tell its story" (Lehr, 2014, 127–29).

*The Birth of a Nation* was an American silent epic drama film directed and produced by Griffith that starred Lillian Gish. The screenplay was adapted from the novel and play, "The Clansman," by Thomas Dixon Jr., and was released on February 8, 1915. It was a commercial success and led to the rebirth of the Ku Klux Klan months later. It also was shown to President Wilson, members of his family, and members of his Cabinet at the White House (Lehr, 2014).

Wilson's attitude toward the movie has been highly disputed. He received many letters protesting his reported endorsement of the movie. When officials called at the White House to add their protests, Wilson's private secretary showed them a letter he had written to Massachusetts Representative Thomas Thatcher on Wilson's behalf claiming that the President had been "entirely unaware of the character of the play [movie] before it was presented, and has at no time expressed his approbation of it." The fact that he had shown it at the White House was described as a gesture toward an old friend. But Dixon quoted Wilson in his autobiography as saying, when Dixon suggested the White House showing, Wilson had told him that he was "pleased to be able to do this little thing for you, because a long time ago you took a day out of your busy life to do something for me." Dixon had suggested Wilson for an honorary degree from Dixon's alma mater, Wake Forest College (Dixon Jr., 1984).

But there is compelling evidence that Wilson knew the character of the play in advance. Dixon and Wilson had both been graduate students in history at Johns Hopkins University, and in 1913 Dodd had dedicated his historical novel about Lincoln, *The Southerner*, to "our first Southern-born president since Lincoln, my friend and college mate, Woodrow Wilson." Considering Dixon's career and the notoriety attached to his play, "The Clansman," Wilson must have known the general tenor of the film. The movie quoted Wilson on American history and mentioned the title of his book, *History of the American People*. Wilson ran for election on a platform of fair dealing with Blacks, but he fired all Black government employees upon taking office (Aptheker, 1971, 159).

General public enthusiasm for the film crowded out voices of protesters and critics. The NAACP had just been organized and a broader civil rights movement barely existed. Screenings in New York City and Los Angeles were highly successful. In Los Angeles, people jumped to their feet and cheered at the climax of the film, which depicted the Klan as rescuing the South from the chaos of Reconstruction. One critic said, "The worst thing about *The Birth of a Nation* is how good it is." President Wilson himself reportedly styled the movie as "history written in lightning" (Brody, 2013; Lehr, 2014, 156).

In Boston, William Monroe Trotter and other Black leaders organized protests to the movie and denounced its version of history. Trotter and others were arrested and the Boston screenings went on as scheduled. The protests, though, were not without effect. After Boston, some theater owners elsewhere demanded significant edits to the film before they'd screen it; occasionally it was even banned outright (Lehr, 2014, Chapter 13).

Griffith thought he was dramatizing history about the Civil War and Reconstruction. The story he told was widely accepted at the time, although it has been completely debunked since. The core of the story was that Reconstruction was a disaster because former slaves were some kind of lower form of life. Griffith portrayed the emancipated slaves as heathens unworthy of being free and uncivilized. They were primarily concerned with passing laws enabling them to marry white women and prey on them. That was the bigoted, racist state of mind of the time.

It is interesting to see how Griffith incorporated racism into his film. The scene where interracial marriage was legalized appears in the movie as an example of a Black legislature. The scene is focused on a Black representative who takes off his shoes while the legislature is in session so the leader has to say shoes are required. But this was still a legal decision. To make a modern comparison, the Congressional passage of the 2017 tax cut showed confusion and turmoil as the Senate leadership rammed the bill through passage. But the tax cut became law even though almost none of the legislators could have read the bill. A neutral observer would have said the Reconstruction act legalized interracial activity; only a racist would say that act was null and void.

Why was the legislative session in the film? It looks like a set-up for the scene often replayed now where KKK members surround a Black man (who was played by a white man in Black-face) who seems terrified. The scene comes in scene 19 of 24 scenes, around halfway through the second half of the movie; it is reproduced in the book about the film. The Black man appears to be a rapist who was caught by the KKK, but he was on trial for having proposed to a white woman. The panel of his declaration said only, "... I want to marry ..." It was not even a full proposal. The white woman is shown as running away and jumping off a cliff to her death (Lehr, 2014, 271).

And the trial scene is echoed later in the film as the elected mulatto lieutenant governor tries to force the daughter of the Radical Republican representative from the North into marriage. She is shown tied up and gagged, while her radical father attempts to discourage the mulatto's plans. Viewers of these scenes clearly see attempted rapes in progress, although they are set up to avoid any actual sexual attacks. Both the lieutenant governor and Gus, played by a white actor in Blackface, "are portrayed as hyper sexed." This is in sharp contrast to the war and later scenes where men routinely shoot and kill each other (Lehr, 2014, 133).

For all its repulsive imagery, the film was a great leap in cinema. Griffith did things that hadn't been done before in silent cinemas, which heightened the power, impact, and drama of the film. Attracted by

Southern California's even climate, Griffith moved his operations there from the East Coast. In time the rest of the industry followed him, leading to the birth of Hollywood. The film's title, *The Birth of a Nation*, echoes the political scientists quoted at the beginning of this chapter who asserted that the 1877 compromise that ended Reconstruction restarted democracy in the United States (Lehr, 2014).

Josephson noted at the end of *Robber Barons* that the robber barons gave generously to Theodore Roosevelt's 1904 re-election campaign. He cited Frick, Harriman, Morgan, Stillman, and several others. Living in the second Gilded Age, we are familiar with the very wealthy influencing elections. No one should be surprised that they were doing this in the first Gilded Age. The results in Figure 3.3 show the geographic spread of the 1904 presidential election. Roosevelt won all the North, while the South went just as uniformly to the Democratic candidate. A picture like this is worth a thousand words. It is as if the Civil War had never taken place or the views represented in *Birth of a Nation* dominated the South (Josephson, 1934, 450).

At the other end of American society, Green Cottenham, a twenty-two-year-old Black man in Alabama, was arrested on March 30, 1908. The sheriff arrested him for a random offense, and a judge convicted him of vagrancy, the all-purpose offense that exploited the loophole in the Thirteenth Amendment: "Neither slavery nor involuntary servitude, *except as a punishment for crime whereof the party shall have been duly convicted,* shall

**3.3.** 1904 United States presidential election.
*Source:* https://en.wikipedia.org/wiki/1904_United_States_presidential_election. A black-and-white version of this figure will appear in some formats. For the color version, refer to the plate section.

exist within the United States." As a modern author amplified this observation:

> Cottenham had committed no true crime. Vagrancy, the offense of a person not being able to prove at a given moment that he or she is employed, was a new and flimsy concoction dredged up from legislative obscurity at the end of the nineteenth century by the state legislatures of Alabama and other southern states. It was capriciously enforced by local sheriffs and constables, adjudicated by mayors and notaries public, recorded haphazardly or not at all in court records, and most tellingly in a time of massive unemployment among all southern men, was reserved exclusively for Black men. Cottenham's offense was Blackness. (Blackmon, 2008, 1)

Cottenham was sentenced to thirty days of hard labor, which then was extended to almost a year because he could not pay the fees levied on all prisoners by the sheriff, deputy, court clerk, and witnesses. He was leased to US Steel in the form of the Tennessee Coal, Iron, and Railroad Company, which would pay off Cottenham's fees by monthly payments. He was sent to a mine near Birmingham where he was chained inside a barracks at night and required to spend most of his time digging and loading coal. His daily requirement was to load eight tons of coal, and he was whipped if he did not meet his quota. He was subject to sexual predation by other prisoners and to diseases that swept through the occupants of the mine. Cottenham lasted less than six months in the mine, and he was buried hastily.

The Texas prisons leased out workers from the end of the Civil War until 1912. The prisons grew rapidly after the war, from about 500 prisoners in 1870 to 3,500 in 1912. The prisoners were close to 60 percent of the total throughout these years. Black Texans, like Cottenham in Alabama, were outside protection of the law. The law acted upon them, and they had no ability to fight back (Walker, 1988).

This harsh form of Jim Crow laws continued up to World War II and was revived by President Nixon as his War on Drugs generated mass incarceration, widely known as the New Jim Crow (Duvernay movie, *thirteenth*; Stokes, 2007; Blackmon, 2008; Alexander, 2010).

# PART II

# THE TWENTIETH CENTURY

# CHAPTER 4

# Wars and the Great Migration

## 4.1 THE GREAT MIGRATION

White Americans became industrial leaders and representatives of the dominant country through world wars and a worldwide depression in the first half of the twentieth century. The peace treaty after World War I led to World War II the same way constitutional compromises led to the Civil War. Meanwhile, Black American families peacefully moved north and west through this aggregate turbulence of the white economy. How did an assassination in Eastern Europe lead to an internal American migration that transformed American race relations from a regional into a national problem? Delving into European history helps us understand how America was caught up in this conflict and continue the beginning of the story that began with French intervention in a conflict between Britain and its colonies.

Conditions before the war are illustrated by a famous quote from John Maynard Keynes in a book on the effects of World War I: "The inhabitant of London could order by telephone, sipping his morning tea in bed, the various products of the whole earth, in such quantity as he might see fit, and reasonably expect their early delivery on his doorstep" (Keynes, 1919, 9). Keynes described London, but his words could have been applied to New York and other large American cities. He went on to say that this person could invest in any part of the world as well. The international trade that started with cotton and progressed to wheat and steel had broadened to include a wide variety of goods and services.

The thirty years from 1914 to 1945 appear in mainstream history as full of conflict, killing, war, and depression. There were two wars so large that they are spoken of as world wars. As a result of World War I, the notable empires of the nineteenth century – Russian, Ottoman, Austro-Hungarian, and German – were all transformed, typically by breaking up. These dramatic events would have large consequences for American domestic and foreign policies over time, but they were overwhelmed in the short run by the Versailles Treaty that ended World War I.

The treaty that ended World War I was based on a nineteenth-century model that distributed blame for starting the war and imposed a large charge on Germany. Germany was forced to pay massive reparations to the victors. These reparations led to a French military incursion into a German hyperinflation and eventually to a worldwide depression. The economic downturn was so large and long-lasting that it is known as the Great Depression. Economic problems led to the rise of Fascism in Italy and Germany. These fascist countries came into conflict with the United States, which resulted in World War II. American history is dominated by these dramatic and draconian events, but the American involvement in these European and ultimately Asian conflicts was gradual.

It makes sense to think of these thirty years as a single war with a temporary truce in the middle. While other countries were involved, the main protagonists were Germany and the United States. And since the "truce" that separates the two world wars was filled with conflicts of various sorts, considering this era as a single conflict clarifies the history of both Europe and the United States. Churchill called it the Second Thirty Years' War, and Lionel Robbins said that the Great Depression in 1934 was not the fourth but rather the nineteenth year of the economic and conflictual crisis (Robbins, 1934; Churchill, 1948; Maier, 1988).

African Americans were not involved in the international relations and political decisions that drove the wars and warlike interlude. They instead were dealing with Jim Crow laws and segregation in the South. For Blacks, the increasing international strife in World War I increased nativist politics and led to dramatic changes in immigration policy. The internal conditions in the United States had changed, and the area of the country with ample industry now had unmet demand for labor. Blacks chose a peaceful way to respond to these white impositions on their lives: They went north.

The North had abolished slavery and fought a civil war to make this a national decision. Surely the North would be a more hospitable place for Blacks than the unrepentant South. Thus was born a migration that would continue into the postwar period. It would be a larger population movement than the gold rush of the 1850s or the abandonment of the Midwest dust bowl in the 1930s. About half the Black population would eventually spread over the North and West as six million Blacks participated in the Great Migration (Wilkerson, 2010, 10).

Note the contrasting reactions to adversity between American whites and Blacks. The whites chose military action; the Blacks chose voluntary migration. The whites chose violence to resolve problems; the Blacks chose peaceful actions to escape their problems. While whites projected their violence onto Blacks, African Americans wanted only to be included in profitable activities. This demographic upheaval may have been the most important event of mid-twentieth-century America, and it demonstrated again that the portrayal of African Americans in *Birth of a Nation* was a projection of white violent fantasies onto people of color.

Ira Berlin argued that this was one of four great migrations that African Americans have made. As noted in Chapter 1, the first one was the Middle Passage where Africans were brought to the Southern US by force. The second was the move to Texas and the West as agriculture expanded in the first half of the nineteenth century and slaves were moved west to grow more cotton. Both of these migrations were made under compulsion by whites and were ones in which the African Americans had no voice. The third and fourth migrations were the result of Blacks migrating by their own volition. The third migration (famously known as the Great Migration) was the greatest one according to Berlin's list because it involved six million people – far more than in any of the other great migrations. The final migration, still in progress, is the recent increase of immigration from Africa and the Caribbean to the United States. Like the Middle Passage, all these dark-skinned immigrants were known as "Africans" only when they reached the United States and were grouped together with previous immigrants (Berlin, 2010).

We can understand the omission of the Great Migration in most American histories by revisiting *Birth of a Nation*. As described in the last chapter, the film portrayed Blacks (played by whites in blackface) as unintelligent and sexually aggressive toward white women, that is, as potential ruffians and rapists. It presented the white version of Reconstruction – which differs greatly from the more balanced view in Chapter 2 – and saw the Ku Klux Klan as heroes. President Wilson called it "history written with lightning." It also presented Black political leaders as incompetent buffoons, implicitly supporting Black disenfranchisement (Lehr, 2014).

This movie would be an interesting episode in economic history if it were not for the opening speech of candidate Donald Trump in 2016, a century after the initial screening of *Birth of a Nation*. As he announced his candidacy he said, "When Mexico sends its people, they're not sending their best .... They're bringing drugs. They're bringing crime. They're rapists. And some, I assume, are good people." The accusation that Latino immigrants bring crime is refuted by data showing that immigrants commit fewer crimes than Americans, and the accusation of them being rapists is baseless.

Trump probably was reaching back to his memory of *Birth of a Nation* and its portrayal of African Americans as aspiring rapists. He revealed two supports of his views that have been borne out in his presidential policies. The first step is to link Blacks and "browns," that is, African Americans and Latino Americans, together. As noted earlier, this aggregation of poor vagrants goes back to eighteenth-century England. The second step is the projection of white violence onto these other populations. It is not unusual for people to project their faults onto others; it is dangerous to race relations now.

The Great Migration was a peaceful response to Southern persecution of Blacks and increasing labor market demand in the North and Midwest. It contrasted sharply with the world wars going on for thirty years and went against the earlier portrait of Blacks as the violent ones. We need to recall not only the violence and depression of the world wars but also the large-scale demographic movement of six million people that transformed racism from a regional to a national problem.

Northern jobs were attractive to Southern Blacks because their agricultural work was declining. The boll weevil was destroying crops, and the weather caused flooding. Black Southerners were an underclass subject to violent attacks justified by Jim Crow laws. Miners leaving

Alabama's steel towns went to coal mining towns of Kentucky and West Virginia. Floating agricultural workers, as opposed to sharecroppers, were much more likely to be driven north by the boll weevil. And most interregional migrants were single men without responsibilities (Wright, 1986, 204–5).

The migrants were not only fleeing agriculture. The nascent industrialization of the South had fallen on hard times. The Southern cotton industry succeeded enough to threaten the health of the New England cotton industry, but it did not expand beyond that. It was a solitary industrial movement without a background of skilled workmen and independent craftsmen. The high-pressure steam engine was produced by many small craftsmen in New England at the beginning of the nineteenth century, but the South did not have the background for industrialization at the end of the century. Railroads were scarce, and cotton planters were not interested in altering their pattern of exporting their crops.

The Southern steel industry faced discrimination from the North through what was known as Pittsburgh Plus pricing, which can be described as follows: Steel companies sold their rolled steel products at prices, freight on board (FOB) Pittsburgh, plus freight from Pittsburgh to the point of delivery. Shipment, however, was made from the mill or warehouse most convenient to the delivery point. In other words, the Pittsburgh Plus freight was a fictitious freight, not actually paid, nor representing an actual transportation cost. To a customer in South Bend, Indiana, rolled steel was sold FOB Pittsburgh, plus the fictitious freight from Pittsburgh to South Bend, less the actual freight to South Bend from Chicago, the point of shipment. In all cases the Pittsburgh Plus price was a "delivered" price, and the amount of fictitious freight added, or actual freight deducted, was not disclosed to the buyer.

At Birmingham, Alabama, a somewhat different practice prevailed. The Pittsburgh Plus system was inaugurated in the Birmingham district, but the Steel Corporation was forced to abandon it in 1908. Instead of the fictitious freight from Pittsburgh to Birmingham, an arbitrary amount, known as the "Birmingham Differential," was added to the FOB Pittsburgh price, although the steel is furnished from the respondent's Birmingham plant. This differential charge originally was $3.00 per ton, and it was increased in 1910 to $5.00 per ton. In the territory surrounding Birmingham, steel was sold on the Birmingham Differential price, unless such price exceeded the Pittsburgh Plus price, in which case the latter was used (Mechem, 1924).

Added to the problems that limited the Southern textile industry, the Birmingham steel industry had to contend with prejudicial pricing. US Steel was formed in 1901 as a trust, and its industrial basis was in and around Pittsburgh. Management had little interest in Southern industrial development, and it favored its main plants. This resulted in an increase in the size of the Great Migration, where workers who could not find jobs in the South moved north.

Northern industries sought workers from the South during World War I because they could not find European immigrant workers as immigration was restricted by warfare, and they were happy to loan Black workers money for the train trip north. They treated Southern Blacks like the European indentured servants that provided labor for eighteenth-century Southern farmlands. The Great Migration did not start earlier, despite the pressure on Southern Blacks, because Northern factory owners preferred to hire white workers. The war forced them to look beyond their preferred sources for workers (Collins, 1997).

The Great Migration was large, and the demand from Northern war industries was large. Migrants went from both rural and urban areas in the South and included freedmen with varied skills and occupations. The Great Migration was a key force decreasing the Black–white differences in earnings. The gains were commensurate with the gains made by late nineteenth-century European immigrants, revealing again the great regional gaps in incomes among American regions. The demand for wartime workers was strong enough that differences between migrants did not affect the gains that each migrant made. And while Northern demand was overwhelming, there were differences between Northern firms. Only some firms hired the Black migrants, and they had to learn how to integrate them into their workforce (Whatley, 1990; Collins and Wanamaker, 2014, 2015).

The Great Migration coincided with an increase in residential segregation in both the South and the North. New evidence of this phenomenon from 1880 to 1940, before and during the Great Migration, comes from a detailed understanding of how the US Census used to be conducted. Census enumerators went door-to-door collecting household data. (Census forms are mailed or even emailed today.) Using the census manuscript, economists were able to discern if adjacent entries were for households of the same race.

This measure has two advantages over more traditional measures for cities or wards. It can be used for rural as well as urban neighborhoods. In addition, the emphasis on neighbors focuses our attention on personal interactions, for it is easier to be prejudiced against Blacks if you do not have any contact with Blacks. If you have Black neighbors whom you see and talk with regularly, it is harder to generalize and lump all Blacks together into an undesirable group.

This measure shows that Southern cities were and remained the most segregated in the nation. And it shows that segregation increased in both the South and the North from 1880 to 1940. This increased segregation was present in both rural and urban neighborhoods. This finding implies that Black migratory patterns not only increased segregation in the North but also allowed increasing separation by race in the South. In essence, while the Great Migration helped close the Black–white gap in income, it also appears to have exacerbated Black–white geographic sorting. White flight from Northern cities would sustain of this continued racial segregation (Logan and Parman, 2017).

Returning to the world wars, it is essential to understand how the European powers in 1914 formed into two competing sets sharing common aims and enemies. These two sets became, by August 1914, Germany and Austria-Hungary on one side and Russia, France, and Great Britain on the other. The Triple Entente involving Britain, France, and Russia is comparable to the alliance between Germany and Austria-Hungary, but the Entente was not an alliance of mutual defense. Britain accordingly felt free to make its own foreign policy decisions in 1914.

The heir presumptive to the Austro-Hungarian throne was shot dead on June 28, 1914, in Sarajevo by one of a group of assassins coordinated by a Bosnian Serb. The assassination of the heir to the throne so close to when the aged Austrian emperor was likely to hand over the crown was seen as a challenge to Austrian policy. It triggered the July crisis in international diplomacy that turned a local conflict into a European, and then a worldwide, war in August (Clark, 2013).

The European war settled down into a trench stalemate in northern France and a German attack on shipping. The United States was initially neutral, but was forced into the war as German U-boats sank the *Lusitania* and some merchant ships. Woodrow Wilson called for war against Germany in early 1915 and began an American military buildup. The expansion of military production at the same time as increased recruiting of soldiers led to an expanded demand for labor in war industries.

Wilson loaned billions of dollars to Britain in 1917 as the war dragged on and Britain ran out of money. Then Wilson took the United States into the European conflict to break the stalemate in the trenches. He acted like the French in our revolutionary war, who entered to break the stalemate between Britain and its colonies as neither side was willing to surrender. As noted in Chapter 1, it is far easier to start wars than to end them. The United States provided the extra manpower and resources to convince the Germans to seek an armistice.

The trenches in northern France commanded a lot of attention, but the war also raged in the East. Churchill's misguided attack on the Gallipoli was a famous disaster. The result was the collapse of several empires. The German Empire survived in truncated form, even though Poland was carved out of its eastern provinces. The Austro-Hungarian Empire – where the assassination that set off the war occurred – collapsed entirely, as did the Ottoman Empire. The Russian Empire was transformed by the victory of the Communists in 1917 and its withdrawal from the war. All of these dramatic and sudden changes had implications for the interwar period, and the rise of communism affected American politics as well (Feinstein, Temin, and Toniolo, 2008).

## 4.2 THE VERSAILLES TREATY

World War I ended with the Treaty of Versailles in 1919. There had been no fighting in Germany, and the German population did not have any experience with the military fighting or defeat. This ignorance played an important role in the subsequent history of the treaty, which blamed

Germany for the initial attack and took full advantage of the German defeat. John Maynard Keynes was a member of the British delegation to Versailles who resigned in disgust and wrote a best-selling book, *The Economic Consequences of the Peace*, denouncing what went on there. The book has become a classic and is still read today (Keynes, 1919).

Keynes focused on the requirement that Germany pay reparations to the Allies as it had received reparations from France after Germany defeated France in 1870. He was very colorful and emphatic in his portrayal of the negotiators. He described Clemenceau as an elder statesman who dominated the negotiations and stayed focused on the long struggle between France and Germany. He wanted a Carthaginian peace that would hobble Germany for the next round, including the return of Alsace and Lorraine, taken by Germany after the 1870 war with France. Lloyd George wanted only to win reelection, advocating that reparations should pay for the entirety of the British war effort. He succeeded in adding Article 231 to the peace treaty: "The Allied and Associated Governments affirm and Germany accepts the responsibility of Germany and her allies for causing all the loss and damage to which the Allies and Associated Governments and their nationals have been subjected as a consequence of the war imposed upon them by the aggression of Germany and her allies." Woodrow Wilson was character-ized as a Protestant minister, proclaiming his Fourteen Points and remaining ignorant of details. One of the points was to form the League of Nations, precursor to the United Nations formed after World War II, which the US Congress rejected after the treaty was signed. Wilson also was a Southerner who liked *Birth of a Nation*.

The Americans refused to forgo repayments of the loans they had extended during the war. The US secretary of the treasury David Houston wrote in a March 19, 1920, letter,

> As to the general cancellation of intergovernmental war debts suggested by you, you will, I am sure, desire that I present my views no less frankly than you have presented yours. Any proposal or movement of such char-acter would, I am confident, serve no useful purpose. On the contrary, it would, I fear, mislead the people of the debtor countries as to the justice and efficacy of such a plan and arouse hopes, the disappointment of which

could only have a harmful effect. I feel certain that neither the American people nor our Congress, whose action on such a question would be required, is prepared to look with favor upon such a proposal. (Finch, 1922, 618)

Keynes worried about the resumption of the German economy under reparations. In order to pay reparations, the Germans would have to restrict domestic consumption to allow some of the production to be used for reparations. Coal and steel would be exported as part of reparations, and any cash payments in German currency would be used to purchase other German goods. The resulting pressure on German consumption would prevent Germany from fully recovering from the loss of the war and defeat peaceful coexistence in Europe. This concern was later recognized as the "transfer problem" that accompanies all foreign obligations (Keynes, 1919).

The leadership of the German army deflected criticism of the army by popularizing what has been called the stabbed-in-the-back accusation. The theory was promulgated by Ludendorff, chief of staff to General Hindenburg, the leader of the German army and future president of the Weimar Republic in 1933. When asked why Germany lost the war, Ludendorff replied with his list of excuses, including that the home front failed the army. His questioner asked him: "Do you mean, General, that you were stabbed in the back?" Ludendorff's eyes lit up and he repeated, "Yes, that's it, exactly; we were stabbed in the back." Ludendorff publicized the phrase in the military, and he let it be known among the general staff that this was the "official" version. Hindenburg proclaimed this phrase in a publicized statement, and it was picked up by right-wing organizations. This publicity led to the stab-in-the-back accusation being disseminated throughout German society, contributing strongly to German anti-Semitism. The accusation set up a conflict that tormented Germany until fascists replaced the republic in the depths of the Depression to avenge this stab in the back (Wheeler-Bennett, 1938).

In the short run, the German government tried to evade paying reparations by expanding their currency. If they inflated their currency, they could lower the amount of goods they sent abroad. The cause of the dizzying acceleration of prices confused many of those who lived through it, but it was in fact relatively straightforward. The Versailles Treaty imposed a huge debt on Germany that had to be paid in gold or foreign currency. With its gold stock reduced, the German government attempted to expand its use of German currency, but the resulting increase in the supply of German marks caused German prices to rise.

German prices of goods rose rapidly, increasing the cost of operating the German government, which could not be financed by taxes because they would be payable in the ever-falling German currency. As the German people realized that their money was rapidly losing value, they tried to spend it quickly. That increased the velocity of money and caused an ever-faster increase in prices, creating a vicious cycle that led to a loaf of bread that cost around 160 Marks at the end of 1922 costing 200,000,000,000 Marks by late 1923. A dollar was worth four trillion marks (Widdig, 2001; Fergusson, 2010).

The German government could not pay reparations in its worthless currency, leading the French to occupy the Ruhr, Germany's coal and steel center. The hyperinflation was ended with the aid of an American loan that was part of the 1924 Dawes Plan to reorganize reparations payments. The plan provided an end to the Allied occupation and a staggered payment plan for Germany's payment of war reparations. Because the plan averted a serious international crisis, Charles Dawes received the Nobel Peace Prize in 1925 for his work (Schuker, 1976).

The Dawes Plan let the United States offset its government war loans to the Allies by a new private loan to Germany. Germany used the Dawes loan to pay reparations to England and France, who then could repay their wartime loans from the United States. This complicated financial circle meant that Keynes' fear of continued German depressed consumption was not realized. It was a far more complicated financial arrangement than the proposal summarily rejected by Secretary Houston described earlier. And it also meant that the prosperity of the 1920s in both Germany and the United States easily could be vulnerable to German anger at paying reparations.

Keynes summarized his argument as follows:

The [Versailles] Treaty includes no provisions for the economic rehabilitation of Europe – nothing to make the defeated Central Empires into good neighbors, nothing to stabilize the new States of Europe, nothing to reclaim Russia, nor does it promote in any way a compact of economic solidarity amongst the Allies themselves; no arrangement was reached at Paris for restoring the disordered finances of France and Italy, or to adjust the systems of the Old World with the New. (Keynes, 1919, Chapter 6)

The end of World War I brought several years of turbulence to America. The first agitators were women. The National Woman's Party focused on the passage of a national women's suffrage amendment in 1916. In 1917 more than 200 supporters were arrested as they picketed the White House. Some protested who were on a hunger strike were force fed after being sent to prison. The two-million-member National American Women's Suffrage Association then made national suffrage its top priority. After an intensely contested series of votes in Congress and in state legislatures, the Nineteenth Amendment became part of the United States Constitution on August 18, 1920. It states, "The right of citizens of the United States to vote shall not be denied or abridged by the United States or by any State on account of sex." Black women, however, did not get to vote until 1965, and their jury duty was deferred until then as a result (Kerber, 1998; Terborg-Penn, 1998; Weiss, 2018).

The destruction of empires noted earlier brought the Soviet Union into being. Fear of communism set off a wave of FBI raids, known as the Palmer Raids, in 1919 and 1920 by the Department of Justice to capture and arrest suspected leftists – mostly immigrants, anarchists, and communists – and deport them from the United States. Attorney General A. Mitchell Palmer directed the raids and arrests, including 3,000 of the latter. Five hundred and fifty-six foreign citizens were deported, including a number of prominent leftist leaders, although officials at the Department of Labor, which had authority over deportations, largely frustrated Palmer (Finan, 2007).

Similar tensions between Black and white people soon after World War I also were active dramatically in the early 1920s, notably in the 1921 race riot in Tulsa, Oklahoma. Tulsa was no aberration. It followed the pattern of the Wilmington massacre of 1898 described in Chapter 3 and was a similar violent white response to Black attempts to prosper.

The riot occurred on May 31, 1921, following the publication of an inflammatory article in a local newspaper about a young Black man allegedly assaulting a white woman. A group of Black Tulsans came to the jailhouse that night to protect the accused. Their presence and their assertion of Black rights threatened white rule, and a group of equally defiant white men met them. A shot was fired, and the riot began (Ellsworth, 1982).

White rioters descended on the city's Greenwood District, a Black community considered so affluent that Booker T. Washington had called it "Black Wall Street." Greenwood had about 10,000 residents and a vibrant commercial district. Soon a local National Guard unit with a water-cooled Browning machine gun aided the rioters. According to eyewitness accounts, planes circled overhead, shooting people as they fled and dropping incendiary devices. Then several thousand white men – armed with guns, torches, and kerosene – invaded Greenwood in the early morning hours. By the end of the rioting, more than 1,200 houses had been destroyed. Most of the institutions integral to Black life in Tulsa – including churches, schools, a library, and many stores – were destroyed.

Some 300 people were killed, but the attack was less about mass killing than the physical and spiritual destruction of a community. The message from Tulsa to Oklahoma and other states was stark: this is what happens to Blacks who get out of line, just like the 1898 Wilmington massacre. No white person was ever held responsible, and the city and state left the Black community to rebuild on its own.

The riot was shrouded in silence for many decades. It was not taught in Oklahoma schools or mentioned in newspapers. It was not acknowledged by state or local officials. Blacks kept the memory alive in their Juneteenth holiday that was nominally about the end of slavery in 1865 Texas. The state of Oklahoma created a commission to study the massacre under pressure from Black leaders and other advocates. The commission generated newspaper investigations, documentaries, and a spate of books around 2000 (Cobb, 2020; Fenwick, 2020).

After the upheaval of fears of domestic and foreign enemies, the United States experienced a decade of prosperity after the war, while Germany enjoyed a shorter period of prosperity after its hyperinflation. The United States used this time to change its immigration system.

Expanding the resistance to equality of African Americans shown in Wilmington and Tulsa, the United States sought to restrict immigration from other non-European countries. The 1924 Immigration Law prevented immigration from Asia, set quotas on the number of immigrants from Eastern Europe and the Eastern Hemisphere, and provided funding and an enforcement mechanism to carry out the long-standing ban on other immigrants. It set a total immigration quota of 165,000 for countries outside the Western Hemisphere, a reduction of 80 percent from the pre-World War I average. Quotas for specific countries were based on 2 percent of the US population from that country as recorded in 1890, and the law provided funding and legal instructions to courts of deportation for immigrants whose national quotas were exceeded. The purpose of the Immigration Law was to preserve the ideal of American homogeneity as a white protestant nation, and Congressional opposition was minimal. Ironically, immigration restrictions encouraged the Great Migration to continue.

Blacks in Chicago organized Black banks during the 1920s, but the banks did not prosper. Their clientele was too poor and too homogenous to provide opportunities for loans in their segregated cities. White banks prospered, while Black ones languished, and migrants coming north in the Great Migration could not borrow from either type of bank (Baradaran, 2017, Chapter 3).

Affluent white Americans enjoyed the boom of the 1920s, thinking it would continue for a long time, while Southern Blacks continued to move north. They discovered resistance, as we will see more in the next chapter, but we can see it here with the struggle for union membership by Pullman porters. Under the leadership of A. Philip Randolph, the Brotherhood of Sleeping Car Porters tried to unionize Pullman's porters. They met fierce resistance from George Pullman's sons and struggled with the company for a dozen years. Randolph named the new union to distinguish it from the company and the company union. The aim of the new union was to raise wages, eliminate tips, which had become a way for the Pullman Company to keep wages down, and reduce work hours, since porters also had to do double shifts without adequate rest.

The new union had to be very secretive about its aspirations as the company had its own union and was brutal against any independent one.

To oppose the new union, the Pullman Company supported Black churches and employed them in more numbers. The company encouraged Black workers to join other organizations, often with payments, to wean them away from the new union. The company also used force, beating up supporters and organizers of the new union. Randolph opposed the company's publicity against the union as represented by a Black Chicago periodical: "The real reason [for opposing us] is the advertising you are getting from the Pullman Company to oppose the movement. ... You are just like the little boy on the knee of the ventriloquist. ... Without the slightest compunction or scruples, you are willing to betray and sell out your race for a miserable mess of pottage" (Tye, 2004, 141).

Randolph appealed to the Interstate Commerce Commission about the Pullman Company's use of tips, but he lost. He threatened a strike against the company in 1927. A mediation board ruled in favor of Randolph's union because of its large membership, but the Pullman Company refused to negotiate. The Brotherhood postponed the strike, and watched its membership decline from over 4,000 in 1928 to 2,000 in 1929 and 1,000 in 1931. Many observers heralded the decline and urged the Brotherhood to admit defeat and disband, but Randolph and his fellows kept on in these lean years.

He appealed to the American Federation of Labor (AFL) for support, which admitted the Brotherhood into its thirteen-union strong conglomerate in 1929. This was how the AFL dealt with Black unions, limiting their jurisdiction and independence. It also vastly increased the unions' dues to the AFL compared to a united union.

After Franklin Roosevelt became the US President in 1933, he passed the Emergency Railroad Transportation Act, but this act was not applied to the Brotherhood because it was not a railroad company. Randolph and his allies went to work, and they generated a law in 1934 that required companies to negotiate with unions chosen by a majority of their workers. The Pullman Company tried to negotiate with its company union, but the Brotherhood demanded a secret ballot. The Brotherhood won the ballot easily, and it also was admitted to the AFL with a single international charter. The company finally agreed to negotiate with the Brotherhood in 1935. Lots of bargaining still lay ahead, but times had changed. And the company had gotten used to Randolph's efforts. A contract finally took effect in 1937.

The Brotherhood was the first Black union to displace a company union. It was the first Black union admitted as a full-fledged member of the AFL, and it was the most successful Black union ever. The Brotherhood had some advantages that enabled this success. It was fighting against a single company, not a whole industry. It represented a homogeneous workforce, and communication was easy among these workers as they traveled around. Nonetheless, this was a great victory over the long odds emanating from Jim Crow laws and other impediments to Black inclusion in the mainstream of the American economy (Tye, 2004, Chapter 4).

Randolph wanted to have a march for Black rights in Washington during 1941 – after World War II started, but before the United States was involved – and he met with President Roosevelt to discuss it. The president did not want the march and instead issued Executive Order 8802 in June 1941, saying: "As a prerequisite to the successful conduct of our national defense production effort, I do hereby reaffirm the policy of the United States that there shall be no discrimination in the employment of workers in defense industries or government because of race, creed, color or national origin." The president formed the Fair Employment Practice Commission to enforce the order, but it had no budget. The march was postponed, and there would not be another executive order desegregating the US government until after the war (Bates, 2001, 160–61).

## 4.3 GREAT DEPRESSION, NEW DEAL, RACIAL PROBLEMS

The depression that started at the end of the 1920s, produced by recessions in both Germany and the United States, came as a surprise. In contrast to the policies recommended by Keynes, politicians did not try to expand the economy when economic activity declined. Heinrich Brüning, the German prime minister, and the US President Hoover held to earlier theories and tried to balance their governments' deficits as taxes decreased. Hoover, to his credit, tried to keep wages from falling, but this band-aid was not effective.

Germany experienced a slowdown before the United States and before American lending to Germany ceased. Wealthy Americans loaned money to Germany coupled with plans for the German economy. The Young Plan of 1930 modified the earlier Dawes Plan by lowering Germany's reparations and making provision for borrowing to pay them in times of economic difficulty. The government of Germany under Chancellor Brüning suffered as a result of its deflationary policies through two elections in 1930 that resulted in strong showings by the Nazi Party. Brüning's government, reappointed by Hindenburg, responded by redoubling its resolve to continue down the path of austerity so resoundingly repudiated by the electorate. Brüning increased taxes and slashed government spending and intergovernmental transfers. Germany raised money by borrowing from French banks.

Confidence in the German economy rose, and the Reichsbank gold reserves rose from 2,216 million Reichsmarks at the start of 1931 to 2,323 million by the end of March. The Nazis walked out of the Reichstag in protest to Brüning's budget, which enabled it to be passed by the remaining members of the Reichstag. Brüning then persuaded the Reichstag to recess until October. All seemed to be going well, and the French banks became eager to loan to Germany.

Then it all fell apart. Many economic historians argue that German banks took on too much risk and collapsed when depositors withdrew money from the banks to avoid a collapse, like the 1937 banking crisis described in Chapter 2. These scared depositors would withdraw sight accounts – what we call demand deposits – because they can be accessed quickly. And banks would call in loans to build up their reserves again. But demand accounts did not fall in the Grossbanken or Kreditbanken that made up almost all of German banking. Time deposits in the Grossbanken fell in June and July 1931, but not in smaller banks. Depositors seemed to be shifting their bank accounts, but there was no evidence of a bank panic. Danatbank, noted by some economic historians, had no deposit changes different from the other Grossbanken.

There was no rush to withdraw the most liquid deposits and no interbank pressure to recoup reserves. Banks were not calling in loans that forced borrowers to withdraw deposits at other banks; the Grossbanken were not acting in a banking panic. They showed no effect of the collapse of the Viennese Creditanstalt in May that caused panic in Austria. And the Grossbanken as a group were not in any observable trouble. German savings banks also did not experience unusual withdrawals.

Instead, politics raised its ugly head. The German cabinet approved in March to a customs union between Germany and Austria. The Versailles Treaty barred Germany from incorporating Austria, and the Treaty of St. Germain that accompanied the Versailles Treaty blocked Austria from making an agreement that might threaten its sovereignty. The customs union scared the French and extinguished their desire to loan Germany money to tide over the current depressed economic activity. American banks sided with France, and the Bank of International Settlements delayed consideration of German plans (Ferguson and Temin, 2003).

The German finance minister quietly told the Chancellor in March that the budget deficit was growing faster than anticipated. It had reached 2.2 billion Reichsmarks in May. Brüning needed support from a fragmented Reichstag for any proposed budget, and street violence was increasing. There seemed only one way out of this budget disaster, and Chancellor Brüning decided that Germany could not pay any more reparations. German newspapers suspected this decision in late May, and Brüning announced it on June 5.

Reichsbank gold reserves are shown in Table 4.1. They had remained constant and increased slightly in the first half of 1931, fell precipitously in the two weeks following Brüning's announcement. The reserves stabilized in July around three-fifths of its previous level. The Reichsbank raised its discount by 2 percentage points in an attempt to sustain its gold reserves.

Brüning's action precipitated a financial crisis, and it stabilized his political support. But the economic calm lasted only a few days. The Nordwolle, a large textile firm that held large cotton inventories, was in trouble with the higher interest rates from the Reichsbank. The Danatbank, which had invested heavily in Nordwolle, was in trouble as well. And the Reichsbank, trying to save the Reichsmark, could not act as a domestic central bank.

The Federal Reserve Bank in Washington, DC, responded to all this by raising its interest rate by 2 percentage points, like the Reichsbank.

Table 4.1 Weekly reserves at the Reichsbank (million RM), 1931

| Date | Gold | Foreign Exchange | Silver |
|------|------|------------------|--------|
| 7.1.31 | 2216 | 400 | 161 |
| 13.1.31 | 2216 | 268 | 200 |
| 23.1.31 | 2244 | 196 | 207 |
| 31.1.31 | 2244 | 199 | 172 |
| 7.2.31 | 2244 | 198 | 178 |
| 14.2.31 | 2254 | 181 | 192 |
| 23.2.31 | 2266 | 175 | 202 |
| 28.2.31 | 2285 | 166 | 160 |
| 7.3.31 | 2285 | 189 | 166 |
| 14.3.31 | 2286 | 209 | 179 |
| 23.3.31 | 2286 | 223 | 196 |
| 31.3.31 | 2323 | 188 | 157 |
| 7.4.31 | 2344 | 166 | 143 |
| 15.4.31 | 2345 | 114 | 187 |
| 23.4.31 | 2348 | 132 | 207 |
| 30.4.31 | 2368 | 158 | 168 |
| 7.5.31 | 2370 | 169 | 175 |
| 15.5.31 | 2370 | 171 | 186 |
| 23.5.31 | 2370 | 197 | 200 |
| 30.5.31 | 2390 | 186 | 174 |
| 6.6.31 | 2300 | 113 | 177 |
| 15.6.31 | 1766 | 104 | 199 |
| 23.6.31 | 1411 | 93 | 214 |
| 30.6.31 | 1421 | 300 | 78 |
| 7.7.31 | 1422 | 371 | 84 |
| 15.7.31 | 1366 | 244 | 79 |
| 22.7.31 | 1353 | 160 | 74 |
| 31.7.31 | 1368 | 246 | 45 |

Source: *Die Bank*, 1931, various issues; Ferguson and Temin, 2003.

It was the single largest rise in the short-term interest rate ever taken. The rise in interest rates deepened the American recession and turned it into the Great Depression; the financial tangle in America and Europe created by the Treaty of Vienna came back to sting the American economy (Ferguson and Temin, 2003).

This view of the German financial crisis was disputed by Isabel Schnabel. She was named professor of financial economics at the University of Bonn in 2015 and became a member of the German Council of Economic Experts in 2014. Her views are worth considering. She stated, "Because deposit withdrawals and reserve losses were tied together in a vicious circle and foreign support was unobtainable, the banking panic translated into a run on the German currency and resulted in the factual abandonment of the gold standard." She continued by saying, "the crisis of 1931 would not have occurred if the banks had acted with caution in the 1920s" (Schnabel, 2004).

As discussed in the last few pages, there is no evidence at all in the banking data of a crisis before the suspension of reparations in early June 1931, and the data in her response in no way contradicts the data presented here. She also singled out the problems of the Danatbank after Nordwolle failed in mid-June. In her words, "When the currency problems came to a head, the Reichsbank could not keep up its liquidity support to the great banks, which triggered the breakdown of the Danatbank." In other words, she claimed that the failure of Nordwolle and the Danatbank resulted from the currency crisis, and not its cause. Schnabel got lost in the identification problem (Schnabel, 2004).

To provide additional evidence that there was a currency crisis in June 1931 that was not caused by German banks, Figure 4.1 shows the price of Young Plan bonds in Paris during that time. These were the bonds issued to loan Germany for its reparations that it could not pay. Their price was stable in May 1931. No sign of a banking crisis. But the price took a nosedive at the beginning of June, when Brüning's plan to renege on reparations became known in late May.

The collapse of the German mark scared bankers and merchants around Europe; which currency would collapse next? Central banks raised their rates as the Reichsbank had done to convince currency traders to hold onto their currencies, but they were not all successful. The Bank of England gave up the struggle in the fall of 1931 and abandoned the gold standard. This decision shortened the depression in Britain. The Bank of England did not understand this immediately and kept interest rates high to rebuild its gold reserves. They abandoned this idea in a few months, reduced interest rates, and started economic

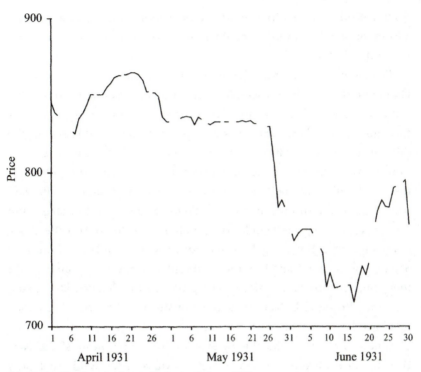

**4.1.** Young Plan bond prices in Paris, April–June, 1931.
*Source:* Ferguson and Temin, 2004.

recovery in Britain a year before the other countries that had designed the Versailles Treaty.

The Federal Reserve Bank in the United States raised its interest rate by 2 percentage points, following the Reichsbank as noted earlier. The Fed saved the dollar, and President Herbert Hoover continued his deflationary policies after the German financial crisis. The economy continued to contract into 1932 and led to Roosevelt beating Hoover in the 1932 presidential election. Roosevelt campaigned on a policy of balancing the budget, like Brüning and Hoover, but uncertainty and bank failures accelerated in the months between the election and his taking office in March 1933. The Fed experienced a run on the dollar as Roosevelt took office, producing a banking crisis that led him to shut down all American banks in what he labeled a "bank holiday" as he took office. Hoover's policies had turned the American recession at the end of the 1920s into the Great Depression of the 1930s. The economic decline produced unemployment that only ended around 1940 with the advent of the last military conflict of World War II (Temin, 1989; Bernanke, 1992).

The Depression led to a change in American leadership, as it led to Hitler and the Nazi Party ascendancy in Germany. President Roosevelt – abandoning his campaign promises – tried to stimulate the economy through his New Deal. (Some contemporaries had trouble seeing the difference between Hitler and Roosevelt in 1933.) But the 1877 Compromise that ended Reconstruction had reinstated the politics of the slaveholding antebellum South as described in Chapter 3. Federal troops had been withdrawn from the South, and the landholding white residents, no longer slaveholders, rapidly moved to control the Black population with Jim Crow laws and Ku Klux Klan violence. Southern Senators were nominated by the landholders without opponents, and they consequently had seniority and power in the Senate. They made sure that Roosevelt's New Deal did not disturb their Southern race relations.

Southern Senators did this by avoiding the application of the New Deal to agriculture and personal service where most Southern Blacks were employed. Instead, they insisted on local administration of the federal laws so that their associates could resist aid to Blacks, and they also refused to allow any anti-prejudice clauses into Roosevelt's bills. The aid that was accepted by the South still applied Jim Crow doctrines, leaving many Blacks out of policies designed to aid them in a depressed agricultural setting. Blacks from the Great Migration also typically were the last hired and first fired, suffering twice from lack of government help and business practices (Sundstrom, 1992; Logan and Temin, 2020).

We can see this process in detail, thanks to the pioneering research of Ira Katznelson. As he wrote: "The New Deal lawmaking would have without the active consent and legislative creativity of these southern members of Congress." And these Southern members of Congress perpetuated Jim Crow and Southern agriculture until after World War II (Katznelson, 2013, 17).

One of the most important laws passed in Roosevelt's New Deal was the National Industrial Recovery Act (NIRA) in 1933. It passed over opposition by some Southerners and Republicans who were not very concerned because industry had not come to the South very much. They saved their fire for the National Recovery Administration (NRA), established to administrate the NIRA. NRA codes were established for all essential industries, but not for domestics or farmworkers. Workers in these sectors consequently never had a minimum wage or maximum hours of work. The definition of agriculture was extended to include canning, which had many Black workers. Roosevelt delegated details to the secretary of agriculture, who excluded citrus packing and cotton spinning from the NRA codes. In Delaware, fertilizer production industries with most Black workers were classified as Southern to permit them to pay lower wages than white workers in other industries that were considered Northern (Linder, 1987).

The Supreme Court, reliving its late nineteenth-century conservatism, declared the NIRA unconstitutional in 1935. Congress replaced it soon by the National Labor Relations Act (NLRA), also known as the Wagner Act, in 1935. That law established National Labor Relations Board that continued and extended the supervision of union formation – which was largely restricted to the North with very few Black members. The CIO, which organized industrial unions, broke off from the AFL in 1935. Black unions were more welcome in the CIO than they had been in the AFL.

Roosevelt signed the Social Security Act in 1935. The bill likely would not have passed if it had included farmworkers and maids as recommended by the president. Committees in both houses of Congress with strong representation from the South deleted these low-paid workers from the bill. The Senate committee even added that this bill "does not relate to employment as a domestic servant or as an agricultural laborer" (Katznelson, 2013, 252–60).

This pattern extended to the Tennessee Valley Authority (TVA), created in 1933 as part of the New Deal to coordinate planning for a river basin that crossed state lines. Southern Congressmen welcomed the support and assumed correctly that the TVA would not upset the existing racial order. A postwar assessment of the TVA found that "the typical position of the TVA agriculturalist is one of white supremacy" marked by references to "good and bad niggers." Blacks were relegated to the most menial positions and barred from vocational schools and training sessions for better jobs. And TVA communities were rigidly segregated with no Blacks at all in a planned model community (Logan and Temin, 2020).

This view emerged visually in a book, *Let Us Now Praise Famous Men*, by James Agee and Walker Evans. Agee and Evans traveled the South in 1936 to provide a photographic and verbal description of "an average white family of tenant farmers." They interviewed three families and wrote a book containing fine photographs and readable prose that is justly famous. However, you cannot tell from either the pictures or the prose that there were any Black tenant cotton farmers at all (Agee and Evans, 1941).

The depressed 1930s turned into the prosperous war years of the 1940s. World War II began on September 1, 1939, with the invasion of Poland by Germany and subsequent declarations of war on Germany by France and the United Kingdom. Japan invaded China in 1937. And in December 1941, Japan launched a surprise attack on the United States as well as European colonies in the Pacific. Following an immediate US declaration of war against Japan, supported by a declaration of war from Great Britain, the European Axis powers quickly declared war on the United States in solidarity with their Japanese ally.

The Western Allies invaded German-occupied France in 1944, while the Soviet Union regained its territorial losses and turned toward Germany and its allies. The war in Europe ended with the invasion of Germany by the Western Allies and the Soviet Union, culminating in the capture of Berlin by Soviet troops, the suicide of Adolf Hitler, and Germany's unconditional surrender on May 8, 1945. President Truman, who had just taken office after President Roosevelt died, decided to drop the atomic bombs on the Japanese cities of Hiroshima and Nagasaki on August 6 and 9, 1945, to forestall a bloody invasion of Japan. After that attack, Japan announced its intention to surrender on August 15, 1945, cementing total victory in Asia for the Allies.

Once the conflicts of the 1930s turned into the warfare of the early 1940s, Blacks joined the American armed forces as if they had not been excluded from many of its benefits. The armed forces were not integrated until after the world wars ended, and Blacks were shuttled into all-Black units. They performed well, as Blacks had done in the Civil War.

And they hoped when they returned to civilian life that their contributions to the American victory would be appreciated. The Allies demanded an unconditional surrender to defeat the Nazis. Instead of waiting for internal political changes among the losers, the Allies demanded that they would supervise a new political structure. This was largely directed at the Nazis in Germany who were widely abhorred for their murder of six million Jews. It seems odd that white Americans could be disturbed by foreign discrimination against Jews while ignoring their own discrimination against Blacks.

Congress passed a bill to introduce a federal ballot in 1943 during World War II that ensured voting rights to all veterans and abolished the poll tax imposed by several Southern states as well. It passed easily in the wartime spirit, but a Southern requirement was added saying that the ballot was required to be provided by states rather than the federal government. The federal ballot was abandoned in 1946 (Katznelson, 2013, 220–22).

When African-American veterans returned to the South, Southerners treated them as if they had never gone away. They were subject to harassment, violence, and even death on their return from the battlefields. In many ways, this reproduced the experience Black Civil War veterans faced when they returned home. Like the Great Migration, these white refusals to accept Black veterans as part of American society are largely missing from mainstream economic histories.

There were waves of violence when the expectations of Black veterans after they left the military met the ingrained habits and beliefs of Southern civilians. Reports of racial violence surged into the NAACP – whose membership increased greatly during the war – and the Department of Justice. Isaac Woodard, Jr., who had worked in a segregated support unit in New Guinea where he was promoted to the equivalent of a sergeant and received several awards for his service, returned to Georgia in early February 1946. He was demobilized and returned by bus to his home. Since buses lacked toilets at that time, Woodward asked to be let off briefly at some stops to relieve himself, which irritated the bus driver. After the driver yelled at him, Woodard said, as he recounted later, "Talk to me like I am talking to you. I am a man just like you."

The bus driver went off to find a policeman to deal with Woodard and found Lynwood Shull, head of a tiny police force in a small city. As Woodard tried to explain things, Shull pulled out a blackjack and hit Woodard over the head. Blackjacks at that time were baton-like weapons, with metal packed into the leatherhead and a coiled-spring handle that gave a great force to the head, frequently causing injuries. After a disputed scene at the jail, Shull stuck Woodard several times in his eyes with the end of the blackjack so violently that he broke his weapon. He blinded Woodard, which led to consequences that will be described in the next chapter.

Another incident happened later in February when a Black veteran complained about poor service from a local business. A white employee objected to the veteran's attitude, and the ensuing fight escalated out of the store and produced efforts to lynch the veteran. He and his family fled from a white mob, and two Black men were killed in police custody. Protests followed, and the federal government tried to prosecute the white mob for ransacking local Black businesses, but Southern juries would not convict them (Gergel, 2019, Chapter 2).

# CHAPTER 5

# Postwar Prosperity and Civil Rights

### 5.1 A BLACK SOLDIER'S HOMECOMING

Let us begin our discussion of the postwar years with the continuation of Isaac Woodard's tragic story, beginning with the song Woody Guthrie wrote about him. Recall that Woodard was a veteran of a segregated army unit in the Pacific during World War II where he had earned several awards for his service.

> My name is Isaac Woodard, my tale I'll tell you;
> I'm sure it'll sound so terrible you might not think it true;
> I joined up with the Army, they sent me overseas;
> Through the battles of New Guinea and in the Philippines.
> On the 13th day of February 1946
> They sent me to Atlanta and I got my discharge pin;
> I caught the bus for Winslow, going to meet my wife,
> Then we were coming to New York City to visit my parents both.
> About an hour out of Atlanta, the sun was going down,
> We stopped the bus at a drugstore in a little country town;
> I walked up to the driver and I looked him in the eye,
> "I'd like to go to the washroom, if you think we got time."
> The driver started cursing, and then he hollered, "No!"
> So, then I cussed right back at him, and really got him told.
> He said, "If you will hurry, I guess I'll take the time!"
> It was in a few short minutes we was rolling down the line.
> We rolled for thirty minutes, I watched the shacks and trees,
> I thought of my wife in Winsboro waiting there for me.
> In Aiken, South Carolina, the driver he jumped out;

He came back with a policeman to take me off the bus.

"Listen, Mr. Policeman," I started to explain,

"I did not cause no trouble, and I did not raise no cain."

He hit me with his billy, he cursed me up and down,

"Shut up, you black bastard"; and he walked me down in town.

As we walked along the sidewalk, my right arm he did twist;

I knew he wanted me to fight back, but I never did resist;

"Have you your Army discharge?" I told him, yes, I had;

He pasted me with his loaded stick down across my head.

I grabbed his stick and we had a little run, and had a little wrastle;

When another cop run up with a gun and jumped into the battle;

"If you don't drop that sap, black boy, it's me that's dropping you."

So I figured to drop that loaded sap was the best thing I could do.

They beat me about the head and face and left a bloody trail

All down along the sidewalk to the iron door of the jail;

He knocked me down upon the ground and he poked me in the eyes;

When I woke up next morning, I found my eyes were blind.

They drug me to the courtroom, and I could not see the judge;

He fined me fifty dollars for raising all the fuss;

The doctor finally got there but it took him two whole days;

He handed me some drops and salve and told me to treat myself.

It's now you've heard my story, there's one thing I can't see,

How you could treat a human like they have treated me;

I thought I fought on the islands to get rid of their kind;

But I can see the fight lots plainer now that I am blind. (Guthrie, ND)

The *NAACP* and others convinced the government to bring a suit against Police Officer Shull, who had blinded Woodard. A prominent forensic pathologist concluded that the crush of both Woodard's eyes required a penetrating injury in each eye, consistent with Woodard's claim that Shull drove the handle end of his blackjack into each eye. The trial was held in South Carolina before an all-white jury in late 1946, which swiftly decided Shull was not guilty. Judge Waring, who was the judge in Woodard's trial, was upset enough to begin reading about the condition of Blacks in the United States.

President Truman was very interested in civil rights for America's African Americans, and he appointed a President's Committee on Civil

Rights in December 1946 that issued its report in October 1947. The report, entitled "To Secure These Rights," focused on four rights: the rights to safety and the security of the individual, to citizenship and its privileges, to freedom of conscience and expression, and to equal opportunity. The report discussed the pattern of lynching in the Gilded Age described in Chapter 3 and covered several cases of police brutality against Blacks, like the violence against Isaac Woodard.

The report also condemned segregated schools, restrictive racial covenants, discrimination in federal services, and racial discrimination in Washington, DC. The harshest criticism was aimed at federal government discrimination against Blacks. *Plessy v. Ferguson* was a prime example of this fault, and the report claimed that the decision was incompatible with the Fourteenth Amendment. The report made many recommendations for federal government actions to secure the rights they listed for all American citizens (Gergel, 2019, 145–49).

Many of Truman's advisors urged him to moderate his support for civil rights, but Truman stayed with his program and made civil rights central to many of his speeches. For example, he received a letter from a Missouri man who had served with Truman in World War I that urged Truman to moderate his view to get reelected. Truman responded in a private letter that was released only after Truman's death. He said he was not asking for equality, but equality of opportunity. He cited the treatment of Isaac Woodard and said, "I can't approve of such goings on and I shall never approve it, I am going to try and remedy it and if that ends up in my failure to be reelected, that failure will be in a good cause."

Truman proclaimed two executive orders in July 1948 that implemented some of the committee's recommendations and made his position clear. The most often-cited executive order outlawed racial segregation in the military and mandated equality in America's armed forces. The other executive order prohibited discrimination in federal employment – extending the prohibition on segregation in civilian parts of the federal government. Despite all of these strong statements and actions, President Truman won reelection in 1948 in an upset victory over the governor of New York, Thomas Dewey.

The military resisted implementation of Truman's desegregation order. Truman therefore appointed a committee to review and approve the desegregation plans of each branch of the military. Truman reiterated in 1949 that his order was desegregation and he was using his power as commander in chief to make these changes. The committee rapidly agreed to plans by the navy and air force, but the army resisted Truman's order. They said Blacks were not suited for combat but rather for manual labor. This argument lost its force as the other branches agreed to desegregate, and the army fell into line and agreed to implement Truman's order (Gergel, 2019, 155–63).

Judge Waring reentered this story in 1951 after reading up on the position of Blacks in the United States and becoming a vocal advocate of civil rights. He was part of a three-judge panel in a suit to protest inferior Black schools in South Carolina in *Briggs v. Elliott*, 342 U.S. 350 (1952). Instead of asking for enforcement of the separate but equal doctrine by bringing the Black schools up to equality with the white schools, the plaintiffs asked that school segregation should be declared unconstitutional. Waring recommended to the plaintiffs that the case should be expanded from an equalization case into a desegregation case.

Judge Waring wrote a minority opinion for the panel that cited research by Kenneth and Mamie Clark that showed separate schools have "detrimental effects on the personality development of the Negro child." They did their standard experiment with South Carolina children. They used four dolls, identical except for color, to test children's racial perceptions. Their subjects, Black and white children between the ages of three to seven, were asked to identify both the race of the dolls and which color doll they prefer. A majority of the children preferred the white doll and assigned positive characteristics to it. The Clarks concluded that "prejudice, discrimination, and segregation" created a feeling of inferiority among African-American children and damaged their self-esteem. Kenneth Clark testified, "The conclusion which I was forced to reach was that these children of Clarendon County, like other human beings subjected to an obviously inferior status in society in which they live, have been definitely harmed in the development of their personalities" and such injuries were "enduring" (*Briggs v. Elliott*, Transcript of Record, 83–90).

Waring used Clark's evidence in his dissent and argued "Segregation is per se inequality." The Supreme Court bundled several local cases into

*Brown v. Board of Education of Topeka*, 347 U.S. 483 (1954). This was the first large decision of Chief Justice Warren, and it ruled unanimously that *Plessy v. Ferguson* was unconstitutional. The decision cited Waring's dissent and used Kenneth Clark's social science as evidence for its conclusion. It followed Truman's executive orders abolishing segregation in the military and federal offices, and it was the final act of the blinding of Isaac Woodard.

*Brown v. Board of Education* reversed the usual set of Black and white models described in Figure 3.1 because it aimed to improve Black education by court action rather than electoral influence. It also would become an isolated decision when the Supreme Court reverted to its usual racist stance in the early twenty-first century.

There are three implications of this long story. First, Jim Crow laws and attitudes continued throughout the first half of the twentieth century and were in full evidence after peace returned. Jim Crow was not an aberration, but a critical part of Southern society. The Great Migration in progress at this time was expanding the reach of this attitude to a national ethos as economic recovery continued. Second, the Supreme Court resisted this view in a decision that reflected the will of the people rather than the aims of the rich and powerful. This turned out to be a temporary shift in Supreme Court decisions despite the wishes of many people that it would be a permanent change. Third, President Truman started the Civil Rights Movements with his desegregation orders a decade before President Lyndon Johnson proposed his more famous extensions of *Brown v. Board of Education.*

Like the Fourteenth Amendment, this decision was honored in the breach, as white legislatures could not bring themselves to provide equal resources for Black students whose parents did not vote. The issue in *Brown,* however, was not the inequality of schools, but the constitutionality of separation. In a pattern that would be repeated in the North as the Great Migration continued, whites in the South moved their children's schools into suburban areas where Blacks were not welcome. As we have seen so many times, whites found ways to nullify the effects of national decisions by preserving the letter of the court's decision while ignoring the spirit and aspiration of the decision (Margo, 1990).

## 5.2 POSTWAR RECOVERY

World War II ended better than World War I, suggesting that the victors had learned from history. Instead of the rancor that ended World War I, there was a feeling of cooperation that led to a generation of economic growth in America and Europe. While many contemporaries thought that a new era was beginning, a lot of the European postwar growth was recovery from the damage and lost opportunities during the war. *Les Trente Glorieuses*, as this period was known in and out of France, was symbolized by international cooperation expressed in the nascent United Nations and the Bretton Woods system for international payments that preserved the fixed exchange rates of the gold standard without relying on gold. The United States was not where fighting took place during the war, and its products were much in European demand during the Reconstruction period. A persistent dollar shortage was the result of this high demand (Temin, 2002a; Neal, 2015).

Instead of an armistice, the United States insisted on unconditional surrender. The lack of communication between Hitler in his bunker and the Allies entering Berlin in 1945 contrasted sharply with the conversation between Grant and Lee at Appomattox in 1865. Instead of supporting a punitive treaty like the 1919 Treaty of Versailles, the United States stepped up to help rebuild Western Europe. In addition, the United Nations, headquartered in New York, replaced the moribund League of Nations in Geneva.

The 1944 GI Bill appeared to offer Blacks more benefits and opportunities than they could have imagined in 1940. But the administration of the bill discriminated sharply against them to the point of mocking them for believing the promise of equal treatment. The administration significantly curtailed the bill's egalitarian promise and widened the country's large racial gap. Yet again, policies designed to transfer and create wealth and economic opportunity were restricted to whites by design.

For example, the GI Bill provided educational benefits for veterans of World War I, but it did not guarantee admission to colleges. Few Blacks were admitted to Northern colleges and universities due to inferior Southern schooling. Blacks therefore applied to Southern Black colleges – being excluded from Southern white colleges – which did not have the capacity to take them. Southern states refused to expand the facilities of Black colleges, particularly dormitories, and much of the Black demand for college education went nowhere. Black veterans also were not helped to get good jobs by the GI Bill. Local employment agencies funded by the bill directed them to traditional Black jobs, ignoring learning that had occurred in the army, and banks often refused loans to Black veterans who lacked capital or credit ratings and lived in undesirable neighborhoods (Katznelson, 2005, Chapter 5).

African Americans responded to the pressure on them in Southern states by moving North and West in the Great Migration. Black workers continued to move out of the oppressive South to better their lives and employment opportunities, but this move was not always successful, and Blacks lost ground relative to whites after World War II. The national unemployment rate for Blacks and whites was the same in 1930; the Black rate was double that of whites in 1965. The unemployment rate for Black teenage boys went from being slightly less than whites in 1948 to being almost twice as high in 1965. Employers did not consider the Black migrants to the North to be full substitutes of their white employees, so the migrants competed largely with earlier Black migrants. While the migrants greatly increased their incomes, this was partly at the expense of earlier migrants (Katznelson, 2005, 14–15).

This was true for several reasons. As explained in the last chapter, most migrating Blacks had poor education and limited skills. White employers continued in the time-honored practice of only hiring the new Black migrants to the worst jobs. This set up competition between new and old migrants and kept their wages down. This not to deny the gains that the new migrants enjoyed, but to explain why Black wages failed to rise relative to white wages. Whites also left cities for the suburbs. For every Black entering a Northern city, almost three whites left. They left both because they did not want Black neighbors and because they expected that more Blacks would lead to higher taxes to provide public goods (Boustan, 2017).

The lower incomes and employment rate of Blacks reduced their accumulation of wealth. Legal structures were created to prevent African Americans from building economic security through homeownership, restrictive deeds that legally enforced segregation, and Redlining denied mortgages to Black neighborhoods. America built a middle class, but systematic discrimination kept most African-American families from being part of it (Rothstein, 2017).

The effects of Redlining are still important today and are harming Blacks and other minorities as temperatures rise in global warming. A spatial analysis of 108 urban areas in the United States today found that 94 percent of Redlined areas display consistent patterns of elevated land surface temperatures relative to their non-Redlined neighbors by as much as 7°C. Southeast and Western cities display the greatest differences, while Midwest cities display the least. Overall, land surface temperatures in Redlined areas are approximately 2.6°C warmer than in non-Redlined areas. These trends derive in part from the relative preponderance of buildings and roads rather than tree canopies in these areas, and historical housing policies are responsible for disproportionate exposure of minority residents to extreme weather caused by global warming (Hoffman, Shandas, and Pendleton, 2020).

Richard Rothstein argued that we all are responsible for the extension of residential segregation to the North. As he noted in *The Color of Law,*

> It wasn't only the large-scale federal programs of public housing and mortgage finance that created de jure segregation. Hundreds if not thousands of smaller acts of government contributed. They included petty actions like denial of access to public utilities; determining, once African Americans wanted to build, that their property was, after all, needed for parkland; or discovering that the road leading to African American home was "private." ... Taken in isolation, we can easily dismiss such devices as aberrations. But when we consider them as a whole, we can see that they were part of a national system by which state and local supplemented federal efforts to maintain the status of African Americans as a lower caste, with housing segregations preserving the badges and incidents of slavery. (Rothstein, 2017, 122)

Thus began a generation of prosperity and economic growth for whites, where the United States dominated the world economy. It has been described as one big wave of United States growth. The innovations that produced this growth occurred earlier, but growth was diverted into

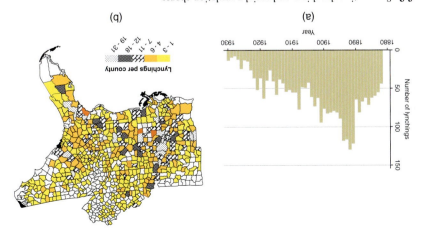

**3.2.** Segregation, lynching, and racial population shares.
*Source:* Cook, Logan, and Parman, 2018; Historical American Lynching (HAL) Data Collection Project. Note that Virginia is not included in the lynching data. (a) Number of lynchings by year, 1882–1930; (b) lynchings per county, 1882–1930.

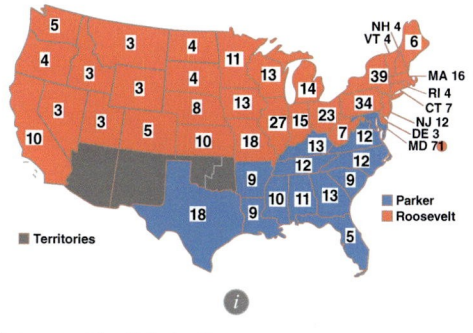

**3.3.** 1904 United States presidential election.
*Source:* https://en.wikipedia.org/wiki/1904_United_States_presidential_election

**7.2.** The army top brass with the President, 2020.
*Source:* Cooper, 2020.

World War II in the first part of this long wave, and the results reached the population at large in the years following 1945.

Four groups of inventions generated this big wave. The use of electricity grew. Electric light extended the length of the day that could be used for all sorts of work and play. It was introduced in the 1890s and extended to many prosperous urban households, but electricity did not revolutionize production until after the wars. Factories needed to be drastically reorganized to benefit from electric motors, and only after war production ceased could new factories be built under the new plans.

The use of the internal combustion engine also grew, making personal and public transport far more attainable. After Ford's introduction of the Model T before World War I and the Model A after the war, the initial use of the internal combustion was limited to tanks and other military vehicles. Trucks were introduced in farms during the Depression, but their spread was limited by low agricultural prices. As with electricity, the full impact of this innovation blossomed after 1945.

The use of petrochemicals to produce plastics and antibiotics also expanded. As petroleum replaced other sources of power for transport, that is, as gas-guzzling cars replaced trains, refiners discovered that petrochemicals could be used for other purposes. Plastics had become popular enough for the college graduate in *The Graduate*, a 1967 movie, to be told to remember only one word to be successful: plastics. Antibiotics, first discovered between the world wars, became generally available only in the 1950s, prolonging the life of children and adults. After new regulations in 1938, most of the new drugs were available by prescription only. The growth of large pharmaceutical companies and hospitals was not the result of technology alone, but of the interaction of new discoveries and government policies.

Finally, communication and information expanded as well. Radios were ubiquitous in the interwar years. Television appeared late in that period, but only diffused after the war ended. They filled a void in earlier life where nothing existed and had as great an impact on daily life as the spread of electricity itself (David, 1994; Gordon, 2000, 2016).

The second and third of these innovations – cars and gas to fuel them – also started the climate change that began to rise around 1970. Many reasons have been given for the slowdown after that time, and global warming will be discussed more fully in the next chapter. It is necessary here to remind ourselves that these innovations were not simply gifts to American society.

White flight was encouraged by the advent of the automobile age. Cars, and in particular farm trucks, made their appearance before the war, but the Great Depression and subsequent war delayed their spread. President Eisenhower signed the Federal Aid Highway Act in 1956, also known as the National Interstate and Defense Highways Act, and set in motion a construction project that is inconceivable today. The new highways were sold as a way to provide access to defend the United States during a conventional or nuclear war with the Soviet Union and its communist allies, a reason that helped obtain Republican support for this large infrastructure improvement. A national plan of highways was constructed with state and federal cooperation, financed by government bonds. Suburbs and suburban living became the symbol of postwar prosperity.

Blacks were omitted from this great remodeling of American city living. As Blacks continued to move North in the Great Migration, they did not have the resources to buy suburban houses. Banks would not lend to them, as they did to whites, to allow them to accumulate real-estate capital. Redlining and job restrictions combined to confine Blacks to the cities being vacated by whites. And, as noted earlier, rural segregation also rose. There was less and less personal contact between the races as time went on.

## 5.3 GREAT MIGRATION CONTINUED

While this pattern rose from restrictions, they also were the results of the Great Migration. Like international migrations, Blacks from the South moved to join Blacks in the North. Family members joined relatives, and unrelated migrants felt more at home with people who were similar to those back home. Migrants were more educated than the group they left, but less educated than the group they joined. The former comparison suggests that more educated Blacks were motivated to seek better jobs in the North. The latter comparison is a result of the poor state of Black education in the South (Margo, 1990; Tolnay, 2003).

The study concluded that it could only be closed by a reversal of past privileges,

> By the 1960s, black poverty was deeply entrenched, but more importantly, it was marked by its stark contrast to the white middle class's prosperity. Not only had the majority of blacks not ridden the postwar boom; conditions in the ghetto had actually worsened. Almost half of black children lived in poverty in contrast with only 9 percent of white children. Black families had less than one-fifth the wealth of white families. A Federal Reserve study concluded that the source of the wealth gap was historic inequalities in income and opportunities. (Baradaran, 2017, 141)

Isabel Wilkerson described the diversity of migrants who left the South in the Great Migration through an intense examination of the varied lives of a few of them. We can note their variety here, but a full appreciation of their individuality requires reading the details in Wilkerson's fine book. Ida Mae Gladney, a sharecropper's wife from Mississippi, lived in Chicago for the next fifty years. Her life revolved around family, church, and work as it would have in Mississippi, but the context was different. She lived a working-class life in the North and eventually had six grandchildren. George Starling moved North, but he had an unhappy wife and two children who ran into legal troubles as teenagers while Starling and his wife were working hard to raise them. Starling did not progress far up the labor ladder in the North, but he was not bitter and warned other migrants to avoid the mistakes that he identified in his career. Robert Foster moved to Los Angeles, became a prosperous doctor, and treated many of the migrants who found their way to his office. He did well enough to host a reception for his far-flung family and his local friends that was luxurious enough to be labeled the Party of 1970 by the *Los Angeles Sentinel* (Wilkerson, 2010, 413–30).

Painter Jacob Lawrence's parents were in the first wave of the Great Migration who met on the way North. Jacob went to school in Harlem as a teenager and enrolled in an arts-and-crafts program after school to keep him busy while his mother worked. He became an artist and painted a sequence of sixty pictures depicting the Great Migration in 1940 when he was twenty-two years old. The pictures now are divided between the Museum of Modern Art in New York and the Phillips Collection in Washington, DC (Lawrence, 1993).

It is clear that the fortunes of members of the Great Migration varied greatly, but there were gains to many migrants from moving North. The problem in identifying these gains is that they showed up mostly in the second generation. Recent research has shown that movement to another neighborhood often helps in the long run, even if not in the short run. Another large change was the expansion of the minimum wage to occupations which were disproportionately held by Blacks. This move away from racist New Deal policy caused a significant closing of the Black/white income gap (Chetty and Hendren, 2018a, 2018b).

The transfer of Southern racial housing segregation to the North went largely unnoticed by the white press. White residents moving out to grass and trees did not seem to be conscious that the suburbs were all white. (They also did not seem to notice that women were left out of the growing economy.) Fifty years later, this period is looked back on as the peak of American prosperity and world leadership, forgetting the legacy of slavery that was being recreated in this new world and the subjection of women that was seen as family disruptions in the new suburbs. Part of this movement was subsidized by the growth of the interstate highway system, which increased suburbanization and led to construction employment among whites (Baum-Snow 2007).

On May 18, 1954, Greensboro, North Carolina, became the first city in the South to announce publicly that it would abide by the Supreme Court's *Brown v. Board of Education* ruling. "It is unthinkable," remarked School Board Superintendent Benjamin Smith, "that we will try to [override] the laws of the United States." The appointment of an African American to the school board in 1953 convinced numerous white and Black citizens that Greensboro was heading in a progressive direction. Integration in Greensboro occurred peacefully compared to the process in Southern states such as Alabama, Arkansas, and Virginia, where "massive resistance" was practiced by top officials and throughout the states.

In Virginia, some counties closed their public schools rather than integrate; many white Christian private schools were founded to accommodate students who used to go to public schools. Even in Greensboro, local resistance to desegregation continued, and in 1969, the federal government found the city was not in compliance with the 1964 Civil Rights Act. Transition to a fully integrated school system did not begin until 1971.

Many Northern cities also had de facto segregation policies, which resulted in a vast gulf in educational resources between Black and white communities. In Harlem, New York, for example, not a single new school was built since the turn of the century, nor did a single nursery school exist – even as the Second Great Migration was causing overcrowding. Existing schools tended to be dilapidated and staffed with inexperienced teachers. *Brown v. Board of Education* helped stimulate activism among New York City parents who initiated a successful lawsuit against the city and state on *Brown's* principles with the support of the NAACP. The parents bolstered the pressure of the lawsuit with a school boycott in 1959. Some of the early freedom schools were established during the boycott. The city responded by permitting more open transfers to high-quality historically white schools. New York's African-American community, and Northern desegregation activists generally, now found themselves contending with the problem of white flight.

On December 1, 1955, Rosa Parks was arrested after she declined to yield her seat on a public bus to a white passenger in Montgomery, Alabama. She quickly became the national symbol of the ensuing Montgomery Bus Boycott and was celebrated as the "mother of the civil rights movement" (Thornton, 2014).

Rosa Parks was the secretary of the Montgomery NAACP chapter. She recently had come back from meeting in Tennessee with Myles Horton and other advocates of nonviolence as a strategy. Following Parks' arrest, African Americans organized the Montgomery Bus Boycott to press demands for equal treatment. Following Rosa Park's arrest, the boycott council mimeographed over 50,000 leaflets calling for a boycott. These were distributed around the city and helped gain attention from civil rights leaders. When the city rejected many of their proposed reform, the NAACP pushed for full desegregation of public buses. The boycott gained support from most of Montgomery's 50,000 African Americans and lasted for more than a year, significantly reducing bus revenue. It ended when the local ordinance upholding segregation of whites and Blacks on buses was repealed. In November 1956, the US Supreme Court upheld a lower court ruling in the case of *Browder v. Gayle,* 353 US 903 and ordered that Montgomery's buses be desegregated. This decision ended the boycott – a decade after Isaac Woodard was blinded for acting like an equal human being on a bus.

Local leaders established the Montgomery Improvement Association to focus their efforts and elected Martin Luther King, Jr. to be president of this organization. The lengthy protest attracted national attention for him and the city. His eloquent appeals to Christian brotherhood and American idealism created a positive impression on people both inside and outside the South.

After the Freedom Rides, local Black leaders in Mississippi asked SNCC to help register Black voters and to build community organizations that could win a share of political power in the state. Mississippi's constitution of 1890 contained poll taxes, residency requirements, and literacy tests. It made voting registration more complicated and led to mass purges of Blacks from voter rolls. These laws and violence during elections suppressed Black participation in elections. Freedom Movement activists thought that all of the state's civil rights organizations needed to unite in a coordinated effort because white opposition to Black voter registration was so intense in Mississippi. In February 1962, representatives from SNCC, CORE, and the NAACP formed the Council of Federated Organizations (COFO). SCLC joined COFO at a subsequent meeting.

By the mid-twentieth century, preventing Blacks from voting had become an essential part of the culture of white supremacy. In June and July 1959, members of the Black community in Fayette County, Tennessee, formed the Fayette County Civic and Welfare League to spur voting. At the time, there were 16,927 Blacks in the county, yet only seventeen of them had voted in the previous seven years. Within a year, some 1,400 Blacks had registered, and the white community responded with harsh economic reprisals. Using registration rolls, the White Citizens' Council circulated a blacklist of all registered Black voters, allowing banks, local stores, and gas stations to conspire to deny registered Black voters essential services. The total number of evictions came to 257 families, many of whom were forced to live in a makeshift Tent City for well over a year. The Justice Department invoked its powers authorized by the Civil Rights Act of 1957 to file a suit against seventy parties accused of violating the civil rights of Black Fayette County citizens in December 1960. In the following year, the first voter registration project in McComb and the surrounding counties in the Southwest corner of the state began. Their efforts were met with violent repression from state and local lawmen, the White Citizens' Council, and the Ku Klux Klan. Activists were beaten, there were hundreds of arrests of local citizens, and the voting activist Herbert Lee was murdered.

In the Spring of 1962, with funds from the Voter Education Project, SNCC/COFO began voter registration organizing in the Mississippi Delta area around Greenwood, and the areas surrounding Hattiesburg, Laurel, and Holly Springs. As in McComb, their efforts were met with fierce opposition – arrests, beatings, shootings, arson, and murder. Registrars used the literacy test to keep Blacks off the voting rolls by creating standards that even highly educated people could not meet. In addition, employers fired Blacks who tried to register, and landlords evicted them from their rental homes. Despite these actions, over the following years, the Black voter registration campaign spread across the state.

SNCC, CORE, and SCLC began similar voter registration campaigns – with similar responses – in Louisiana, Alabama, southwest Georgia, and South Carolina. By 1963, voter registration campaigns in the South were as integral to the Freedom Movement as desegregation efforts. After the passage of the Civil Rights Act of 1964 protecting and facilitating voter registration despite state barriers became the main effort of the movement. It resulted in the passage of the Voting Rights Act of 1965, which had provisions to enforce the constitutional right to vote for all citizens (Morris, 1984; Payne, 1995).

Philip Randolph, chair of the Brotherhood of Sleeping Car Conductors, and Bayard Rustin were the chief planners of a march on Washington, which they proposed in 1963. The Kennedy administration initially opposed the march because they thought it might negate their drive for passage of civil rights legislation. Randolph and King announced firmly that the march would proceed, and the Kennedys decided it was important to work to ensure its success. Concerned about the turnout, President Kennedy enlisted the aid of white church leaders and Walter Reuther, president of the UAW, to help mobilize white supporters for the march.

The march took place on August 28, 1963. The planning of the 1963 march was a collaborative effort of all of the major civil rights organizations, the more progressive wing of the labor movement, and other liberal organizations. The march's major focus was on passage of the civil rights law that the Kennedy administration had proposed after the upheavals in Birmingham. The march was a success, although not without controversy. An estimated 200,000 to 300,000 Black and white demonstrators gathered in front of the Lincoln Memorial, where King delivered his famous "I Have a Dream" speech.

Many speakers applauded the Kennedy administration for the efforts it had made to obtain new, more effective civil rights legislation to protect the right to vote and outlaw segregation, but John Lewis of SNCC took the administration to task for not doing more. After the march, King and other civil rights leaders met with President Kennedy at the White House. While the Kennedy administration appeared sincerely committed to passing the bill, it was not clear that it had enough votes in Congress to do so. However, when President Kennedy was assassinated on November 22, 1963, the new President, Lyndon Johnson, decided to use his influence in Congress to bring about much of Kennedy's legislative agenda.

### 5.4 LYNDON JOHNSON'S GREAT SOCIETY

The 1960s opened with the Beatles startling the white world and Freedom Riders trying to escape the traditional Black world. The progress of television increased the awareness of both new ventures among Americans of all sorts. President Kennedy seemed more interested in the former than the latter, but pressure from his brother and others forced him to pay attention to the latter. His attempts to help the Freedom Riders and other Southern protestors were cut short by his 1963 assassination. Lyndon Johnson asked Congress to declare unconditional war on poverty in Kennedy's honor. Congress passed the Economic Opportunity Act (EOA) that created the Office of Economic Opportunity (OEO) in 1964. It followed with bills that transformed American schools, created

Medicare and Medicaid, and expanded many ongoing federal efforts to relieve poverty. Despite the many contributions Johnson made while president, his reputation has suffered partly because he expanded the Vietnam War and partly because he did not leave a coherent political legacy to the Democratic Party (Bailey and Duquette, 2014).

Segregation was encouraged by the solid Democratic South before President Johnson's Great Society led them to switch parties. The Democratic South excluded Blacks from the force of federal legislation by limiting the laws to manufacturing workers, excluding farm workers and domestic maids. They insisted that the administration of laws be placed in the hands of local officials who were antagonistic toward Black progress. And they refused to allow Congress to insert antidiscriminatory language into any social welfare programs, including local hospitals and school lunches (Katznelson, 2005, 22–23).

The way the EOA and OEO were set up illustrates Johnson's struggle with the Democratic Party. The OEO distributed funds to states, but local administrations managed the distribution within states. Poverty rates and the share of non-whites were the primary determinants of where the funds were used. Rather than employing these funds to help local politicians, OEO funds circumvented the local elite. The OEO apparently wanted to supplant the old leadership to avoid the legacy of Jim Crow that they were presumed to honor. But this attempt to provide new leadership did not lead to political support. It was a serious attempt to alleviate poverty, but it did not stimulate political change that would maintain the new and increased support (Bailey and Duquette, 2014).

President Johnson signed into law legislation establishing Medicare and Medicaid programs in 1965. The new law required states to "buy-in" to the Medicare system by using Medicaid funds to cover Medicare premiums and cost-sharing for impoverished Medicare beneficiaries. These programs have protected the health of millions of American families, saving lives, and improving the economic security of our nation for fifty years. Medicare spending accounted for 18 percent of *total federal spending* by 2018, up from 15 percent in 2017. Medicare per capita spending grew at a slower pace in recent years, averaging 1.5 percent between 2010 and 2017, as opposed to 7.3 percent between 2000 and

2007 (Federal Hospital Insurance and Supplementary Medical Insurance Trust Funds, 2019).

President Johnson also steered through Congress what he called the Kennedy Bill to restore the voting rights of Blacks. The Civil Rights Act of 1965 re-established the voting rights of Black citizens of the United States that had been guaranteed in the Fifteenth Amendment. As we have seen, the Supreme Court nullified the Fourteenth and Fifteenth Amendments in the 1880s as a sort of gravestone for Reconstruction that had died in 1876. Johnson restored the dynamics of the Politics and Race and Class Model in Figure 3.1 that shows Blacks wanting the vote to improve their schools.

These domestic events were accompanied by foreign events that would come back to haunt civil rights at home. Indeed, the involvement of the United States in World War II made them susceptible to attacks that their ideals about democracy and protection of rights was a myth. One view from the Kennedy administration tied them together by linking support for the Civil Rights Act from conservative congressional representatives to Johnson's continued support for the Vietnam War. Johnson supported the war in return for congressional warmongers voting for civil rights at home.

There were about 75,000 American troops in Vietnam in mid-1965. There were few American casualties and the war seemed destined for resolution in Saigon. Then, after some military reversals, General Westmoreland in Vietnam requested an open-ended American commitment to the war, turning it into an American war. Johnson adopted Westmoreland's program in substance if not detail in order to preserve congressional support for his Great Society programs, including the 1965 Voting Rights Act. He believed he was in a honeymoon with Congress after Kennedy's death, and he could not abandon Vietnam and preserve his domestic program (Bator, 2007; Bacevich, 2016).

Johnson's Great Society programs were an attempt to broaden President Roosevelt's New Deal during the Depression. Blacks were excluded from much of the New Deal and GI Bill by Southern Congressmen, and Johnson tried to broaden the scope of federal government assistance. Blacks were ruled out of Social Security by the exclusion of agriculture from its coverage, and Black GIs were restricted to Black colleges that were too poor to build dorms for them. Johnson took account of the Great Migration that was transforming the oppression of Blacks from a regional to a national problem. He tried to provide health care for Blacks by including them in Medicare and Medicaid.

One of the effects of Johnson's Great Society program was to convince Southern voters that the Democrats were no longer looking after their interests. A succession of Democratic presidents from Truman to Johnson had acted to promote the rights of Black Americans and destroy Jim Crow laws. Southern voters began to turn from being Democrats to Republicans (Kuziemko and Washington, 2018).

The late 1960s were chaotic. There were civil disturbances and race riots in many cities around the country: Harlem in 1964, Watts and Chicago in 1965, and Newark, Detroit, and other cities in 1967. Martin Luther King, Jr. and Robert F. Kennedy were assassinated in 1968. Crime suddenly had risen all over. People were scared, and President Johnson appointed a National Advisory Commission on Civil Disorders, known as the Kerner Commission, in 1967 to help understand what was going on. The Kerner Commission's report concluded: "What white Americans have never fully understood – but which the Negro can never forget – is that white society is deeply implicated in the ghetto. White institutions created it, white institutions maintain it, and white society condones it" (Harris and Wilkins, 1988, 19; Kerner Commission, 1968, Chapter 16, Summary).

The report concluded that policies should move toward a single integrated society, and it sold well. But the government had rushed the report into publication, and it vanished from public discussions as a concern as opposition to the Vietnam War rose. President Johnson signed the Safe Streets Act (1968) after all the urban disturbances shifted political views from social welfare to law enforcement. The War on Poverty always had an ambiguous meaning as wars are inherently violent, and this aspect of Johnson's efforts rose to primacy as conservatives acquired more influence. The act created the Law Enforcement Assistance Administration that expanded punitive supervision and control in low-income urban areas throughout the 1970s. Conservatives increasingly saw Johnson's extension of civil rights as the cause of crime and lawlessness, reversing the direction stated in the Kerner Commission Report (Hinton, 2016).

The urban disturbances of the late 1960s scared many people and set the stage for militarization of the police. The Warren Supreme Court was on both sides of this issue. It helped defendants against the police in its 1966 *Miranda v. Arizona* decision and encouraged the police in approving their stop-and-frisk policies in 1968. While the assignation of Martin Luther King, Jr. set off riots in Los Angeles, the police started the riots in Chicago during the Democratic Convention later in 1968. Nixon expanded the Law Enforcement Assistance Administration in the 1970s to support local police and SWAT forces. The first time SWAT forces were used was to ambush the Black Panthers while they slept in 1969. By 1975, there were 500 SWAT teams (Balco, 2014, Chapter 4).

Increasingly opposed by conservative whites, Johnson's civil rights laws were observed in the breach for a few decades and then nullified by the Supreme Court. More than a century after Blacks were freed from slavery and declared citizens of the United States, they still had only limited voting rights. They did however achieve some educational gains.

Unlike Reconstruction, African-American education expanded greatly during the Civil Rights Movement and had a lasting impact. School desegregation significantly increased educational attainment among Blacks exposed to desegregation during their school-age years, increasing the likelihood of graduating from high school, Completing years of school attending college, graduating with a four-year college degree, and college quality. Statistical estimates indicate that school desegregation and the accompanied increases in school quality also resulted in significant improvements in adult labor market and health status outcomes, and reductions in both the annual incidence of adult poverty and incarceration for Blacks. The significant long-run impacts of school desegregation found for Blacks with parallel findings across a broad set of socioeconomic outcomes and health status indicators of well-being, with no corresponding losses found for whites, is striking (Johnson, 2011).

Twenty percent of Black men had graduated from high school by 1970, compared with 7 percent in 1950. And 4 percent of Black men had graduated from college by 1970, compared with less than 3 percent in 1950. The Black college graduates in 1950 were from poor Southern colleges; they were largely from predominantly white colleges by 1970. Aspiring Black students were in demand during the 1960s in both desegregated Southern colleges and Northern white colleges (Freeman, 1976, 41–52).

This educational progress has been analyzed, starting from Head Start and going through high school, providing Black students for colleges, and separately for Black college graduates. Head Start was started in 1964 as part of Johnson's War on Poverty. It has been renewed and improved several times since, not without some hazards. When President George W. Bush renewed funding of Head Start in 2007, he used code words that showed his opposition to the program, "I am pleased that this bill addresses several longstanding Administration priorities, such as increased competition among Head Start providers, improved coordination of early childhood delivery systems, and stronger educational performance standards." "Competition" was code for looking for private charter Head Start programs. "Coordination" was code for reducing the multidimensional focus in very young children, and "performance standards" meant tests for short-run impacts rather than the important long-run impact. President Bush was trying to privatize the predominantly Black educational system. President Obama reversed this direction in subsequent years, looking to evaluate Head Start teachers on their relationships with the students rather than focusing on multiple-choice tests (Bush, 2007; US Department of Health and Human Services, 2015).

Rucker Johnson adopted a research strategy to identify changes in Black and white students during integration that took place at different times in different places during the decades after *Brown v. Board of Education.* He started from the Panel Study of Income Dynamics (PSID) that followed 18,000 Americans starting in 1968 and tracked life outcomes of cohorts from birth to adulthood across several generations. He merged these annual observations with educational data on desegregation and Head Start in every school district across the country, focusing on three cures to inequality: integration, school funding, and high-quality preschool investments.

In order to change from observation to testing the effects of desegregation, Johnson needed to have a control group similar to those used in proving new medicines. Each participant in the PSID had too many variations on family and social indicators to differentiate treatment and control groups. Johnson turned to school districts and assumed that the distribution of students was unrelated to the politics of desegregation orders. He found 868 judicial orders enacted between 1954 and 1980 and created parallel universes for affected and segregated school districts. This enabled him to see the effects of integration by contrasting students in these two kinds of districts, treated by integration and controls (Johnson, 2019, 10–11, 54–57).

Johnson chronicled six effects of school desegregation on student outcomes on Blacks and whites. It had cumulative effects on Black students that increased with the number of years students continued their education after desegregation orders. Black students had improved educational attainment, that is, years of education, and higher likelihood of graduating from high school. They had higher wages and reduced probability of being incarcerated. They had better health and reduced probability of poverty as adults. In each case, they were more included in the mainstream economy as a result of desegregation – without in any way diminishing the effect of education on their white cohorts. Court-ordered desegregation had no measureable effect on white student outcomes at all.

Using a similar approach to study school financing, Johnson examined court-ordered school financing reforms and found similar effects, identified here as poor rather than Black students. For low-income students, an increase in per-pupil spending had cumulative effects like those of integration on years of completed education, higher earnings, and less poverty. A 25 percent increase in per-pupil spending throughout a student's school years eliminated the attainment gaps between poor and rich children.

Head Start had similar effects that changed all of these outcomes in favorable directions. More importantly, well-funded Head Start programs and well-funded schools had larger effects on poor students than the sum of the effects of the two increases separately. Other economists have found varied effects of Head Start because the long-term effects of Head Start are affected strongly by the schooling that follows. Future policy changes need to see Head Start and K-12 education as joint activities that need to be integrated to affect students. They are not alternatives nor competitors for funding, but rather parts of the educational process to educate poor

students so that they can use their talents productively in later life. President
Johnson started before neuroscience developed to show the effect of early
education, but his creation of Head Start was prescient and showed how
important early education is to changing lives (Johnson, 2019).

Black college graduates after 1950 were more often from white
Northern universities than before, although they were still a small minor-
ity of African Americans. They were in high demand as a result of the
Civil Rights Movement, and these Black graduates went into good jobs.
They were a Black Elite, in Richard Freeman's apt title. This highly
educated elite was fully absorbed into the white economy, as a few
Black individuals had been previously. This was a big step, but limited
by the inadequacies of early education.

Only around 60 percent of nonwhite college graduates were professionals or managers in 1950, compared with three-quarters of all graduates. The nonwhite graduates caught up to the 1950 level of all graduates
by 1970, which had increased to 80 percent by that time. Non-whites
gained absolutely and relative to whites. Most of the gain was in management, a new field for Blacks, and it continued into the 1970s. The relative
incomes of the Black Elite rose at the same time. Black professional
incomes rose from 58 to 72 percent of white professionals, and Black
manager's incomes rose from half to two-thirds of white managers
(Freeman, 1976, Tables 5, 11).

These gains did not arise from magic. They came from the increase in
Northern college attendance. The Black students not only gained from a
better education than their predecessors in Southern colleges, they also
gained access to information about the job market that awaited them.
Southern Black colleges were still part of the backward South, and they
lacked the ties to Northern firms that Northern colleges had. Stimulated
by the Ford Foundation, organizations were formed and funds were
raised for placement programs. It is hard to disentangle the effect of
these efforts from straight economic opportunities, but interviews suggested that they were a significant influence. The careers of the new
Black college graduates were helped by a new labor market in response
to economic incentives (Freeman, 1976, Chapter 3, 57–85).

The federal government under Lyndon Johnson also made discrimination illegal in these markets. The Civil Rights Act of 1964, amended in

1972, and Executive Order 11246 imposed heavy fines and other punishments for discrimination in professional and management hiring. The Civil Rights Act ruled out discrimination by employers, employment agencies, and unions. It applied to hiring, firing, compensation and the terms and privileges of employment, and union membership. It established the Equal Employment Opportunity Commission (EEOC) to administer the law. The EEOC had a budget of about $45 million and brought over 34,000 cases, mostly dealing with Southern discrimination. Regression analysis showed that the EEOC had a significant and large effect on Black professional and managerial incomes (Freeman, 1976, 130).

The government also helped Black professionals by hiring them. The federal government hired Blacks as managers, while state and local governments hired them as teachers. The market of teachers shows the interactions between the elite and other Blacks experiencing the integration of schools. School integration meant that fewer Black teachers were needed in integrated schools than had been needed to staff Black schools. But the demand for new Black teachers, predominantly in the North, offset this fall in demand, keeping the total demand for Black teachers high. The demand for Black college professors grew as well, and the wages of Black teachers and professors grew. Freeman, writing in the 1970s, concluded, "If the developments of the 1960s and early 1970s continue into the future, the decade will mark a major turning point in black economic history" (Freeman, 1976, 215).

Alas, these developments did not continue. As in the late nineteenth century, there was a racist reaction to the progress being made by African Americans in the late twentieth century. In both cases, the reactions came as income inequality increased. The wealthiest people sought political power, and they followed the British colonial pattern of divide and conquer. They encouraged racism as a way of dividing working people, although we do not know if the very rich were and are racists themselves. Education suffered as the flight to suburbs to avoid the African Americans who came North in the Great Migration recreated segregated public schools. The Black Elite held onto their positions, although it became harder for poor Blacks to replenish the elite. Black incomes in the United States still are extremely unequal.

## CHAPTER 6

# The New Gilded Age and Mass Incarceration

## 6.1 THE GREAT MIGRATION ENDED

The lives of African Americans had changed, not always for the better, in the century since the death of Reconstruction, as recounted in previous chapters. Freedom without human or physical capital, that is, education or land, did not dramatically improve Black living conditions. And the Republican Party that aggressively championed for freedmen rights after the Civil War morphed into a party of robber barons that used racism to win elections, as illustrated in the election of 1896.

The Republican Party became the party of the rich who were supported by rural folks who thought the Democrats had abandoned them by supporting free trade and losing with this jobs. As noted already, the increasing disparity between rich and poor happened for complex reasons. But the rich Republicans supported a simple model that said that Japan and China had stolen ordinary jobs. This story appeared to satisfy poorly educated people in distress and, as noted already, they switched parties to vote for Republican candidates.

The Voting Rights Act of 1965 was part of Johnson's Great Society, and it set the federal government on a path that conservatives did not want to tread. The organizations formed by Charles Koch, with help from the Southern economist James Buchanan, were opposed to Black inclusion in political decisions, and their opposition to the Voting Rights Act grew as the organizations grew. The Heritage Foundation was started in 1973. The Federalist Society, the future source of President Trump's judicial nominees, was started in 1982 (MacLean, 2017).

Economic and political changes in the 1970s ended the Great Migration and reduced migrants' gains as the white American economy leapt ahead. When candidate Richard Nixon said he was adopting a Southern Strategy in 1968, he was signaling that he would continue the Republican tradition of using Jim Crow laws to separate African Americans from the white economy.

The Great Migration ended in 1970 because the jobs that Blacks hoped to find in the North were vanishing. This change can be seen in the original division of activity that was introduced when national income accounting originated in the 1930s. Economist Simon Kuznets organized economic activity into three groups: agriculture, manufacturing, and services. The industrial revolution led workers to switch from agriculture to manufacturing. They moved into towns to find work, studied at schools, and increased their incomes. Starting in the 1970s, economic activity moved from manufacturing to services. The change was subtle because new manufactured objects were involved, but the services – television, iPhones, Facebook, Google, and the like – were more prominent than the manufactured delivery devices. Jobs in manufacturing declined, and jobs in the new electronic services grew. "Financialization ... is today widening the gap between rich and poor." Wages stagnated, and inequality grew as shown in Figure 6.1 (Foroohar, 2016, 5).

These new jobs required a college education. As we have seen, some Blacks completed college and found jobs in these new industries, but most Blacks did not. We will see what happened to them shortly. For now, we observe that the wage premium for college graduates, which had been decreasing earlier in the twentieth century, increased dramatically after 1980. The return from a year of K–12 schooling showed little change after 1980. But the return from a year of college education rose from 0.076 in 1980 to 0.126 in 2000 and to 0.141 in 2017. The returns from a year of postcollege education (graduate and professional) rose from 0.067 in 1980 to 0.131 in 2000 and to 0.176 in 2017. The primary reason for this rapid growth in the wages of college graduates was due to a slowing down of college attendance after 1980. It also was accompanied by increased spread of wages within college graduates, suggesting that different kinds of education led to different wages. But the returns of the Black Elite were high (Autor, Goldin, and Katz, 2020).

## 1.1 THE RISE OF INEQUALITY IN THE UNITED STATES, 1978–2018

(Share of national income earned by the top 1% vs. bottom 50%)

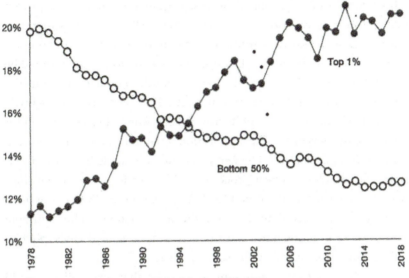

**6.1.** The rise of inequality in the United States, 1978–2018.
*Source:* Saez and Zucman, 2019, 7.

Southern Blacks migrating northward had only limited education, and they could not find work in the new economic activities. They found themselves adrift in Northern cities and looked around for jobs that did not require much education. Younger migrants also looked for education to qualify themselves for better jobs. Education in Northern cities was more available than in the rural South, but the migrants typically did not have access to good schools due to residential segregation.

Blacks increasingly lived in cities vacated by whites as suburbia grew, but urban property values fell as Blacks moved in. Blacks running from Southern Jim Crow policies lacked the income and capital of unionized white workers. And an important decision by the Supreme Court in 1974 condemned urban school systems to growing poverty. The case came from Detroit, which had absorbed many Black families seeking work. They were excluded from white neighborhoods by restricted access to mortgages and the opposition of white neighbors. The Detroit school district was two-thirds Black by the 1970s, and the NAACP filed suit against Michigan Governor William Milliken and others, charging direct discrimination against Blacks in the drawing of school districts.

The Supreme Court held in *Milliken v. Bradley* (418 US 717) that school districts were not obliged to desegregate unless it could be proven that the lines were drawn with racist intent. Historical lines that produced segregated districts were not illegal. In other words, if the population is stable and officials used race to draw school districts, that would be illegal. But if school districts were stable and the population changed – particularly if it changed from white to Black – there was no illegality.

Intent is a familiar concept in criminal law, where it has been used for many, many purposes. The application to public policy, however, is fraught with problems. Public decisions often are made by people interacting in complex political processes. The records of their discussions typically are brief and often bland. It is harder to find intent in a committee's actions than in an individual's actions. The Supreme Court used a traditional indicator in a way that accepted cities' policies without inquiring into their causes or effects.

The 1974 *Milliken* decision made it clear that white flight would successfully separate white suburbanites from their new dark-skinned neighbors. The decision ensured that Black urban communities would lack an adequate fiscal base. The Supreme Court would not combine or otherwise alter existing school districts, and whites fleeing cities for suburbs would be able to separate their children from those of urban Blacks. The decision also mandated poverty conditions for the urban school districts, which became poorer and Blacker over time. The tax base for urban schools decreased as urban factory jobs decreased, and fleeing whites avoided paying for urban schools. The Supreme Court limited school busing across city boundaries and encouraged rising racial segregation between inner cities and suburbs. The result was segregated schools with inadequate resources for urban schools attended by the children of the Great Migration. Separate and unequal, one might say.

*Milliken v. Bradley* was brought by the NAACP to further the implementation of *Brown v. Board of Education*. The decision meant that integrated education could be avoided by white flight from cities. *Brown v. Board of Education* was effectively dead after only twenty years.

The 1974 Supreme Court repeated the actions of the 1880s Supreme Court in voiding the first section of the Fourteenth Amendment roughly twenty years after the Amendment was adopted in 1868. Justices Powell and Rehnquist, two years after becoming Supreme Court Justices, made Nixon's Southern Strategy into a national policy (Temin, 2017).

President Nixon was a pivotal figure in a tumultuous period. He adopted a Southern Strategy for his domestic program as he ran for president in 1968. But he approached the expanding Vietnam War very differently. The Tet Offensive had been painful, and the North Vietnamese wanted to bargain with the South to see if they could share power in Vietnam. Nixon urged the Vietnam government to stall the peace negotiations that President Johnson had started. A recent biographer commented, "Under federal law, which bans private citizens from undercutting the government by negotiating with foreign powers, Nixon's actions were potentially felonious" (Farrell, 2017, 342n).

The American economy was in turmoil in the late 1960s. The expansion of the Vietnam War under presidents Johnson and Nixon led to rising prices in the United States and changed the dollar shortage after World War II into a dollar glut. The Nixon Shock in 1971 took the United States off the gold standard and out of the Bretton Woods agreement that supported prosperity and trade in the 1950s, fixed prices temporarily, and imposed some tariffs. While Nixon's actions did not formally terminate the existing Bretton Woods system of international financial exchange, the suspension of one of its key components effectively rendered the Bretton Woods system inoperative (Neal, 2015).

Then the Organization of Petroleum Exporting Countries (OPEC) raised oil prices dramatically in 1973. And various other actions changed inflation to "stagflation." This was a new term in macroeconomics, since economists were used to inflation caused by full employment. The combination of unemployment and inflation required new thinking. President Carter asked his economic advisor not to use the word "recession" in the late 1970s. The economist called it a banana. We face similar conditions in the COVID-19 coronavirus pandemic of 2020; we may face a new kind of stagflation, possibly with another cute label.

Race riots occurred in many cities around the country in the late 1960s in response to the growing Vietnam War, as discussed in Chapter 5.

Nixon ignored the Kerner Report on the riots, and it was forgotten. He then transformed Johnson's War on Poverty into his War on Drugs. His two top policy advisors recalled later how Nixon determined to deal with the urban riots. John Ehrlichman, President Nixon's domestic adviser, later revealed how Nixon hoped to exploit the domestic turmoil:

> The Nixon campaign in 1968, and the Nixon White House after that, had two enemies: the antiwar left and Black people. You understand what I'm saying? We knew we couldn't make it illegal to be either against the [Vietnam] war or blacks, but by getting the public to associate the hippies with marijuana and blacks with heroin, and then criminalizing both heavily, we could disrupt those communities. We could arrest their leaders, raid their homes, break up their meetings, and vilify them night after night on the evening news. Did we know we were lying about the drugs? Of course, we did. (Baum, 2016)

H. R. Haldeman, Nixon's Chief of Staff, confirmed Nixon's attitude in his diaries. He described views of President Nixon, "P" in the diaries, as follows:

> P emphasized that you have to face the fact that the whole problem is really the blacks. The key is to devise a system that recognizes this while not appearing to. Pointed out that there has never in history been an adequate black nation, and they are the only race of which this is true. Says Africa is hopeless. The worst there is Liberia, which we built. (Associated Press, 1994; Haldeman, 1994)

President Nixon's position was inconsistent. He prolonged the Vietnam War in 1968. Blacks rioted against the war and the conscription it entailed. Yet Nixon had no trouble blaming them for the violence instead of owning it himself. As conservative presidents often do, he diverted attention from his own faults by projecting his violence onto African Americans and to achieve other aims he had in mind.

President Nixon replaced President Johnson's War on Poverty with a new War on Drugs. The rate of incarceration in the United States started to rise soon after the Great Migration ended. It had stayed constant near 100 people per 100,000 residents from 1925 to 1970 and then grew rapidly after 1980. The incarceration rate rose rapidly for the next

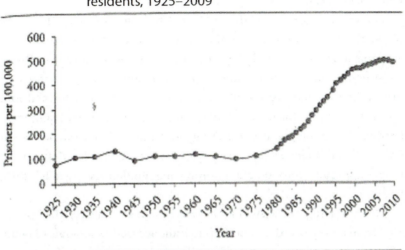

State and Federal prison inmates per 100,00 US residents, 1925–2009

*Source:* Authors' compilation based on Bureau of Justice Statistics, *National Prisoner Statistics* (various years).

**6.2.** State and Federal prison inmates per 100,000 US residents, 1925–2009.
*Source:* Raphael, Steven, and Michael A. Stoll. 2013, 5.

30 years, although more slowly after 2000 as shown in Figure 6.2. The incarceration rate in the European Union, Canada, and Mexico stayed near 100 per 100,000 residents, the American rate before 1980. The current American incarceration rate around 600 is the highest in the developed world, beating even Russia's incarceration rate. (Raphael and Stoll, 2013, 5–10; Carson and Anderson, 2016).

Federal and state laws were expanded, ranging from three-strike laws to harsh penalties for possession of small amounts of marijuana. The laws also shifted the judicial process from courtrooms to offices where prosecutors put pressure on accused people to plea bargain. The threat of harsh minimum sentences gave prosecutors the option of reducing the charge to a lesser one if the accused was reluctant to languish in jail – if he or she was unable to make bail and face the possibility of long years in prison. The number of inmates grew primarily from the increase in convictions rather than the length of sentences. "Few people in the criminal justice system are as powerful, or as central to prison growth, as the prosecutor" (Stuntz, 2011, 286; Pfaff, 2017, 127).

The crack epidemic of the 1980s led to policy changes that combined the two movements of the 1970s. The changes originated in attempts to reform the judicial process to lower prison terms, promote consistency among courts and encourage alternative sanctions to prison. By the time various bills were combined and transformed into the Sentencing Reform Act of 1984, however, the aim had shifted to become a part of the War on Drugs and the national toughness on crime. It was followed by a series of laws that translated the new, tough approach into detailed sentencing guidelines (Lynch, 2016, Chapter 2).

The Anti-Drug Abuse Act of 1986 was passed after a basketball player died from a drug overdose and Republicans accused Democrats of being soft on crime. Democrats wanted to take credit for an antidrug program in the November elections, so the bill had to pass Congress in October. That required action on the House floor in September, and committees had to finish their work before the August recess. Since the idea was born in July, committees had less than a month to develop the ideas, write the bills to carry out those ideas, and get comments from the relevant government agencies and the public at large.

The House Judiciary Committee considered a new idea that was "tough on drugs" for the first time four days before the recess began. The idea was to create mandatory minimum sentences in drug cases, which had tremendous political appeal. It was a type of penalty that had been removed from federal law in 1970 after extensive and careful consideration. But no hearings were held on reviving this idea in 1986. No experts on the relevant issues, no judges, no one from the Bureau of Prisons or from any other office in the government provided advice on the idea before it was rushed through the committee and into law. After bouncing back and forth between the Democratic House and the Republican Senate as each party jockeyed for political advantage, the Anti-Drug Abuse Act of 1986 passed both houses a few weeks before the November elections (Sterling, 1999).

The Anti-Drug Abuse Act of 1986 mandated a minimum sentence of five years without parole for possession of five grams of crack cocaine, while it mandated the same only for possession of 500 grams of powder cocaine. This 100:1 disparity clearly criminalized Blacks, who favored crack cocaine far more than whites did. The result was that by the 1990s, one of three Black men could expect to spend time in prison (Bonczar, 2003; Alexander, 2010).

The racial disparity between whites and Blacks under the new rules can be seen in the contrast between this estimate and the estimated one of seventeen white men who could expect incarceration. Despite the racial disparity of incarceration, poor whites outnumber them in prisons, echoing the violence against poor whites in the 1840s and the first Gilded Age. As in the depressed 1840s, poor whites suffer along with Blacks (Lynch, 2016, 26; Temin, 2018).

The Anti-Drug Abuse Act of 1986 also allowed prosecutors to seek a doubling of the mandatory minimum sentences if the defendant had a prior conviction. Another law passed in 1988 allowed prosecutors to ask for life imprisonment without parole for defendants who had two or more prior drug convictions. The War on Drugs became a New Jim Crow (Bonczar and Beck, 1997; Bonczar, 2003; Alexander, 2010; Lynch, 2016, 26).

Congress similarly determined the shape of another crime bill a decade later. President Clinton proposed another crime bill to allay fears as the crime wave of the 1980s reached its peak with a bill that would put 100,000 more police on the streets and expand prisons. These punitive measures were offset by a ban on assault weapons and a variety of social programs aimed at crime prevention and social intervention. Clinton's centrist approach gave solace to advocates of both punishment and rehabilitation.

The bill seemed on the way to passage when it was upset by racial conflict. One of the social programs in the bill provided for the midnight basketball program to occupy errant youths and reduce the danger they posed on the nighttime street. Midnight basketball rapidly became associated with helping Black youths and a code word for racial benefits. It raised deeply entrenched images and ideas associating crime with young African-American men that heightened the threat of crime and raised serious questions about preventative programs. The social programs were stripped from the bill, and it passed containing only the punitive parts.

Clinton signed it, an action he later regretted (Wheelock and Hartmann, 2007; Raphael and Stoll, 2013).

The disparity in the minimum sentences for crack and powder cocaine lasted until 2010, when the illegal possession of crack cocaine was increased to 28 grams (1 ounce) by the Fair Sentencing Act of that year, decreasing the racial ratio from 100:1 to 28:1. The larger disparity had continued for a quarter century, supported by the backlash from the Civil Rights Movement in Nixon's Southern Strategy, and the belief that Black prisoners were inherently criminal – not ordinary people who had done criminal things (Raphael and Stoll, 2013, 115–20).

Todd Clear, a prominent criminologist, argued that the growth of mass incarceration disrupted families, social networks, and other forms of social support. After a certain point, the collateral effects of high rates of incarceration contributed to more – not less – crime. The resulting crime fueled a public call for ever-tougher responses to crime. The politics of race and justice sustained an ever-growing policy base that guaranteed new supplies of penal subjects in a self-sustaining manner. This feedback made it harder to reverse mass incarceration, and we are now in an equilibrium with high incarceration (Clear, 2007, 175; Temin, 2018).

Bruce Western, writing at about the same time, spelled out the varied ways in which mass incarceration affected the lives of poorly educated Blacks. Incarcerated poor men found it hard to find good jobs, and their annual incomes were about one-third lower than nonconvicts with similar education. Incarceration also inhibited the formation of stable two-parent families, which pool resources, socialize and supervise children, and provide networks of mutual aid. Mass incarceration diminished the ability of incarcerated men from enjoying these social resources. Western concluded, "First, that mass imprisonment has significantly sealed the social immobility of poor Blacks. Second, if we view the effects of the prison boom in the context of its causes, mass imprisonment has significantly subtracted from the gains of African American citizenship hard won by the civil rights movement" (Western 2006, 163, 191).

These findings have been confirmed by recent research on income differentials between Black and white men. In the heart of the Great Recession, almost 40 percent of prime-age Black men at the bottom of

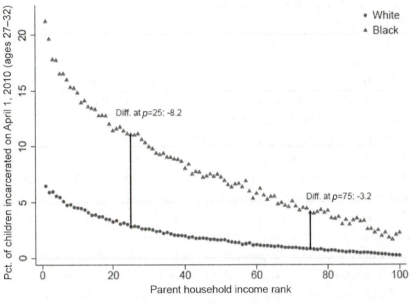

**6.3.** Incarceration rates by income and race, 2010.

the income distribution where mass incarceration takes its toll were unemployed compared with less than 20 percent of white men. Blacks at the top of their income distribution found that their incomes reduced the Black–white income gap, largely through greater college employment (Bayer and Charles, 2018; Western, 2018).

The effect of all these laws and convictions can be seen in Figure 6.3, which shows the incarceration rate for Blacks and whites in 2010. The upper line for Black incarceration rates was above the rate for whites, but much further above for poor families. This clear difference shows that race was dominant, even though income also was important in the aftermath of growth of a Black Elite described in the last chapter. College-educated Black men were far safer from drug convictions than working-class men (Chetty and Hendren, 2018a, 2018b).

This graph shows that race and class are intertwined. Poor Blacks are much more likely to be incarcerated than members of the Black Elite. Education is key, as incarceration upsets the path of children toward education and condemns them to a life of poverty. Poor Blacks are thought of as criminals, and rich Blacks try to separate themselves from this group. The problem for Blacks today is how to escape from this cruel system of mass incarceration.

The American criminal justice system holds almost 2.3 million people in 3,000 local jails, 2,000 state prisons, 200 juvenile correction facilities, and 100 federal prisons. Blacks are three times as likely to be sent to prison as whites because 40 percent of prisoners are Black while Blacks are only 13 percent of the population. See Figure 6.3 for an illustration of racial disparity in incarceration. In addition, three-quarters of jail prisoners have not been convicted of any crime; they are poor and often Black victims of our monetary bail system. That is why the line for Blacks in Figure 6.3 slopes down as family income increases. The war on drugs is the center of mass incarceration, and nonviolent drug convictions dominate federal convictions. However, most state prisoners are convicted of other offenses, and an additional 3.6 people, such as Meek Mill (identified in Chapter 7), are on probation (Sawyer and Wagner, 2020).

Black banks helped prosperous Blacks, but they were limited in what they could do

> Insofar as there is segregations and widespread poverty in the black community, banks that exclusively serve this community cannot be successful. ... Self-help microfinance cannot overcome macro inequality and systemic racism. Policy-makers have been placing the weight and responsibility of centuries of wealth inequality on these tiny economic engines, and the results have been failure and frustration. (Baradaran, 2017, 278–79)

Even well-off Blacks face anger from whites that seems to transcend class. Trayvon Martin was shot by a white man when he went out to buy something for his mother at the corner store in 2012 Florida. His killer was found innocent, recalling the treatment of lynching a century earlier. Ahmaud Arburg was shot while jogging for exercise in 2020 Georgia. His killers are currently awaiting trial. Killings and incarceration are different, but they come from the same racist impulses (Alvarez and Buckley, 2013; Fausset and Rojas, 2020).

Prejudice against people of African origins is also evident in Western Europe., while not as prominent as in the United States with its history of slavery. A Black Belgian student was killed in a fraternity initiation, and a

Swiss banking expert who rescued Credit Suisse was abruptly fired from his CEO position at the bank after objecting to a racist program (Apuzzo and Erlanger, 2020; Kelly, 2020).

As mass incarceration grew, it put pressure on state governments. About 90 percent of prisoners are in state prisons. And the fiscal weight of these prisoners put pressure on state budgets, which reduced education expenditures. State universities lost funds whenever there was a fiscal crisis, and primary and secondary schools lost funds more smoothly. Mass incarceration thus lowered economic growth in two ways. Prisoners were not educated while in prison, although we do hear of occasional prison schools. More importantly, the funds for the schooling of all children has been reduced (Mitchell and Leachman, 2014; Temin, 2018).

The effects of incarceration on the individuals involved can be seen in Figure 6.4. This model distinguishes three human modes. Customary behavior is simply doing today what you did yesterday and possibly earlier times as well. Instrumental behavior, beloved by economists, is to further aims that the individual has. Economists often label this mode as rational. Command behavior is doing what you are told by whatever authority is commanding you.

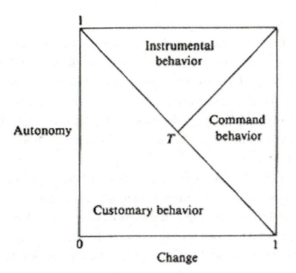

**6.4.** Modes of behavior.
*Sources:* Temin, 1980.

When in prison, you adhere to command behavior unless you are eager for penalties from the prison administration. Schooling, almost by definition, teaches instrumental behavior. These modes of behavior are opposed to each other. Prisoners are not supposed to choose instrumental actions; they are to follow orders. And prison guards are not prepared to honor choices that prisoners might make to improve their welfare, date of release, or any other aim. Prison schooling therefore is an oxymoron.

The changes described so far – the end of the Great Migration, the start of mass incarceration, and reduced educational expenditures – were roughly coincident in the 1970s. It is hard to separate cause and effect in simultaneous changes, and economists use what they call identifying strategies to make the distinction. The strategy here is to assume that members of the Great Migration tended to join African-American communities that were already established in the North. More migrants meant more prisoners in the War on Drugs. Examining local variations in the rate of Black settlement in the North, we can identify mass incarceration as a cause of reduced school spending.

Several economists have tried to examine the tumultuous events of the late twentieth century to decide which things were cause and which effects. They examined both the wage stagnation and the civil rights of African Americans. They found that while the federal government was the prime mover for improving Blacks' civil rights, they could not identify specific government actions that were most effective. And Blacks now are so diverse that no single cause can be found for the economic changes that Blacks have experienced. Black college graduates lost earnings while Blacks with less education lost jobs. No single factor can explain all these outcomes (Donohue and Heckman, 1991; Bound and Freeman, 1992).

The story can be summarized as follows. Black migration increased white suburbanization. The introduction of automobiles and new highways increased whites moving to the suburbs, and almost three whites left cities for each added Black resident in addition. The Supreme Court determined in *Milliken*, 1974, that the Black cities would be poor. Presidents Reagan and Bush reduced federal funding for cities in addition. As urban manufacturing work disappeared, Black and white urban working-class communities deteriorated. Drug use increased, and mass incarceration gathered steam. The disappearance of good urban jobs set this process off, and that is the third of the changes that occurred around 1970 and could be the ultimate cause of these interrelated changes (Wilson, 1996; Boustan, 2010; Derenoncourt, 2019).

Nixon converted federal programs into block grants to states in order to give states more choice in how to spend the money, calling his move a New Federalism. Reagan then reversed fifty years of American domestic policy by cutting back federal grants to local and state governments that the federal government used to help poor people. Public service jobs and job training were reduced sharply, and the share of federal funding for large cities fell from 22 percent to 6 percent of their budgets. The decline of both private and public sources of employment in inner cities greatly reduced employment opportunities for white and Black urban residents alike (Temin, 2017).

## 6.2 FROM REAGAN TO A BLACK PRESIDENT

President Reagan continued Nixon's Southern Strategy by initiating his presidential campaign in Philadelphia, Mississippi. Why in such a small town? Because every Southerner and sympathizer knew that three civil rights workers, Chaney, Goodman, and Schwerner, were murdered in Philadelphia during the 1964 Freedom Summer while attempting to register Blacks to vote. Reagan did not need to say a word for this effective claim to sympathize with white supremacists and be effective. He supported states' rights and condemned the Federal Government as an enemy of the (white) people.

The long-run effects of the New Federalism can be seen in the 2015 crisis of lead pollution in the public water supply to Flint, Michigan. Flint had been an auto manufacturing center, but employment in the auto industry declined soon after Blacks came to Michigan for good jobs during the Great Migration. Blacks arrived to find reduced employment, and the city of Flint was unable to pay its bills as manufacturing continued to decline through the 1990s. Republican Governor Rick Snyder was elected in 2011 and supported a controversial law that allowed him to appoint emergency managers of cities in financial trouble. Flint suffered from white flight that destroyed urban tax revenues as automobile jobs disappeared. Governor Snyder put Flint into receivership and appointed an emergency manager in 2012. There were four different managers in the next three years, an arrangement that was not likely to yield comprehensive plans.

An emergency manager took Flint off the Detroit water system to save money in April 2014. He decided to take Flint's water from a local river instead. The immediate result was brown water pouring out of the faucets in peoples' homes, and lots of complaints from residents about the new water supply. Detroit offered to reconnect Flint to its water system in January 2015, and to forego a substantial connection fee. A different emergency manager refused.

The complaints became sharper when high levels of lead were found in Flint's water in February and March 2015. This was known in the governor's office, but no action was taken. In September of that year, several doctors made a public statement that many Flint children had elevated levels of lead in their blood. Soon after the doctors' news conference and a year and a half after the switch to river water, the state began to act. Flint was reconnected to the Detroit water system in October.

The residents of Flint, who by then had high levels of lead in their blood and pipes in their homes that were damaged by the river Water; they needed help. The state government brought fresh bottled water to Flint for emergency help, but that was all it did. State funds for reconstruction were blocked by political objections, and federal emergency funds were blocked as well. The residents of Flint were unable to move, locked in by homeownership and other constraints, and the needed investment in Flint's water pipes was being made very slowly. (Bosman, 2017; Davenport, 2019; Smith, Bosman and Davey, 2019).

A 2020 rule by the Environmental Protection Agency rejected the urging of top medical and scientific experts to require replacing the country's 6 million to 10 million lead service lines, an expensive but effective way to avoid crises like that in Flint. Some experts said the new rule actually weakens the current rule by more than doubling the amount of time utilities have to replace water systems with serious levels of lead contamination. Dr. Mona Hanna-Attisha, the Michigan pediatrician whose research exposed the Flint water crisis, called the new rule heartbreaking (Friedman, 2020; Gray, 2020).

Conservative rich people considered Johnson's Great Society to be harmful to the unregulated competition that they desired. They want a limited government that does not care for working people. That explains why the funds needed to restore damaged water pipes in Flint and provide help for children whose brains were damaged by bad water have been so hard to find. Betsy DeVos, President Trump's Secretary of Education, is a Michigan resident, and her family has a great deal of political interest in the state. She convinced the Republican legislature to favor charter schools over public schools, and Michigan went from a middle state for educational success to a very poor state (MacLean, 2017).

Returning to events around 1970, various forces starting then resulted in a change in the demand for specific jobs that created an hourglass job profile, splitting the American labor market into a low-wage part of laborers and service workers and a higher-wage part of professionals and managers. A college education is needed to get hired into the top group. Lower-paying jobs often barely allow workers to get by and do not provide enough income for people to save for retirement, which seems farther away than many current needs. And to compound the issue, low-wage sector jobs began to disappear.

The changing face of jobs was the result of technological change, but technology is only part of the story. Several causes can be distinguished, and they can be divided into domestic and international. All of them were results of governmental decisions. Advances in technology and electronics were promoted by government, primarily military, spending. The growing interest in and deregulation of finance shaped firms and industries. Globalization was accelerated by policies opening international capital markets, promoting American foreign investment and American economic influence.

The development of computers increasingly substituted for labor in routine tasks, that is, tasks that can be accomplished by following explicit rules. Factory jobs were the basis of unions in the twentieth century, and unions lost members and influence as these trends continued. The Great Migration ended in the economic confusion of the 1970s and left the new Northern urban residents scrambling for good jobs as the nature of work changed (Autor, 2019).

The percentage of the labor force in unions declined from close to 40 percent in 1954 to 10 percent today. Unions lost effectiveness as well. In the 1970s, strikes involved more than 950,000 workers every year; in the 1990s, by contrast, strikes never involved half a million workers, despite a larger labor force. Many more strikes were broken, with employees losing their jobs. Unions had diminishing political influence within the Democratic Party and increased Republicans Party dominance. Explanations of these changes focus, respectively, on demographic changes, the role of the union itself, the state, especially the legal system, globalization, and neoliberalism, and the employer anti-union offensive (Clawson and Clawson, 1999).

As jobs and unions disappeared, wages stagnated for both whites and Blacks. This wage stagnation came from diverse causes and has lasted for at least fifty years. It came from both technical and organizational changes in business and from both domestic and foreign developments. Unions disappeared as jobs vanished, and the loss of labor bargaining power broke the connection between increasing labor productivity and wages. This new pattern differs dramatically from the shared benefit of economic growth before 1970 (Temin, 2017).

The shifts that began around 1970 altered the distribution of income. Labor's share fell while capital's share grew. The fall of labor's share of GDP in the United States and many other countries in recent decades is well known, but its causes are still obscure. One approach to this problem is to examine differences among business firms. Since globalization and technological changes led the most productive firms in each industry to expand and antitrust issues were not pursued, market concentration rose as superstar firms grew. They have high markups and a low labor share of value-added. It was not simply trade and technology, but also the policy decision not to constrain the new, large, and even monopoly firms that led workers to lose out in the postindustrial economy. Financialization of industries intensified this process (Autor, Goldin, and Karz, 2020; Lazonick, Moss, and Weitz, forthcoming).

The rise in inequality since 1960 is shown in Figure 6.1. It has been very dramatic and has subjected us all to a new gilded age. The tax rate

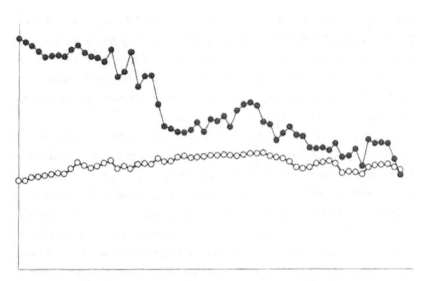

**6.5.** Taxes on the richest 400, 1960–2000.
*Source:* Saez and Zucman, 2019, 23. The horizontal axis is years, 1960–2000. The vertical axis is percentage tax for the richest 400 Americans (solid circles) and the bottom 50 percent (hollow circles).

on the very rich also has decreased drastically since 1960 as shown in Figure 6.5. The fall in the tax rate for rich people should be included in the reasons for inequality growth since taxes on the rich were reduced as the rich gained political power. Their tax rate fell dramatically under Reagan, and inequality rose sharply during that period (Saez and Zucman, 2019).

Some Black men and women who had been educated in the postwar prosperity were absorbed into this new and changing economic structure on almost the same terms as white workers with similar training. This new Black Elite is a durable result of the Civil Rights Movement. But less educated Blacks did not do so well. They were the last to be hired in many factories and therefore the first to be fired as foreign competition grew. The upward mobility that they had shared with their more educated white peers turned to downward mobility as the economy and the political environment changed (Freeman, 1976).

Educated Blacks and whites were able to educate their children for good jobs in the new economy, but fired factory workers could not. Affirmative action disappeared under President Reagan. Blacks also could not buy houses or new cars or move into better neighborhoods. Working-class Blacks fell behind whites both in salaries earned and wealth accumulated. And even those Blacks who graduated college wanted to avoid discriminatory experiences at work and to help other Blacks. They chose to work in nonprofits, governments, and civil rights law (Lazonick, Moss, and Weitz, forthcoming).

Japan and then China increased their exports, imitating the export-led growth path of England and Germany a hundred years earlier, and American jobs were hurt. As computers took over repetitive tasks, more jobs were lost. And as finance expanded in the late 1970s, companies were encouraged to specialize in their core activities, that is, the activities that they were known and patronized for. This would increase their value on the stock market, and outside firms and services could be hired to do menial jobs. The same computers that reduced factory jobs also made it easier to create instructions for service jobs and to monitor them (Temin, 2017).

Johnson's Great Society ushered in a decade of two-party Southern governments. Manufacturing prospered, particularly in North Carolina, and led to good race relations. As the boom ended in the 1980s and 1990s, union membership began to fall, particularly in Alabama. Between the Voting Rights Act and the mid-1990s, the median white Southerner voted for liberal-to-moderate Democrats, no doubt conservative by outside standards but well within the spectrum for the national party.

Class-based partisan voting emerged during this period, which observers saw as a sign of diminished role for race and for regional distinctiveness. But changes in economic conditions, attributed by voters to removal of long-standing barriers to import competition in industries that were fundamental to regional prosperity, destroyed this racial harmony. Many votes against Democratic legislators in 1994 were direct retaliation against President Clinton for his trade policies. The longer-term trend more likely reflected the loss of manufacturing jobs, associated with stagnant or falling real incomes, increased joblessness, and the decline of formerly robust industrial communities. Poor whites changed from being treated like Blacks to opposing Black equality. The return to antebellum Southern attitudes started in response to Johnson's Civil

Rights Movement and continued in response to Clinton's free trade programs (Wright, 2013, 2020).

The company supervisor was replaced by a contract with a separate company that monitored workers. For example, most hotel employees used to work for the hotels they worked in. Today, over 80 percent of a hotel's employees are hired and supervised by a separate management company. They no longer have a path to advancement within the hotel company, they typically also lack vacations and pension plans, and their economic mobility has decreased greatly (Weil, 2014).

The shift from paying wages to hiring subcontractors was a momentous change in the place of workers in a business enterprise. When workers were wage earners, there was a social component to their work. Workers saw themselves as a group, and being a member of a stable group fostered morale. Most successful firms gain from the identification of workers with the firm and the extra care and effort that produces. When workers are hired instead by a competitive service company, they have no identification with the parent firm. They have low morale and will not exert extra effort for the parent company's benefit. Intrusive monitoring replaces morale, and antagonism replaces cooperation. This change particularly affected Blacks who had missed the opportunity to get an education in the prosperous years (Temin, 2004).

More importantly, Blacks who attempted to upgrade their skills became victims of for-profit education. The increasing returns to skill made a market where firms created educational programs of high cost and little value, and where they preyed upon Black workers looking to increase their skill in the market. These schools left Blacks with high amounts of debt and few marketable skills at a time when more modest investments in skills from lower-cost options would have had a higher return. Even when trying to adapt to the new economy, Blacks found themselves victimized again (Cottom, 2017).

The share of national income of the richest members of the economy increased as the share of income captured by workers with unchanging wages fell. The United States and other English-speaking countries have the most unequal incomes in the world. American inequality was increased further by tax cuts for the rich under Reagan and Trump. A book on tax evolution summarizes these results: "The wealthy have seen their taxes rolled back to levels last seen in the 1910s, when the government was only a quarter of the size it is today. It is as if a century of fiscal history has been erased" (Saez and Zucman, 2019, xi).

The 2008 financial crisis proved to be one more nail in the coffin of racial equality. While Blacks made significant gains in income and home-ownership from the 1950s to the end of the twentieth century, the housing market collapse reversed the vast majority of that progress. In some American cities, Blacks have average wealth of less than $100. Nationally, a white household who did not finish high school has more wealth on average than a Black household with a college education. The policies which historically excluded Blacks from wealth building cannot be solved by education or labor market policies which concentrate on income. It is the product of a historical legacy.

The 2008 financial crisis resulted in the election of the United States' first Black president, Barack Obama. This election was the most exciting result of the Black Elite that had grown in the Civil Rights Movement. It was one thing to have Black doctors, lawyers, and businessmen; it is quite another to have a Black president. Obama's election shows that it is bad education, not innate inferiority, that condemns most Black people to poverty in America. Education is not simply formal schooling, but also growing up in a stable environment where students can absorb and learn.

President Obama was a beacon of success to part of the American population. But his election also was a sign of imminent danger to the racist part of the population. The population of the country is polarized along several dimensions, but the racial division dominates the discussion of political fortunes. This Janus-like result of Obama's administration needs to be kept in mind as we analyze resulting events. He is married to Michelle Obama, who was a descendant of American slaves. She helped him in his campaign and was accused by the racists of being an angry Black woman – revealing both faces of educated Black people in the United States (Obama, M., 2018).

Obama had an ideal upbringing in Hawaii where there were mixed races and few Blacks. He went to Harvard Law School and became editor of the *Harvard Law Review* while there. Then he went to Chicago and worked with poor Black communities before entering politics. He served in the Illinois House of Representatives and then the United States Senate. He gave a stunning speech at the 2004 Democratic convention and was selected to be a presidential candidate in 2008. He might have been elected in any case, but he was helped by his Republican opponent's apparent ignorance of what was happening in the financial crisis as the election approached in the fall of 2008. Race fell into the background as the economy tanked, only to resurface quickly after the financial crisis (Obama, 2007).

Obama wanted to alleviate the suffering that followed the crisis, but he was hampered by his limited command of economics. He therefore followed the advice of his economics teachers and staff members. The two most important advisers were Robert Rubin, Secretary of the Treasury under President Clinton, and Lawrence Summers, a senior Treasury Department official throughout President Clinton's administration, who was appointed director of the National Economic Council by President Obama. Rubin had been head of Goldman Sachs before entering the government, and he was Summers' boss during President Clinton's administration.

The flavor of their advice can be seen in negotiations that preceded Obama's inauguration. Christina Romer, the prospective head of Obama's Council of Economic Advisors, showed how three alternative sizes of fiscal expansion should stimulate the economy: "What happens if we do $600 billion, $800 billion, and $1.2 trillion of stimulus? If you want to keep unemployment below 8 percent you do $800. But if you want to get it down quickly to below 7 percent you need to do something really big like $1.2 trillion." Summers deleted the $1.2 trillion from the memo to the president-elect. His argument was that he did not think the new administration could get that much through Congress, and it would not be good for the president ever to be seen as losing (Hundt, 2019, 132–33).

Unemployment went up to 10 percent in 2009, and $1.2 trillion fiscal policy stimulus would have been better. Even if the president did not get all he wanted, he would have been better off starting high and ending near $800 billion. In fact, the president lost by not asking for the larger amount. The administration thought about a second stimulus package in the summer of 2009, but the Republicans would not consider more spending. One chance was enough. Was Summers being conservative or too cautious to engage Republicans with a larger stimulus?

Blacks and Hispanics suffered the sharpest fall in wealth in the 2008 financial crisis and the Great Recession. The median wealth of white households only fell from $135,000 to $113,000 between 2005 and 2009, while the median wealth of Black households fell from $12,000 to $6,000 and Latino households' wealth fell from $18,000 to $6,000. While white households' wealth fell less than 20 percent, Black households' wealth fell by half, Latino wealth, by two-thirds (Pew Research Center, 2011, 13).

After the economic crisis calmed down a bit, President Obama started to negotiate with Republicans about his plan for what would become the Affordable Care Act. He did not realize how opposed the Republicans are toward poor people, and spent several months dickering with them. The reform act passed in March 2010. It was dubbed Obamacare by the Republicans, and Obama was flattered. He did not realize that the nickname would remind poor whites that this was a Black man's plan, and it has become the expression used most often for the organization that administers the Affordable Care Act.

Obamacare was a great success. It reduced the uninsured by half and did not allow discrimination based on previous illnesses. Together with the Health Care and Education Reconciliation Act of 2010 amendment, it was the most significant regulatory overhaul and expansion of the American healthcare system since the passage of Medicare and Medicaid in 1965. The 2010 act retained the existing structure of Medicare, Medicaid, and the employer market, but overhauled parts of the markets within these programs. Insurers were required to accept all applicants without charges based on preexisting conditions or demographic status (except age). To combat the resultant adverse selection, the act mandated that individuals buy insurance (or pay a fine/tax) and that insurers cover a list of "essential health benefits."

Obamacare faced strong political opposition before and after enactment, with calls for repeal and legal challenges. In *National Federation of Independent Business v. Sebelius,* the Supreme Court ruled that states could choose not to participate in Obamacare's Medicaid expansion, although it upheld the law as a whole. Republican states typically did not expand

Medicaid even though the federal government would pay almost all the added costs. The map of states that did not expand Medicaid looks like the 1904 election and the Confederacy, although some Midwest cities are included too. Polls initially found that a plurality of Americans opposed the act, although its individual provisions were generally more popular and the law gained majority support by 2017.

The law caused a significant reduction in the number and percentage of people without health insurance. The percentage of people without health insurance fell from 16 percent in 2010 to 9 percent in the first half of 2016. Approximately 12 million people were covered by the exchanges (10 million of whom received subsidies) and 11 million added to Medicaid. Another million were covered by Obamacare's "Basic Health Program," for a total of 24 million. The uninsured rate dropped in every congressional district in the United States from 2013 to 2015 (Barry-Jester and Ben, 2016).

As in the 1880s, the Supreme Court stepped in soon after the 2008 Financial Crisis to promote corporations' progress in several landmark decisions. Early in 2010, the Supreme Court decided *Citizens United*, 558 US 310, ruling that the government could not restrict independent political expenditures by nonprofit companies because money spent by corporations was the same as speech. This decision followed *McConnell v. Federal Election Commission* (2003) in greatly easing the flow of campaign contributions from rich individuals and large corporations. The opinion defined corruption as bribery only when it had an explicit quid pro quo, which means the explicit exchange of something of value for a specific and identifiable government action. This is a much narrower definition of bribes than the Supreme Court held in prior cases where a variety of gifts were ruled illegal, although it was introduced earlier in *Buckley v. Valeo*, 424 US 1 (1976). As the opinion in *Citizens United* expressed the new, narrow standard, "Independent expenditures, including those made by corporations, do not give rise to corruption or the appearance of corruption" (Teachout, 2014, 7, 232).

This decision extended the Supreme Court's favoritism toward corporations that started in the 1880s when they turned the Fourteenth Amendment around to apply to corporations instead of freedmen. This and following decisions would replay the Supreme Court's vision from the 1880s that corporations were people and deserved much more consideration than African Americans (Winkler, 2018, Chapter 10).

*Citizens United*, decided in January, changed the political landscape. The Democrats were discouraged after the fight for the Affordable Care Act and the slow recovery from the financial crisis of 2008, and they did not understand how quickly the Republicans would act on the Supreme Court's decision. Charles Koch and his secret organizations were quick to seize the opportunity. Reasoning that their money would have more impact in smaller markets, they poured money into state races for governors and representatives in the 2010 mid-term elections. Democrats were slow to take advantage of this opportunity. They were neither disciplined nor under centralized control, and they had far fewer liquid resources at their disposal than the Kochtopus (Mayer, 2016; Page, Seawrite, and Lacombe, 2019).

Republicans put into operation its REDMAP, a plan to redistrict in favor of Republicans. Gerrymandering is a traditional American practice, but REDMAP was the first set of state actions orchestrated in a national effort. The first step was to jam voters likely to favor your opponents into a few throwaway districts where the other side could win lopsided victories, a strategy known as "packing." The second step was to arrange other boundaries to win close victories, "cracking" opposition groups into many districts. As a result of lopsided political spending, Republicans emerged from the 2010 election with just shy of thirty Republican state governors and almost as many Republican-controlled state legislatures.

As a result of REDMAP, Democrats received 1.4 million more votes than Republicans for the House of Representatives in 2012, yet Republicans won control of the House by a 234 to 201 margin. Democrats would have had to win the popular vote by 7 percentage points to take control of the House (assuming that votes shifted by a similar percentage across all districts), a magnitude that happens in only about one-third of congressional elections. The ability of Democratic voters to change the leadership of the House of Representatives is very limited; plutocrats – the 1 percent – sharply hampered their access.

The role of money in politics has grown since then, although readers may recall that money mattered in the 1896 presidential election. Candidates are ranked by how much money they have raised, and scholars have found a linear relation between money and votes. The new technology just described shows how money was transformed into votes through various electronic channels (Ferguson, Jorgensen, and Chen, 2019).

Fundraising for politics also has been affected by the reluctance to apply the antitrust laws to large companies and particularly electronic innovators. This has generated rich executives who feel they should wield political power as well as economic power. Although they do not have much contact with Blacks, they use racial divisions to divide the working class, a familiar American practice. As a result, "Race and corporate power are totally intertwined" (Teachout, 2020, 139).

In the aftermath of Watergate in 1974, an attempt was made in Congress to pass a law providing for public funding of political campaigns. Alas, it did not pass, even though this was before the rapid increase of inequality shown in Figure 6.1 took place. We now have to contend, as a result of this failure and the Supreme Court with the dominant effect of the very rich on our politics (Mandle, 2008, 138–39).

The Voting Rights Act of 1965 incorporated provisions to deal with the legacy of Jim Crow laws in the South. The Supreme Court ruled that its most effective provision was unconstitutional in *Shelby County v. Holder* (570 US 529) in 2013, just as the Supreme Court had eviscerated the Fourteenth Amendment in the 1880s. The Voting Rights Act required selected states, mostly in the South, to preclear proposed voting arrangements with the federal government. In other words, the federal government would decide whether voting arrangements would violate the Voting Rights Act before they went into effect. The Supreme Court held this provision to be unconstitutional because the coverage formula was based on data over forty years old, rendering it no longer responsive to current needs and therefore placing an illegitimate burden on the constitutional principles of federalism and equal sovereignty of the states (Overton, 2006).

Despite the Supreme Court's assertion that all states are alike, the states that had been listed in the original bill immediately rushed to impose voting restrictions that otherwise would not have passed preclearance. While it seems clear that these restrictions are racially motivated, they can no longer be phrased in that way. The difficulties of voting therefore affect low-wage whites and Blacks. Between growing inequality and continuing race prejudice, democracy seems to be on a downward trajectory. Jim Crow laws are reviving.

The Supreme Court more recently accelerated this decline in another case, *Rucho v. Common Cause* (588 U.S. ___ 2019), by ruling that states could not be sued in federal courts for partisan gerrymandering congressional districts. The court said it still had jurisdiction over racial gerrymandering, but it failed to draw any connections between partisan and racial gerrymandering. Since modern Republican look increasingly like Southern Democratic in the original Gilded Age, future partisan gerrymanders will shrink the effects of Black votes. This is not as violent as Jim Crow laws a century ago, but it may be as effective in reducing Black votes.

By delegating voting right to states, the Supreme Court replicated the practice of late nineteenth- and early twentieth-century Southern senators. As noted earlier, the Southerners used this practice repeatedly to reduce the impact of federal programs on the Jim Crow practices of the South. The Great Migration has changed a Southern problem to a national one, and the Supreme Court has now signed into the opposition to Reconstruction.

# PART III

# THE TWENTY-FIRST CENTURY

## CHAPTER 7

# Racism Rose and America Declined

### 7.1 DONALD TRUMP'S BUSINESS

Donald Trump had no prior experience in politics when he defeated Hillary Clinton in 2016 to become president. Her campaign slogan was "Better Together," as she looked to the future, but she failed to get started. His aim was to divide the country and split his opposition. This chapter tells how Republicans sought to destroy racial equality and the future of the United States.

It is useful to see how Donald Trump acted as a businessperson since he continued his private behavior into his political life. He was in the real-estate part of the finance sector, and he borrowed extensively from the financial services industry. He started in New York buildings in 1980, as the city was recovering from its brush with bankruptcy in the tumultuous 1970s. He wanted to build a large residential building in a choice location. He convinced Bonwit Teller to sell their lease on a building on Fifth Avenue just south of Central Park for $25 million. He acquired the air rights to build a large building on that spot by paying off New York City commissioners and hired undocumented Polish laborers earning almost nothing to demolish the old building.

Trump wanted more. New York passed Section 241a in 1971 to promote buildings in areas that were too depressed for normal investors by subsidizing construction in these marginal neighborhoods. Trump wanted to receive a $25 million subsidy from taxpayers – exactly as much as he paid for the lease. Central Manhattan is hardly a depressed neighborhood, but Trump applied to the city housing commissioner for the abatement, whose staff laughed at the presumption. The commissioner denied the application, and Trump called him dishonest and threatened retaliation. The threat came in a phone call to the commissioner's house saying someone was going to kill him for his decision.

Trump turned to the courts and won a favorable decision in the lower court. The city appealed, and the appeals court overturned that decision and ratified the commissioner's initial decision. The court said, "Trump Tower's enormous bulk was achieved by means of multiple zoning variances, including the transfer of air rights and the use of a special Fifth Avenue District zoning bonus. ... This has nothing to do with encouraging residential housing by means of a tax exemption." Trump and his lawyer, Roy Cohen, appealed to the New York Supreme Court, which said in a unanimous decision that the badly written law was so broad that even a building on Fifth Avenue was eligible for the tax abatement (Bernstein, 2020, 84–88).

When Trump's Atlantic City casinos began to fail in the early 1990s, he deducted the full value of his business losses from his income even though he had borrowed most of the money invested in the casinos. His niece, Mary Trump, described his mood after his Atlantic City fiasco: "Nothing was ever fair to him. That struck a chord in [his father] Fred, who nursed his own grievances and also never took responsibility for anything other than his successes. Donald's talent for deflecting responsibility while projecting blame onto others came straight from his father's playbook" (Trump, 2020, 140).

Trump's businesses filed for bankruptcy several times under Chapter 11 of the bankruptcy code. Unlike bankruptcies under Chapter 7, which liquidate businesses, Chapter 11 bankruptcies put debts on hold while negotiations take place between the failing businesses and their creditors. Trump was an aggressive bargainer and forced his debtors to allow forgiving payment terms and provide him with additional loans to keep his properties afloat. He rapidly became too big to fail.

Real estate investors often avoid paying taxes when they sell properties. If they sell at a loss, they carry the loss forward to offset future income because the loss is classified as an ordinary loss. And if real estate investors make a gain, they avoid taxes by reinvesting the proceeds in another property. This like-kind exchange can be used over and over again to delay taxes. Trump advocated the special treatment for real estate to Congress, saying that new buildings create other expenses for furnishings. Trump and his fellow real estate investors were permitted to fully deduct a variety of losses, sometimes only on paper, against their income (Ashkenas, Dance, and Gates, 2016; Drucker and Stewart, 2020).

Trump started with a million dollar advance from his father with the promise of more if needed. By 1990, he was $3.4 billion in debt, with over $800 million of that being his personal responsibility. In addition to owning casinos, he had purchased a yacht for $29 million, New York's Plaza Hotel for $407 million, and an airline for $365 million. All were losing money in 1990 and 1991.

Trump's cash fell below $1.7 million at the end of 1991 and was expected to fall below a million in a few months. He fell behind on property taxes and turned to his family for help. His father purchased $3 million in chips from one of Trump's casinos and did not cash them in, providing Trump with needed cash. Trump was still in financial trouble in 1993. He asked his siblings if he could borrow $10 million from the family trust. They agreed to this and an additional $20 million the following year. (President Trump later denied that he borrowed from his siblings.)

Trump gave up his money-losing yacht, airline, and hotel. He sold stock in his casinos and shifted his personal debt into a new public company. He also took a business loss of $916 million that freed him from paying income taxes for the foreseeable future, helped by a law that loosened regulations in the real estate industry that he had testified for. Tax experts observed that Trump's losses should have offset his gains from the reduction of his debts, but this income was not reported (Buettner and Bagli, 2016b; Barstow, Craig, and Buettner, 2018).

Trump's new company filed for bankruptcy in November 2004. Bondholders took a $500 million loss, and the company lurched toward bankruptcy again in 2009. Bondholders gave up another $1.3 billion in exchange for control of the company; Trump gave up any official role in his company and owned less than 10 percent of it (Buettner and Bagli, 2016a).

Trump often had unsuccessful projects where other people lost money while he walked away with profits. An example is his 2010 plan to build Trump SoHo, an apartment building in a part of New York that had lots of culture, but no tall buildings. The building was never built, and there were many suits by people who lost money accusing Trump and his family of false statements about the building that were settled in the fall of 2011. Cyrus Vance, the New York District Attorney, declined to open a criminal suit, and Trump's attorney contributed gifts that totaled $50,000 to Vance's reelection campaign in 2012 (Bernstein, 2020, 213–15).

Trump had been a celebrity since the 1980s, but his business had foundered, and he had become a garish figure of local interest by 2003. His performance in the TV series, "The Apprentice," mythologized him on a much bigger scale, turning him into an icon of American success. The program's legacy was to have cast a serially bankrupt carnival barker in the role of a man who became the leader of the free world.

Trump starred in fourteen seasons of "The Apprentice." He then appeared in the gilded atrium of Trump Tower, on Fifth Avenue, to announce that he was running for President. Only someone "really rich," he declared, could "take the brand of the United States and make it great again." He also made the racist remarks about Mexicans quoted in Chapter 4, which prompted NBC, the network broadcasting "The Apprentice," to fire him (Keefe, 2019).

President Trump's 2016 electoral victory was a cliffhanger rather than a landslide, far smaller than he asserted on many occasions. Trump's margin in the Electoral College ranked 46th among the fifty-eight presidential elections in United States history. His margin in the popular vote was 47th among the forty-nine presidential elections for which we have data. Only Rutherford B. Hayes in 1876 and John Quincy Adams in 1824 had smaller proportions of the popular vote and still became president. Hayes, as explained earlier, was only declared the winner in the 1877 Compromise that ended Reconstruction (Patel and Andrews, 2016; Baker and Haberman, 2020).

These rankings echo the 2000 election of President George W. Bush, who also was far down in the electoral rankings, 52nd in Electoral College votes and 45th in the popular vote. Both elections resulted in the election of a president who failed to attract a majority of the voters. Both elections generated evidence that some people's votes had not been counted, but Democrats did not try aggressively to reverse the initial results, favoring a smooth transition to the new president over support for the programs they supported.

For example, keeping people waiting in line to vote costs them greatly, reduces their income if they are paid hourly, and discourages poor voters from voting. In addition, several studies showed that Wisconsin's Voter-ID law suppressed enough votes in 2016 to substantially aid Trump's win in the state. Votes typically were suppressed in urban, Black, and Democratic districts (Stewart and Ansolobehere, 2013; Krotoszynski, 2016; Lithwick and Cohen, 2016; Berman, 2017; Wines, 2018).

President Trump continued his prior business activities in his administration. He refused to put his business into a trust while in office, and Trump's properties played host to at least 13 foreign government–sponsored events, 143 foreign government officials, and officials from the state of Maine. Since his inauguration, Trump took close to 500 trips to his private properties, including 272 trips to his golf courses. The cost of those alone was estimated in May 2019 at more than $100 million. These boondoggles were taxpayer-funded advertisements because Trump traveled with the media in tow and misused his official position to promote his properties. Trump made his administration a customer of his businesses, and the Secret Service regularly paid the Trump Organization up to $650 per night for rooms at his Mar-a-Lago club (Haberman and Lipton, 2019).

Trump's conflicts of interest extended to his intervention in the relocation of the Washington headquarters of the FBI in early 2018. The government spent a decade and $20 million preparing to move the FBI out of its aging building, whose façade was deteriorating enough to be outfitted with netting to catch falling chunks of concrete. The building is catty-corner across Pennsylvania Avenue from the Old Post Office building, which the Trump International Hotel leases from the GSA. Trump suspected that moving the FBI could have opened space for a competing hotel.

The administration proposed a new plan to Congress to demolish the building and erect a new one on the site. The GSA's inspector general found that the FBI and GSA had been in previous communication with the White House regarding the long-planned move. This new plan misrepresented the costs of rebuilding on the site as the most cost-effective option, but it would have been cheaper to stick to the original plan of moving the FBI's headquarters to the suburbs (Shaub, 2020).

Trump fought subpoenas for his tax records, possibly to hide other thievery. The *New York Times* obtained Trump's tax returns in late September 2020. Mr. Trump long fought to keep private his tax returns because they tell a story fundamentally different from the one he sold to the American public. His reports to the IRS portray a businessman who took in hundreds of millions of dollars a year, yet racked up chronic losses that he aggressively employed to avoid paying taxes. He paid no income taxes at all in ten of the previous fifteen years before his election because he reported losing much more money than he made. After he took office, the records show that he depended more and more on making money from businesses that put him in conflicts of interest with his job as president. He paid only $750 in federal income taxes the year he won the presidency, and he paid another $750 in his first year as president (Buettner et al., 2020; Kelly, Goldmacher, and Kaplan, 2020; Weiser and Rashbaum, 2020).

Key Republican members of Congress announced even before President Trump took office that they suddenly were not afraid of enlarging the national debt at all. In a dramatic reversal from their position opposing a second Obama stimulus in 2009, many members of the Republican House Freedom Caucus said on January 5, 2017, that they were prepared to support a tax cut to rich people that would top the Reagan and George W. Bush tax cuts. It also would explode the deficit and increase the public debt to more than $29 trillion by 2026. The proposal did not come until later, but the deficit hawks again did not protest (Kaplan, 2017; Waldman, 2017).

A tax cut to the rich – possibly with small cuts for low-wage people – was part of the Republican fiscal policy of those two presidents. The other part was to spend more on the military, all the while saying that the tax cuts would stimulate economic growth fast enough to balance the federal budget. This is a Republican claim with no evidence behind it. The economy did not grow as fast as hoped in the 1980s, and it took twenty years to pay down Reagan's deficit. Bush's policies led to the

2008 financial crisis that added to the federal debt. Reagan managed to avoid getting into a large war with his military buildup, but Bush fatefully invaded Iraq in 2003 (Clarke, 2004; Bacevich, 2016).

The Supreme Court upheld in *McConnell v. Federal Election Commission*, 540 US 93 (2003), the 2002 Bipartisan Campaign Reform Act known as McCain–Feingold Act, which prohibited large contributions by wealthy individuals and corporations to national parties whose receipts were publicly disclosed. The ban on so-called soft money left individual and corporate donors free to direct their funds to outside groups where donations are concealed from public scrutiny.

The Republican and Democratic parties aired two-thirds of all advertisements in the 2000 presidential general election. That figure dropped to one-third in 2004, and it was less than one-fourth in 2008. By 2012, the political parties sponsored just 6 percent of all advertisements. Both major national parties now outsource their basic activities, including research about their opposition and voter list management. The parties have become dependent on outside groups, and they cede power to organizations that operate with little or no disclosure and that frequently have narrow political agendas.

The result in 2016 was that two-thirds of states ended up under Republican control, including both governors and state legislator bodies. While national publicity focused on the presidential race, the *McConnell* decision paved the way for the top of the income distribution to take control of state and local governments around the country. To the extent that very rich people control state political money, we are living in a plutocracy (MacLean, 2017; Ferguson, Jorgensen, and Chen, 2019).

The election of 2016 recalls the election of 1896. There are uncomfortable parallels even though these elections were over 100 years apart. Republicans used racism as an electoral tool in both elections as an effective way to blunt the power of ordinary working people. Divide and conquer was their model. Rich Americans who had won their fortunes in the economic sphere thought they should have political power as well as economic power. Inequality of income, that is, Gilded Ages, are all alike. Despite a difference of one hundred years, racism and wealth still go together.

Poor white workers value their superiority over Black and brown low-wage workers more than programs that improve their lives. They have been Trump supporters since the 1990s as explained in Chapter 6. This is the same racist behavior that was seen in the reactions to Reconstruction, the Great Migration, *Brown v. Board of Education*, the Civil Rights Movement, and President Obama (Fields and Fields, 2012; Anderson, 2016).

The rapidity of this backlash was anticipated from President Trump's first venture into politics: his "Birther" assertion that President Obama was illegitimate because he was not born in the United States. Trump impugned President Obama's legitimacy because Obama was the first African-American president. As usual since the Civil Rights Movement, this was expressed in code words, but the meaning was clear. The proper place of African Americans is below those of European descent, not above it. Trump also showed that he was willing to lie in public and insist on his position even after others pointed out the falsehood. Only when his lies about President Obama's birth had outlasted their usefulness did he reluctantly admit they were mistaken. Trump revealed that he would do anything to become the center of national attention. He has been addicted to receiving it for many decades, and his TV experience taught him how to expand his influence from local to national (Abramovitz, 2018; Temin, 2019).

President Trump repeated this lesson as president in the aftermath of the bloody Charlottesville demonstration on August 12, 2017. He expressed his racism by supporting the Ku Klux Klan and neo-Nazis after the demonstration – this time without using code words. He told lies by equating Robert E. Lee to George Washington and Thomas Jefferson as if they were all builders of the United States. He conflated the Revolutionary and Civil Wars, or perhaps he thought the Civil War was about building his mythical all-white country. And he drew attention away from Heather Heyer, the dead civil rights victim of the demonstration (Dyson, 2017; Shear and Haberman, 2017; Thrush and Haberman, 2017).

Trump's appeal can be seen in the model in Figure 6.4 used earlier. Trump draws a lot of his support from people in the customary mode of thought. Racial prejudice is so common after two hundred years with and without slavery and Jim Crow laws that still echo today that people vote for him without thinking. The decline of education in the United States encourages that kind of customary nonthinking action. Many in Trump's "base" of evangelicals have fallen into command behavior. Trump is behaving like a cult leader, and his audience believes in him so much that they willingly harm themselves. This cult culture explains why so many poor whites who would benefit from Democratic policies harm themselves by voting for Trump. As the model shows, the more rapidly the economy changes, the more likely that this command behavior and cult following will continue (Hassan, 2019).

The polarization of politics can be seen in President Trump's impeachment trial in early 2020. It was the third impeachment trial of a president and the third acquittal in American history. The Republicans and Democrats disagreed over Trump's conduct and his fitness for office. Some members of his own party conceded the allegations that Trump sought to pressure Ukraine to smear his political rivals, which were the main impeachment charges. But the Republican senators refused to see the evidence against the president, and they voted for acquittal.

Several Republican senators acknowledged the heart of the House impeachment case after voting for his acquittal. They confirmed that Trump undertook a concerted pressure campaign on Ukraine to secure politically beneficial investigations into his potential rival, primarily former Vice President Joe Biden, using nearly $400 million in military aid as leverage. But most Republicans argued that the conduct was not sufficiently dangerous to warrant the Senate removing a president from office for the first time in history and certainly not with an election near. Others dismissed Democrats' arguments altogether, insisting their case was merely an attempt to dress up hatred for President Trump and his policies as a constitutional case (Kaplan, 2018; Fandos, 2020).

Trump was not deterred by his impeachment from committing other potentially impeachable actions with foreign countries. For example, President Erdogan of Turkey pressed Trump to quash an investigation of Halkbank, a Turkish bank, by a federal prosecutor in Manhattan that threatened members of Erdogan's family and political party. When the prosecutor sat down with Trump's attorney general, he was stunned to be presented with a settlement proposal that would give Erdogan a key concession. It allowed Halkbank to avoid an indictment by paying a fine and acknowledging some wrongdoing. The Justice Department then would end investigations and criminal cases involving Turkish and Halkbank officials who were allied with Erdogan and suspected of participating in the sanctions-busting scheme.

Trump's sympathetic response to Erdogan was problematical because it involved accusations that the bank had undercut Trump's policy of economically isolating Iran, a centerpiece of his Middle East plan. Trump also was discussing an active criminal case with the authoritarian leader of a nation in which he does business; he reported receiving at least $2.6 million in net income from operations in Turkey from 2015 through 2018. Trump was doing impeachable actions again for violating the separation of powers (Buettner et al., 2020; Lipton and Weiser, 2020).

Racist policies discussed in Chapter 6 resulted in mass incarceration. A comprehensive study of race and opportunity in the United States found that the Black–white income gap is entirely driven entirely by sharp differences in men's, not women's, incomes. The Black–white gap is not immutable: Black boys who move to better neighborhoods as children have significantly better outcomes. Mass incarceration of Black boys and men clearly has an effect on the income distribution. The study found that Black boys do better with fathers at home, but they cannot be home if they are incarcerated. As shown in Figure 6.3, Black men are far more likely to be incarcerated than white men if they are poor (Chetty and Hendren, 2018a, 2018b).

This will not change soon. It took more than thirty years to get into our current equilibrium of mass incarceration; we may not be able to get out of it in lesser time. Current policies in immigration enforcement do not support optimism. The government spends more on immigration than on all federal criminal law enforcement agencies combined. Much of this money goes to house people waiting for judicial hearings, which could not keep up with increased enforcement of immigration rules (Temin, 2018).

Detainees are housed in containment facilities that are increasingly run by for-profit prison companies. These facilities house immigrants, while mass incarceration typically houses citizens. They focus on Latinos rather than Blacks, and they are largely separate from the War on Drugs. They nevertheless reinforce the image of inborn criminality and complicate the problem of justice and prison reform within the United States (Meissner et al., 2013).

The Trump administration is blurring the distinction between these two systems because the rapidly increasing number of immigration inmates is forcing the administration to look for space in existing jails. Illegal immigrants factor into mass incarceration as prisoners awaiting a civil procedure that could end in deportation, while the prisoners awaiting trials are in criminal procedures that could lead to possible prison sentences.

The Clinton, Bush, and Obama administrations tried to separate these two groups by adding specific requirements for the treatment of immigration detainees. These standards grew into more than 400 pages specifying, for example, the number of toilets available for the detainees. The Trump administration replaced these requirements with a much shorter list of general questions, such as whether the facility is "clean and in good repair," to persuade local officials who run jails to provide accommodations for immigrants. The changes appeal to companies operating jails for profit; over half of immigration detainees are in private jails, contrasting with far lower proportions of criminal detainees held in private jails. As one Ohio sheriff who had about 300 inmates facing a mix of criminal and immigration charges said, "Jail is jail" (Dickerson, 2018).

It gets worse. The Trump administration reported that it could not find the parents of 545 incarcerated Latino children who were separated from their parents or tried to enter the United States on their own. Some of these children had been in their mother's arms when incarcerated. In late October 2020, the administration began to ship all these children to Mexico regardless of their countries of origin, claiming they were protecting the children from COVID-19 coronavirus infection. They also were violating American laws and agreements with Mexico by the children's incarceration and then their expulsion (Dickerson, 2020a, 2020b; Shear et al., 2020).

Latino immigrants were lumped in with African Americans and started out with no education or physical assets. Radical Republicans failed to give new freedmen forty acres and a mule in Reconstruction, as noted in Chapter 2. Almost two centuries later, most African Americans have not been able to acquire either education or physical capital. While some Blacks have got education and succeeded in acquiring some wealth, many more have ended up in prison. And in the early twenty-first century, poor people of all colors may find themselves in the same position. This lack of investment in our poor citizens may signal slow economic growth to come.

By neglecting them education, access to favorable banking, and access to good jobs, the United States is depriving itself of the skilled labor that might otherwise develop within the poor, Black and brown communities. These people, given the opportunity, might also be innovators in business, the arts, and government who would help the entire population.

Larry Krasner, Philadelphia's District Attorney who took office early in 2018, instructed his assistants to start their plea bargaining at the lower end of mandatory sentencing guidelines, decline charges for both marijuana possession and sex workers who had two or fewer prior convictions, and reduce retail theft under $500 to the lowest possible misdemeanour. Krasner is a pioneer for judicial reform at the local level of enforcement, a promising path that will take a long time to become national even though it has been adopted by several other reform district attorneys. It has taken a generation to produce mass incarceration; it may take a long time to eliminate it (Temin, 2018; Krasner, 2021).

## 7.2 ALL KINDS OF INVESTMENT ARE DOWN

Economists studying economic growth distinguish four kinds of capital that increase economic growth: Keynesian capital, that is, physical assets, financial capital introduced by Thomas Piketty, human capital, that is, education, and social capital. Only the first of these appears in the National Income and Product Accounts (NIPA) produced by the Bureau of Economic Analysis (BEA) of the Department of Commerce. We need to examine the incomplete standard data to understand how our changing economy may be working against the people who live and work here (Piketty, 2014).

The BEA summarized its current practice of calculating the output of the financial sector, and specifically credit intermediation and related activities, the same way as it does for other kinds of firms, that is, by looking at profits. But the BEA does not have a comprehensive measure of the output of the financial sector to use as its output. William Nordhaus explained why this problem arose: "The problem in a nutshell is that there are no observable values or prices that are the analogs to prices the Bureau of Labor Statistics finds to write down and tabulate. . . . Valuation techniques that are largely subjective and based only on survey information alone . . . are difficult to validate and should be avoided where possible" (Nordhaus, 2006, 150–51).

The BEA talks frequently about the difference between national product and national income. They must be equal, taking taxes and transfers into consideration. And if they are equal, then it does no harm when calculating national product to use estimates of national *income* in place of absent data on national *product.* The BEA publishes an "error" when national income and product do not come out equal (Rassier, 2012).

The BEA therefore uses profits as a measure of output, adjusted in a variety of ways to accommodate different industries. Philippon used an estimate of value added, that is, profits plus wages, in his historical estimate of the size of the financial sector. As he defined it, "I therefore use the GDP share of the finance industry, i.e., the nominal value added of the finance industry divided by the nominal GDP of the US economy" (Philippon, 2015, 1416).

This is a bit of a problem since profits often are taken as wages, as Piketty reminded us. The meaning of value added consequently is not as clear in finance as in manufacturing. Which wages are intermediate services? Secretaries, if there are any in modern offices, clearly are supplying intermediate services, but the wages of finance people clearly are not limited to clerks. The wages are largely coterminous with the value added in finance. The *number* of employees only is available for nonsupervisory employees and imputed to all employees; any wages paid to them in finance may be imputed similarly (Dean and Kunze, 1992).

The United States' de-industrialization has as its counterpoint the rise of services by definition. Agriculture, mining, construction, and manufacturing occupied only a quarter of the labor force in 1990 and fell below one-seventh in 2016. The rest of the labor force works in services (Carter et al., 2006; US Department of Labor, Bureau of Labor Statistics, 2017).

The BEA acknowledged this problem in 2009: "While all countries account for investment in tangible assets in their gross domestic product (GDP) statistics, no country currently includes a comprehensive estimate of business investment in intangible assets in their official accounts." The authors noted that the BEA has included some kinds of intangible investments, but they acknowledged that progress was slow. There is a paucity of information, and the BEA has to search for sources of relevant data (Aizcorde, Moylan, and Robbins, 2009, 10).

The BEA added R&D investment as reported to the National Science Foundation after considering how to deflate R&D for estimates of real GDP. They also added investment in artistic originals into investment by shifting them from current expenses to an investment account. And they are conducting research into measuring investments in human capital. They admitted that the measure under study would only include investments in traditional education, not on-the-job training that might be important, and that the measure would focus on market-based investments in education, not individuals' investment of time (Aizcorbe, Moylan, and Robbins, 2009, 12; Soloveichik, 2010).

Even though we cannot measure intangible investments well in the NIPA, they are important in economic growth. Consider the various kinds of capital listed earlier separately, starting from Keynesian investment, which can be measured and ending with social capital that can only be inferred from isolated examples. In between, financial and human capitals have some quantification. There also are connections between them that illustrate how these divergent forms of capital interact.

Keynesian physical investment fluctuated widely as the economy experienced recessions and prosperity, but it did not return to its previous level after the 2008 Financial Crisis. Various reasons have been proposed to explain this lack, but no one disputes the low level of Keynesian investment in recent years (Foroohar, 2016, 13; Alexander and Eberly, 2018).

Political support for public physical investment has flagged despite the great need for infrastructure investment. Republicans did not support any Democratic proposals during the Obama presidency. President Trump stressed his intention to invest in our infrastructure during his presidential campaign, but no plans emerged during his presidency. It appears that any plan to invest in public assets foundered on the rocks of privatization and low taxes. Physical capital investment as a share of the domestic economy fell to zero during the pandemic and has not yet recovered to its low post-2008 level (Mayer, 2016; MacLean, 2017; Temin, 2017; Bellafante, 2018).

The Koch brothers extended the fight against public transit to cities and counties across the country. For example, the business community in Nashville, Tennessee, had ample public support for a comprehensive plan to improve the local infrastructure with coordination between plans for light rail, buses, and a traffic tunnel underneath the town center. But house-to-house campaigning against the taxes needed for this plan by the Kochs' Americans for Prosperity organization defeated the plan at a local election. "The Kochs' opposition to transit spending stems from their longstanding free-market, libertarian philosophy. It also dovetails with their financial interests, which benefit from automobiles and highways" (Tabuchi, 2018a).

The result of this neglect is that the American Society of Civil Engineers gave American infrastructure a D+ in 2017, repeating the grade in their previous report. Bridges retained their C+ grade, but public transit systems received a grade of D-, down from D in 2013. The new report from the civil engineers was very much like their report of four years earlier; the overall picture of an aging and underfunded infrastructure remains (American Society of Civil Engineers, 2017; Temin, 2017).

The lack of infrastructure harms urban growth, but ignoring and denying climate change harms the whole economy. Dramatic reports in late 2018 showed that climate change harms our economy and needs at least as much attention as roads, bridges, and subways. Scientists noted that the government was required to release the most comprehensive report; it did so on the day after Thanksgiving to minimize its public impact. The report predicted that climate damage will reduce the

American economy by 10 percent at century's end if significant steps are not taken to rein in global warming. This startling conclusion grabbed the public press despite the administration's efforts to hide it. The report detailed some of the ways climate change would impact the United States economy: $141 billion from heat-related deaths, $118 billion from sea-level rise, and $32 billion from infrastructure damage by the end of the century, among others (Davenport and Pierre-Louis, 2018; Davenport, 2019).

More than half of the carbon dioxide in the air today has been exhaled in the past thirty years. The United Nations said that we will have 4.5 (Celsius) warming by 2100 if we continue to follow the path we are on now. This is twice as big as the Paris accord aim of only a two-degree rise (Wallace-Wells, 2019, 4, 14).

While the public was aroused, the federal government rolled back climate protections imposed by the Obama administration. The Koch network and other large oil companies like Marathon Petroleum pushed back on fuel-efficiency standards for cars and trucks, which use one quarter of the world's oil. Their advocacy resulted in national presidential directives and draft legislation for states from the American Legislative Exchange Council (ALEC), another part of the Koch network. The draft described the existing fuel-efficiency rules as "a relic of a disproven narrative of resource scarcity" and says "unelected bureaucrats" shouldn't dictate the cars Americans drive (Davenport and Pierre-Louis, 2018; Levenson, 2018; Tabuchi, 2018b; Tarullo, 2019).

Climate change has grown more and more obvious as Trump continued to deny its existence – in western forest fires and southern hurricanes. The progress of global warming is shown in Figure 7.1, where it can be seen that it began to be a major problem in the 1970s at the same time that wages stagnated and mass incarceration accelerated. This will harm economic growth cumulatively as temperature rises (Davenport, 2019; Cramer, 2020; Flavelle and Friedman, 2020).

Turn now to financial investment, where we find some of the same problems. Rajan and Zingales argued that finance consistently has been at the mercy of politics. That surely is true, but finance has been slowly deregulated. Deregulation began with airlines and Savings and Loan Associations to deal with stagnation in the 1970s and continued with

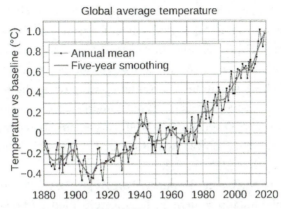

**7.1.** Global average temperature, 1880–2020.
*Source:* Wikipedia. https://en.wikipedia.org/wiki/Global_temperature_record

the repeal of the Glass–Steagall Act that separated commercial and investment banking in the Depression in 1999 – both under Democratic administrations – that set the stage for the 2008 financial crisis. There can be too much of a good thing (Warf and Cox, 1996; Winston, 1998; Rajan and Zingales, 2003).

Since the election of 2016, politics puts the interests of large corporations and rich anarchists in charge of financial policies, leading to fiscal and financial policies that help only this part of the population. Piketty defined financial capital as

> the sum total of nonhuman assets that can be owned and exchanged on some market. Capital includes all forms of real property (including residential real estates) as well as financial and professional capital (plants, infrastructure, machinery, patents, and so on) used by firms and government agencies. . . . In practice, capital can be owned by private individuals (in which case we speak of "private capital") or by the government or government agencies (in which case we speak of "public capital"). (Piketty, 2014, 46)

The Federal Reserve asked people how they would pay for an unexpected emergency expense for $400. Sixty-three percent of people interviewed in 2019 said they would use cash, but 37 percent said they could not. More than a third of people could not pay this unexpected expense. Most Black people fit into that category. Educated Black people and the

Black Elite earn good money and could pay easily for such an expense. But the people in Flint, Michigan, still suffer from the absence of safe drinking water. They undoubtedly fall in the one-third of people who could not pay this expense. And Black urban workers in many cities who live from paycheck to paycheck in rental housing or on the street could not pay cash for a $400 emergency. That a middle-class Black woman had trouble cashing a $200 check at her Wells Fargo bank shows that even the Black Elite can have problems raising cash (Bosman, 2020; Federal Reserve, 2020, 21–22; Flitter, 2020).

The state of Michigan announced on August 20, 2020, that it had reached a $600 million settlement for the suits filed on behalf of Flint residents against the state. Four-fifths of the settlement is destined for children who were harmed during the water crisis, much of that for those what were infants at the time. Residents were pleased at the news, but they were concerned about the time it would take to get the state aid (Gray, 2020).

This settlement was criticized as inadequate, but it was the largest the residents could get from the state where rich families like Devos and Koch retain influence. At least a third of the settlement will go to lawyers, and additional expenses will go to agencies dealing with the children damaged by the bad Flint water. This meager settlement will be helpful, but it will not end the Flint water crisis, which will continue. What amount of compensation is adequate to compensate for permanent brain damage, which will stay with some victims for the rest of their lives? (Scofield, 2020).

The 2017 tax cut was a substantial financial *dis*investment because it increased the national debt of the United States by $1.5 trillion or more for the next decade. It will be hard for private financial investment to overcome this negative contribution. And the share of gross domestic investment is *smaller* than in recent years. What is going on?

Republicans sold the 2017 tax cut as restructuring the incentives in the American economy that would unleash more investment, better efficiency, and higher wages, stimulating enough growth to offset any revenue lost to the government from lower tax rates. That clearly did not happen. Business investments typically are for short-run gains, and changes in the tax rate have little incentive effects. Almost half the tax cut to large corporations and rich individuals went into tax havens to lower taxes even farther. Much of the rest went into stock purchases to raise the stock price and spread the gain among companies' rich friends. Physical investment likely is low because of globalization as well. Businesses are not investing in the old economy because the old products can be imported from advanced developing countries like Japan and China. Our place in this new globalization will depend on some of the intangible investments discussed below, chiefly human capital. The 2017 tax cut did not have the advertised effect of increasing investment (Koo, 2018, Chapter 5; Tankersley and Phillips, 2018; Tørsløv, Weir, and Zucman, 2018; Kopp et al., 2019).

The tax cut had one clear effect; it increased the United States debt. That debt can be carried indefinitely, but may have to be paid off at some future time by the citizens of the United States. Who would pay this tax increase? As shown in Figure 6.5, the tax rate on the richest people has gone down continuously since World War II. Any tax increase therefore would be paid by the rest of us, including almost all Black citizens. The bottom third of the income distribution that could not pay cash for a $400 emergency, including most American Black people, may well pay for the 2017 tax cut in some form (Flitter, 2020).

The effect of finance on growth is nonlinear. There are diminishing returns from finance as it gets larger and becomes negative for large financial sectors. International comparisons show that higher growth of the financial sector can reduce economic growth. Credit booms harm industries that have intangible investments or high R&D intensity because they lack collateral for loans. And the resources that go into finance crowd out other economic activities. (Rajan and Zingales, 2003, 31–33; Cecchetti and Kharroubi, 2019).

Private equity firms have grown in recent decades to raise capital from wealthy individuals and institutions to make risky investments that promise high returns. Private equity firms buy companies and use high leverage to make these high returns. The debts, which have fixed interest payments, provide high returns on the capital invested by rich investors since all the profits go to them. If the company fails, the debts default and investors walk away without loss. Society picks up the tab (Davis, 2009–2010; Foroohar, 2016; Sullivan, 2019).

The typical setting is shown by the treatment of Simmons Bedding in a small Wisconsin town. Simmons filed for bankruptcy protection in 2009 as part of an agreement by its current owners to sell the company – the seventh time this 133-year-old firm was sold in a little more than two decades. Simmons workers lost their jobs (Creswell, 2009).

A larger example is shown by the 2018 bankruptcy of Sears, America's largest retailer. The problems at Sears Holdings, as the company is known on Wall Street, were more than a decade in the making because a Mr. Lampert stayed convinced of his own deeply flawed thinking. Mr. Lampert began his fifteen-year odyssey in 2003 after he bought the bonds of the failing discount retailer Kmart and converted those bonds into a controlling position in Kmart's equity. In 2005, he merged the revived Kmart with Sears, then a conservatively run thriving nationwide retailer.

Mr. Lampert decided *not* to invest the capital needed to refurbish the Sears and Kmart stores to keep their inventory and appearance fresh. Instead, he made a huge gamble that did not pay off to invest in Sears's website and online shopping. But Amazon ate Sears's lunch (and dinner) until Lampert threw in the towel in 2018 and joined forces with Amazon to allow it to sell Kenmore appliances, something that he had long refused to do. Sears workers may find jobs at Amazon. But Sears was an old company that treated its workers well, and Amazon is a new company that is less generous (Cohan, 2018; Schwartz and Corkery, 2018).

A more recent example is in the failure of two well-known retailers: J. Crew and Neiman Marcus. They shared an increasingly common problem for retailers in trouble: an enormous debt burden from leveraged buyouts organized by private equity firms. Like many firms in their industry, J. Crew and Neiman Marcus paid hundreds of millions of dollars in interest and fees to their new owners in the past decade, when they needed to spend money to adapt to a shifting retail environment. When the pandemic hit and wiped out much of their sales, neither store could go anywhere for relief except court.

"Much of the difficulty that the retail sector is experiencing has been aggravated by private equity involvement," said Elisabeth de Fontenay, a professor at the Duke University School of Law who specializes in corporate finance. "To keep up with everybody's switch to online purchasing, there really needed to be some big capital investments and changes made, and because these companies were so debt strapped when acquired by private equity firms, they didn't have capital to make these big shifts" (de Fontenay quoted in Maheshwari and Friedman, 2020).

Consider now the third kind of capital, human capital. Teacher pay and state support for public universities have been lagging for decades when the pill allowed them to plan their children's timing. Teacher pay was not raised when women were able to get better paying jobs in the 1970s because they could plan when to have their children, and pay stayed low as average wages stopped growing. Public universities lost support after every financial crisis when state expenditures needed to be reduced. The trends now are the continuation of these patterns. Public colleges typically suffer reductions in state funding during economic crises; they may disappear entirely in the coming recession (National Science Board, 2012; Temin, 2002b; Carey, 2020).

Teacher pay declined relative to other jobs now open to women for the last half-century. State support for state universities has declined so far that they look more like private universities than public ones. State universities have raised tuition to survive, and college attendance ceased to grow in the 1980. Macroeconomic thinkers say that education is the key to national success in the world where developing countries like China and Japan challenge United States economic leadership. Letting our human capital decay may be the most important problem for future generations (Goldin and Katz, 2008; Allegretto and Michel, 2018; Koo, 2018, Chapter 5).

The low pay of teachers led to a teacher shortage, which is now becoming acute. Since our superior education in the nineteenth and twentieth centuries attributed greatly to the growth of the economy, it is great shame that we are encouraging women who used to be teachers to consider other occupations. The shortage of qualified teachers is worst, as might be expected, in high-poverty schools – where many Black students go (Temin, 2002b; Garcia and Weiss, 2020).

The decline in human capital accelerated after Betsy DeVos was confirmed as Education Secretary in 2017 by a single vote delivered by the vice president, who was brought in to break the first tie on a cabinet nomination, because her antipathy toward public schools was well known. She, however, had a longer time in office than many other members of Trump's initial cabinet and personal advisors, revealing that her views and program had the approval of the current Republican administration. The first education budget of the new administration in 2017 cut funds from federal education initiatives, including work–study programs, loan forgiveness, and mental health while adding money to expand charter schools, education vouchers, and public-school activities to promote choice-friendly policies (Huetteman and Alcindor, 2017; Ravitch, 2017; Tanenhaus, 2018).

The decline of public education has severe effects on Black people. As noted already, there is now a Black Elite who have education and good jobs. But most Black children even now are not getting adequate education. The causes have been described earlier, as the Great Migration led to white flight to suburbs and the Supreme Court in 1974 ruled the fleeing whites did not have to pay to support urban public schools. Historically, it was illegal to educate slaves; Frederick Douglass was the exception that proves the law. Then Jim Crow laws deprived freedmen education because they could not vote, as shown in Figure 3.1. Finally, *Brown v. Board of Education* had only a brief effect as white families moved to new suburbs, stranding Black families in city centers.

The problems created by this history appear at all levels of education today. Head Start began in 1965 as part of the Civil Rights Movement. The need for early education grew out of this history because Black parents typically had little education to pass on to their children. As many studies have shown, an absence of books at home places beginning students at a sharp disadvantage at school. Head Start helped beginning grade scholars, but the effects appeared to disappear over the next few years.

Further research showed that Head Start had durable effects if adequate grade-school education followed. Head Start did not guarantee college admission. Head Start is the beginning of a long process that needs personal attention along the way. With generations of relatives who have been denied education, children often think they are unable to learn. When a teacher asked a young boy to go to the board to work out a math problem, he replied that he was mentally retarded and not supposed to be in regular school. The teacher responded that someone else's opinion did not have to become his reality. This encouragement freed the student to progress in school and graduate in due time (Delpit, 2012, 79; Temin, 2017).

Black students need stimulus and encouragement as shown in Figure 6.3. The student needs to be shaken out of his customary reluctance to think by teachers who lead him or her into new areas. The figure shows the problem created by current political advocates of arming teachers to combat school shootings. Armed teachers represent authority and move students into command behavior where they cannot think for themselves. Only a friendly teacher can stimulate a student into independent thought without scaring him or her to death.

The results of all this history are sharpest in college education. Almost half of undergraduates leave college before graduation. Graduates are burdened by student debt. Eighty percent of Black students graduate with college debt, and they have on average 70 percent larger debt than white students. Debt is particularly prevalent in for-profit colleges that attract students by their ease in getting government Pell grants and providing for daily costs of studying.

As in earlier education, attention by teachers is all important. An experiment at the University of Texas put low scoring SAT students into smaller sections of some classes with more peer tutors and faculty advisors. The proportion of students graduating rose from 50 to 70 percent, and poor and minority students made the biggest gains. But getting faculty to help poor and minority students is hard as most professors want to publish more than they want to encourage poor Black and brown students. The professors value their own advancement above the advancement of their students (Kirp, 2019, Chapter 5; Tough, 2019, Chapter 6; Zimmerman, 2020).

Finally, consider social capital. This is a new name for the old idea of community, and it has spread through the social sciences. No way has been found to include it in GDP, and the BEA has its hands full trying to put an imperfect measure of human capital into our national accounts, as noted above. Various proxies have been introduced to add social capital into growth theory and to note whether it appears to be increasing or decreasing. A few examples show what has been happening recently to American social capital (Putnam, 1993, 2000).

Consider first the effects of mass incarceration, which has grown to the point where we look more like the autocratic regimes of Eastern Europe and the Middle East than the democracies of Western Europe. The recent stability in the number of American prisoners indicates that we have settled into a new balance of mass incarceration and it will be hard to dislodge ourselves from this apparent equilibrium. New Jersey did free about 2,300 prisoners, who were released in November 2020 to avoid COVID-19 coronavirus infections in prison. It marked one of the largest single-day reductions of any state's prison population. The released prisoners were only prisoners within a year of completing sentences for crimes other than murder and sexual assault (Temin, 2018; Tully, 2020; Tully, Schweber, and Armstrong, 2020).

Criminologist Todd Clear noted that young, poor, and dominantly minority men and (to a lesser extent) women cycle through jails, prisons, and then back into the community. They disrupt families, weaken social networks, and other forms of social support, putting children at risk and promoting delinquency. The collateral effects of these high rates of incarceration contribute to more crime that fuels a public call for ever-tougher responses to crime. The increasing presence of people of color contributes to a public sense that race and crimes are closely linked, sustaining an ever-growing policy base that guarantees new supplies of penal subjects in a self-sustaining and self-justifying manner (Clear, 2007, 175).

Diminished returns and reversal of returns are becoming clear in both financial and social capital investment. At lower levels of financial investment, the results are beneficial to national income and product, but they decrease until they now are doing more harm than good for most people. Similarly, incarceration helps keep order for ordinary people, but mass incarceration destroys social capital. There is a self-reinforcing pressure here where participants in finance and in criminal justice and private prisons acquire what they consider property rights to their activities and resist limits on their growth. They want to expand even though they are having diminishing or even negative social returns.

Business schools echoed these government actions in the 1970s by adopting new principles that became the basis of business thinking. Two famous finance articles argued that financial markets were efficient and that managers should be linked to the market more than to production. This focus on finance led them to regard excess taxes and regulations as a danger to American efficiency and human costs of economic activity as irrelevant (Fama, 1970; Jensen and Meckling, 1976).

Pearlstein took issue with this framework and proposed a new "Pearlstein graph." Patterned after the Laffer curve, the Pearlstein graph showed efficiency increasing with inequality at low levels of inequality, but decreasing with too much inequality. The result is an upside-down U that shows we could enjoy the most efficiency with more equality of income. Wu drew this relation as a right-side U by graphing costs. Pearlstein and Wu concluded that business schools and now businessmen produced a kind of capitalism that corrodes social capital by undermining trust and discouraging socially cooperative behavior. Business focus on economic efficiency destroys social capital. Like modern finance and mass incarceration, too much emphasis on efficient firms makes the economy work worse, not better (Pearlstein, 2018, 137; Wu, 2018, 70).

Social capital also is destroyed every time there is a mass shooting in the United States. The FBI reports that hate crimes increased for the third year in 2017, and easy access to guns has made many of these crimes lethal. Crazy people have been allowed to express their anger by shooting up churches and schools with alarming frequency. They are not helped by comments that churches and schools should have armed guards to protect themselves or by National Rifle Association (NRA) claims that the Second Amendment should apply to all, not just to members of a government militia. Just as the Supreme Court weaponized the First Amendment, the NRA literally has weaponized the Second (Eligon, 2018; Goodstein, 2018).

Gun violence has been turned toward places where people congregate: churches, synagogues, and – most notably – schools. Students cannot learn, that is, cannot acquire human capital, while using their attention to avoid suffering from gun-toting lunatics. Yet the NRA position parroted by many politicians is to advocate arming teachers and schools to prevent violence – further distracting students from their education (Mazzei, 2018).

Dasgupta succinctly defined social capital as the confidence that contracting parties will fulfill their contracts, that is, uphold their obligations to one another, which is a result of belonging to a community. He argued in his *Very Short Introduction* to modern economics that social capital was the primary factor differentiating the prospects of ten-year-old girls living in the American Midwest and in southern Ethiopia. Ordinary children growing up in the United States today may be very adversely affected by the lack of social capital – which has been declining for several generations (Dasgupta, 2007).

Various economists have attributed the decline in American social capital to TV, working women, growing economic inequality, and the demise of the pedestrian urban shopping core in American cities. The assault on social capital by the government and the business establishment, if not checked soon, will make a very inhospitable environment for our children and grandchildren to grow up into (Putnam, 2000; Costa and Kahn, 2003; Rae, 2003).

Social capital also diminished from the government's actions, but by a very different path. President Trump frequently lied, changed his mind, and called people by disparaging names. He acted against the rules of the presidency, for which courts frequently condemned him. He provided a very bad example for defeating the pandemic by refusing to wear a mask to prevent the spread of virus infection. And his racist corrupt administration consistently lied, stole, and stole, particularly from Black people. All of these things became regarded as normal, diminishing the expectation that someone agreeing to a contract will actually fulfill his or her obligation of the contract – that is, reducing social capital.

The decline in social capital accelerated with President Trump's claim of an invasion of Latino immigrants appealed for asylum from Central American violence.

Since January, [2019,] Mr. Trump's re-election campaign has posted more than 2,000 ads on Facebook that include the word "invasion" – part of a barrage of advertising focused on immigration, a dominant theme of his re-election messaging. A review of Mr. Trump's tweets also found repeated references to an "invasion," while his 2016 campaign advertising heavily featured dark warnings about immigrants breaching America's borders. (Kaplan, 2019)

Invasion is a military term, which describes a foreign army invading our soil, as in *The Guns of August.* President Trump apparently had trouble distinguishing Latino armed fighters from women and children seeking asylum. This conforms to the model of a dual economy, where the upper class cannot distinguish individuals in the lower class. If rich people cannot recognize minorities as individuals, how are they to know who to trust? The inability to trust others destroys social capital (Temin, 2017).

If investment in human and social capital does not recover soon, our future could be like Argentina's past as it went from one of the richest countries after World War II to a poor country subject to periodic crises today. This decline was a result of bad policies that came in turn from a fractured society and divisive politics. The Social Progress Index records the fall in these kinds of investment; the United States is not the leading country in the world (Lewis, 2009. 19–34, 191–92; Social Progress Index, 2020).

The fate of many Black boys today is shown by Bruce Western, a noted author in incarceration studies, who followed 122 prisoners in Boston, MA, for a year after they were released from prison. Two-thirds of his sample had only poverty incomes, and half made less than $6,000, which researchers conceptualize as deep poverty. These felons are not included in prison or poverty data as they are too poor and scattered to be in a general sample. It is worth quoting Western's conclusions on race:

> Africans and Latinos make up less than one-quarter of the city's population but were about 75 percent of the formerly incarcerated sample of the reentry study. The white respondents we interviewed were mostly in their forties or older, were high school graduates, and had histories of addiction, mental illness, and homelessness. The Black and Latino respondents were more often in their twenties and more likely to be high school dropouts with little work history. They experienced more unemployment, and their incomes were only half the incomes of whites after incarceration. Because kin connections were stronger among Black and brown respondents compared to whites, Black and brown families were drawn into the orbit of the prison through visits, phone calls, canteen payments, and the provision of housing after release. In short, the new racial inequality was visible in Boston through the association between the incarceration of

young Black men and the deep economic disadvantage woven into the structure of their economic opportunities. (Western, 2018, 176)

These conclusions show the effect of the discrimination against poor Black boys described in this book as the second Gilded Age continues. What would it cost to fix or even ameliorate these conditions? Do not ask the rich people of the Gilded Age. Their only interest is in low taxes, as revealed in Figure 6.4, while poor Blacks suffered under their radar. As a New York District Attorney said in the previous Gilded Age, "The rich can go practically unpunished, unless their crime is so glaring ... while the poor have to receive the penalty of their offense in every instance" (Taub, 2020, 118).

Earlier, I described Trump's experience in real estate. He exhibited the same behavior as president. He spoke to his base and ignored everyone else. He did not negotiate with others; he only threatened and bullied. As his niece Mary Trump described him, "Donald today is much as he was at three years old: incapable of growing, learning, or evolving, unable to regulate his emotions, moderate his responses, or take in and synthesize information" (Trump, 2020, 197).

The urge to continue the New Jim Crow laws that put poor Black boys in jail will cost the United States as times go on. Neglecting the absence of investment in the future, in physical, educational, and social investment will cost us dearly in the next generation. We will see ourselves falling behind other postindustrial countries and slipping backward into what economists used to call a less developed economy.

Kleptocracy is a hallmark of the Trump administration, and it is very hard to eliminate once it is established. Corrupt firms buy out honest firms, often using harassment, forced payments, and physical violence. Liberal groups lack the cohesiveness to supplant kleptocracies; elections usually bring chaos and then a return to kleptocracy (Dawisha, 2014; Teachout, 2014).

## 7.3 THE COVID-19 PANDEMIC

Over 400,000 Americans died from the COVID-19 coronavirus pandemic of 2020. What did Trump do to combat the epidemic? Nothing! He started out by denying its existence and ended up leaving all responsibility to the states. If his actions had any effects, they were harmful, leading to competition between states for vital healthcare supplies. He chose to deny an imminent danger to the American public and to do nothing to alleviate their suffering when it arrived. He acted like a dishonest real estate salesman, not the President of the United States. The following quotes from Trump and his staff illustrate his evolving apparent blindness of the coronavirus pandemic (Krugman, 2020a).

Privately, Trump called Bob Woodward on January 7, 2020, and said, "It [COVID-19] goes through air. That's always tougher than the touch. You don't have to touch things. Right? But the air, you just breathe the air and that's how it's passed. And so that's a very tricky one. That's a very delicate one. It's also more deadly than even your strenuous flus." On March 19, Trump stated, "I always wanted to always play it down, I still like playing it down, because I don't want to create a panic" (Woodward, 2020, xviii ff).

Trump said publicly on February 27, 2020, that we had a total of fifteen infected. "We took in some from Japan because they're American citizens, and they're in quarantine. And they're getting better too. Of the 15 people – the 'original 15,' as I call them – 8 of them have returned to their homes, to stay in their homes until fully recovered. One is in the hospital and five have fully recovered. And one is, we think, in pretty good shape and it's in between hospital and going home. So we have a total of 15 people, and they're in a process of recovering, with some already having fully recovered" (Krugman, 2020a).

Trump said on March 9, 2020, "So last year 37,000 Americans died from the common Flu. It averages between 27,000 and 70,000 per year. Nothing is shut down; life & the economy go on. At this moment there are 546 confirmed cases of CoronaVirus, with 22 deaths. Think about that!" (Krugman, 2020b).

Paul Krugman wrote in late August,

If I had to pick a single day when America lost the fight against the coronavirus, it would be April 17. That was the day when Trump proclaimed his support for mobs – some of whose members were carrying guns – that were threatening Democratic state governments and demanding an end to social distancing. "LIBERATE MINNESOTA," he tweeted, followed by "LIBERATE MICHIGAN" and "LIBERATE VIRGINIA," and save your great 2nd amendment. (Krugman, 2020c)

Trump and his administration grossly minimized the pandemic and its dangers every step of the way, week after week over a period of months. Reporters from the *New York Times* recreated how this happened in July 2020. Policy was made in early morning meetings with Trump's chief of staff and his aides. Their ultimate goal was to shift responsibility for leading the fight against the pandemic from the White House to the states: "They referred to this as 'state authority handoff,' and it was at the heart of what would become at once, a catastrophic policy blunder and an attempt to escape blame for a crisis that had engulfed the country – perhaps one of the greatest failures of presidential leadership in generations" (Shear et al., 2020).

Trump's chief of staff would tell people of their ideology: "Only in Washington, D.C., do they think that they have the answer for all of America." An examination of the policy shift in April and its aftermath shows that the approach Trump embraced was a deliberate strategy that he stuck to doggedly as evidence mounted that the virus would continue to infect and kill large numbers of Americans without strong leadership from the White House. White House officials did not begin to recognize that their assumptions about the course of the pandemic had proved wrong until June (Shear et al., 2020).

Recommending opening up the economy in April and May with the pandemic in full force was very poor advice. It led to much more illness and gross economic damage. Epidemiologists emphasized the role of testing in opening up the economy to prevent new outbreaks of the deadly virus. Congress asked the president in May to present a plan for national testing in a month. The report, however, only said that individual states were responsible for planning and carrying out all coronavirus testing. This absence of federal leadership greatly increased mortality from the pandemic. Blacks and Latinos suffered the most. Trump finally announced on July 22 that the pandemic was getting worse, not better. He recommended masks, but he did not wear a mask in his announcement, admit any errors he had made, or refer to any health professionals (Baker, 2020b; Mandavilli and Edmondson, 2020).

Trump opened areas to commerce prematurely, aided by support groups that appear spontaneous as shown on the evening news. They, like the Tea Party members at election time, are supported by Richard Koch and Betsy DeVos. DeVos also diverted funds for education in the CARES Act from public to private and religious schools, using the COVID-19 coronavirus pandemic to further her agenda against public education (Graves, 2020; Green, 2020).

Notice how odd the ideology that the federal government should not act – even in a national catastrophe – fits this elected president of the federal government. If Trump did not want power, did he run simply to earn more money? That would be consistent with his actions as president. Or did he adopt the mantra of the Chicago economics doctrine that governments should not do anything to mitigate economic depressions without asking if there were exceptions? That also is consistent with actions as president when he resisted efforts to help states survive and offer education and other services to their inhabitants.

President Trump also changed the date for the completion of the 2020 census in August. Federal law requires the bureau to send population totals to the president by December 31 of every census year. But the pandemic forced census officials to rewrite that timeline in April, pushing delivery of population totals to next April in 2021. The House approved the new deadline in May, but the Republican-controlled Senate did not follow suit at Trump's behest. The Census Bureau then had to try what officials said it could not do: accurately count the nation's hardest-to-reach residents – nearly four of every ten households – in just six weeks. The deadline returned to December with the risk of losing many poor, Black, and immigrant people (Wines, 2018; Wines and Fausset, 2020).

COVID-19 coronavirus has claimed more than 400,000 lives in the United States, aided by an absence of federal action to protect the citizens. Mortality among Black people has been particularly frequent, as a result of the denial of economic opportunity detailed in previous chapters. They have been denied mortgages to move to the suburbs, denied education to get better jobs, and denied freedom in mass incarceration – which has become a "hot spot" for the coronavirus. Free Black people are forced to take public transportation, which has proven fatal for many. Latinos trying to better themselves are in prison as well. We are not told of the status in private prisons, but it no doubt is as bad or worse than public prisons. It is almost as if our racist president wanted to kill anyone with a dark skin (Friedman, 2020; Rabin, 2020).

For example, Rana Mungin, the first in her Black family to attend college, quickly stood out for her work on race and class. She majored in psychology at Wellesley College, where she wrote about her family and her childhood in Brooklyn. She later studied creative writing at UMass Amherst, where her work added to the national discourse about institutional racism. But Mungin died at thirty from COVID-19 coronavirus complications after she was twice denied coronavirus tests during trips to a Brooklyn hospital: The very biases that Mungin sought to bring attention to in her work played a role in her premature death (Arnett, 2020).

Mungin was just one person, but state data indicate that her early death was not unusual. In Illinois, over 40 percent of people who died from the disease were African Americans, who were just 15 percent of the state's population. The proportions were similar in Michigan. And in Louisiana, about 70 percent of the people who died were Black, though only a third of that state's population were Black. In other words, Black people died three times as frequently as white people (Bouie, 2020; Eligon and Burch, 2020; Rabin, 2020).

Trump embraced policies recommended by Scott Atlas, a Fox News commentator who he brought to the White House in the course of his reelection campaign, particularly the idea of "herd immunity." This is the claim that if enough people have immunity for COVID-19 as a result of a mild case, then the risk of infection will decrease. Trump first advocated this in an ABC interview in early September, where he referred to it as "herd mentality." The United States population is around 300 million, to stay with rounded figures. People estimate that about two-thirds of people need to have had COVID-19 to provide herd immunity, that is, about 200 million. At the current death rate of 3 percent, that would yield six million deaths. (A lower death rate would produce fewer deaths, but a death rate of one percent still would cause two million deaths.) This should be compared with the over 350,000 deaths caused by COVID-19 by that time – many orders of magnitude smaller. Trump's support for herd immunity shows a disregard for the health and safety of ordinary American citizens, and particularly of Black and brown people who are the primary victims of the coronavirus (Baker, 2020a; Mandavilli, 2020).

The *New York Times* summarized why Black lives are so vulnerable:

> First, they work jobs that limit their ability to quarantine. Black people account for 12 percent of workers overall, but 17 percent of front-line workers. Second, they live in overcrowded housing. Black renters are twice as likely as white renters to live in a household with more than two people per bedroom. Third, they live closer to environmental hazards. Black people are exposed to almost twice as much air pollution as white people. Fourth, they have limited access to health care. Black people are twice as likely to be uninsured as white people. Fifth, they interact with a largely white medical establishment. Black people make up 13 percent of the country's population but only 5 percent of physicians. (Wezerek, 2020)

This characterization of Black lives today shows the effects of their historical treatment since they were slaves and then subject to Jim Crow laws for many years. It is tragic that the pandemic hit Black people so hard, and it shows the reprehensible effects of racism. The white racists are not simply killing Blacks in Wilmington and Tulsa; they are killing far more of them during the COVID-19 coronavirus pandemic.

An ACLU research report estimated that prisons were important contributors to the premature deaths of Black people, doubling their death rates. As noted in Chapter 6, one-third of Black men go to prison during our mass incarceration. Inmates cannot social distance from each other in prison, and Black inmates often have complicating illnesses due to poverty or lack of medical attention. Yet states, where the great majority of prisoners are held, have been very reluctant to free prisoners – even those awaiting trial but not yet convicted of any crime – because of the pandemic. The rate of incarceration did not fall during the COVID-19 pandemic. Was this due to mass incarceration practice, represented by customary behavior in Figure 6.3, or fear of facing a "Willie Horton ad" in the next election? We cannot know (ACLU, 2020; Aviv, 2020; Gertner, 2020; Rabin, 2020).

Dr. Fauci, the epidemiologist who was a center of public interest, said in June, that the COVID-19 pandemic was a double whammy for Black people: "First because they are more likely to be exposed to the disease by way of their employment in jobs that cannot be done remotely. Second, they are more vulnerable to severe illness from the coronavirus because they have higher rates of underlying conditions like diabetes, high blood pressure, obesity and chronic lung disease" (Grady, 2020).

## 7.4 2016 REDUX AS TRUMP LOST HIS REELECTION

The Republican Party used its 2016 program for the 2020 election. It therefore is appropriate to recall the three causes of Trump's 2016 victory I listed in the epilogue to *The Vanishing Middle Class* to see how they affected the 2020 election. The three causes were racism, money from large donors, and Russian help. I discuss them in turn before turning to the outcome of the election (Epstein and Karni, 2020; Epstein, 2020).

Racism runs deep in the United States, as this book has shown. President Truman desegregated the army in 1948, as described earlier. But a recent picture of army commanders, Figure 7.2, shows an all-white group. President Trump did not say a word about the failure of integration a half-century after army racial integration was ordered. Almost half of the men and women on active duty in the United States military are people of color. But the picture of the president surrounded by a sea of white faces in military uniforms is a vivid portrait of the top commanders who lead this diverse institution. The people making critical decisions are almost entirely white and male. Only two senior commanders in the military with four-star rank in the military's five branches are Black, and there is only one woman in the group, who is white.

There are few people of color at the top of the army a half-century after desegregation because of the history and culture of the US military. The armed forces were not fully integrated until after World War II, as noted in Chapter 5. The elite service academies that educate the officer class have increased their enrollment of minority recruits in recent years, but they remain largely white. And African Americans who become officers often are steered toward logistics and transportation rather than

**7.2.** The army top brass with the President, 2020.
*Source:* Cooper, 2020. A black-and-white version of this figure will appear in some formats. For the color version, refer to the plate section.

the marquee combat arms specialties that lead to the top jobs (Cooper, 2020a, 2020b).

Candidate Trump exploited these persistent biases to arouse racist sentiments around the country. Many people in Wisconsin small towns feel that someone or something was responsible for the decline of their communities. They believe that wherever their tax dollars are going, they are not staying in their towns. Cities often are shorthand for people who are not white in rural language since the urban–rural divide includes race. It is very likely that when rural people refer to "those people in Milwaukee," they refer to racial minorities (Cramer, 2013, 85).

Trump drew his base from white rural folks, as noted earlier, and he catered shamelessly to them. W. J. Cash explained that violence was an integral part of the Southern mind. As he said in *The Mind of the South*, "The individualism of the plantation world would be one which, like those of the backcountry before it, would be far too much concerned with bald, immediate, unsupported assertion of the ego, which placed too great stress on the inviolability of person whim, and which was full of the chip-on-shoulder swagger and brag of a boy" (Cash, 1941, 42).

The Great Migration brought many freedmen to the North, and the reaction to that brought the Southern mind to northern white people as well. Eric Garner famously gasped, "I can't breathe," eleven times while lying face down on the New York City sidewalk in 2014. The medical examiner ruled Mr. Garner's death a homicide caused by the compression of his neck from a chokehold and the compression of his chest held on the ground in a prone position. The policeman who held Mr. Garner in a chokehold was fired but not charged, inciting protests nationwide.

What was Garner's offense? It was a misdemeanor. Cigarettes are far more heavily taxed in New York City than in neighboring states. Garner had cigarettes from Virginia that he was selling below the local price, which earned a profit to him. This kind of arbitrage is illegal, but it is only punished when poor Black people try it (Taub, 2020, 125–26).

George Floyd repeated Garner's complaint many times before dying in Minneapolis six year later. The manual of the Minneapolis Police Department states that neck restraints and chokeholds are only to be used when an officer feels caught in a life-or-death situation. There was no apparent threat of that nature in Mr. Floyd's detention. Instead, experts viewing the footage suggested that it was more likely a case of "street justice," when a police officer seeks to punish a suspect by inflicting pain for something done to the officer during the arrest.

The Democratic Mayor of Minneapolis, Jacob Frey, said that the rioters were right to protest 400 years of racism and that we all must strive for equal treatment. The police officer was arrested and accused of third-degree murder four days after Floyd's death. Third-degree murder exists in only three states and is closer to manslaughter than murder. The Attorney General of Minnesota upgraded the accusation to second-degree murder and accused the other policeman helping as well. However, he added, "Trying this case will not be an easy thing. Winning a conviction will be hard" (Eligon and Burch, 2020; MacFarquhar et al., 2020).

President Trump then issued an angry ultimatum to protesters in Minneapolis and inserted himself in a harshly divisive fashion into the growing crisis there, attacking the city's Democratic mayor, accusing the protesters of being THUGS (Trump's capitalization), and suggesting that the military could use armed force to suppress riots that erupted after the death of George Floyd. "I can't stand back & watch this happen to a great American City, Minneapolis," Mr. Trump tweeted, "A total lack of leadership. Either the very weak Radical Left Mayor, Jacob Frey, get his act together and bring the City under control, or I will send in the National Guard & get the job done right." Mr. Trump's mix of threats and attacks, unfolding on Twitter through Friday morning, came despite the fact that the Governor of Minnesota had already activated and deployed the National Guard in response to a request from local leaders.

The president inflamed sensible people even more in a disastrous attempt to improve his image on June 2, 2020. After a weekend of protests for the Minneapolis police killing that led to his own front yard and forced him to briefly retreat to a bunker beneath the White House, President Trump arrived in the Oval Office on Monday agitated over his television images, annoyed that anyone would think he was hiding and not eager for action. Trump wanted to send the military into American cities, an idea that provoked a heated, voices-raised fight among his advisers. But by the end of the day, encouraged by his daughter Ivanka Trump, he came up with a more personal way of demonstrating toughness; he would march across Lafayette Square to a church damaged by fire the night before.

The only problem was that a plan developed earlier in the day to expand the security perimeter around the White House had not been carried out. When Attorney General William P. Barr personally surveyed the scene early Monday evening, he discovered that protesters were still on the northern edge of the square. They would have to be cleared out if the president were to make it to St. John's Church. Mr. Barr gave an order to disperse them (Baker et al., 2020).

This resulted in a burst of violence unlike any seen near the White House in generations. As he prepared for his surprise march to the church, Mr. Trump went before cameras in the Rose Garden to declare himself "your president of law and order" but also "an ally of all peaceful protesters." However, smoke, flash grenades, and chemical spray deployed by shield-bearing riot officers and mounted police routed peaceful protesters a block away and clergy on the church patio.

The president crossed the street and held high the Bible – upside down – as a sign of his support for white evangelicals. He did not open the Bible or refer to anything in it. He did not argue for unity and cooperation in combating racial prejudice and police brutality. Instead, he berated the demonstrators remembering the Minneapolis police killing of George Floyd a few days earlier. We do not know how evangelicals responded to this photo op, but New Yorkers saw our dyslexic president attempting to divide our nation (Baker et al., 2020; Poniewozik, 2020).

To emphasize that division, the White House was transformed after this event into something resembling the Green Zone in Iraq during our war there. Every day, more fences went up and more concrete barriers were put in place as the security perimeter expanded farther and farther. Trump showed no discomfort with the increasing security. He embraced the idea of military units in the streets of the capital, seeing it as a demonstration of strength and berating governors for not using the National Guard more in their states (Baker et al., 2020a).

President Trump transformed peaceful urban protests into a national wave of riots that resulted in gunfire and several deaths. We need a president who will bring us together instead of pulling us apart. African Americans were made citizens of the United States in the Civil War, and several constitutional amendments specified their right to participate in the economy and vote. These amendments have suffered from Supreme Court decisions in the 1880s and again in the 2010s. Nevertheless, we cannot be a unified country until we accept the new status for freedmen for whom we fought the Civil War (Dewan and Baker, 2020).

Police unions have emerged as the largest obstacles to change. The greater the political pressure for reform, the more defiant the unions are in resisting it, and few city officials, including liberal leaders, are able to overcome their opposition. The unions aggressively protect the rights of its members accused of misconduct, often in arbitration hearings that they have battled to keep behind closed doors. And they have been effective at fending off broader change, using their political clout and influence to derail efforts to increase accountability.

That is due in turn to the surplus military that has been given from the American army to city police forces. As Radley Balko concluded his book on the militarization of the police: "Police are armed, dressed, trained, and conditioned like soldiers. . . . In short, police today embody all of the threats the Founders feared were posed by standing armies, plus a few additional ones they couldn't have anticipated." And the Senate in July 2020 rejected a bipartisan bid to bar the Pentagon from transferring a wide range of military-grade weaponry to local police departments (Balco, 2014, 334–35; Edmondson, 2020).

For example, New York City's police unions have been among the most vocal opponents of reforms in Albany, including calls to reform the state's tight restrictions on the disciplinary records of officers. The city's police unions joined statewide police groups on Friday in urging the Legislature to keep the law in place. And a memo of opposition from the police groups asserted that rational policy discussions cannot take place before a backdrop of burning police vehicles and looted store fronts. The city's patrol officers' union and another representing police sergeants have been sharp critics of Mayor Bill de Blasio, who took office in 2014 on a wave of discontent over stop-and-frisk policing. The mayor promised reform, but the fatal shooting of two uniformed officers in Brooklyn by a man who invoked the police killing of Eric Garner generated a revolt by rank-and-file officers. Other, smaller cities face similar problems (Scheiber, Stockman, and Goodman, 2020).

President Trump collapsed into his White House refuting all claims of Black people equality in the early summer. He sounded like someone from the 1950s rather than most Americans after Floyd's murder. Trump denied the pandemic and returned to his statements of February that were out of date even then. He held his first public campaign rally in Tulsa, Oklahoma, the site of the famous 1921 race conflict that killed 300 Black people. He also muzzled the Center for Disease Control (CDC) and Federal Emergency Management Authority (FEMA) so that his faithful supporters would not be aware of the danger. Someone must have had a little hold on reality, and the Administration did not want rally attendees to be able to sue the government if they got sick at the convention (Cottle, 2020; Shear, Haberman, and Herndon, 2020).

Turning to the role of dark money in presidential elections, Figure 7.3 shows political contributions to various national political leaders during the 2016 election cycle. The size of political contributions is shown on the horizontal axis. The leaders are drawn from both parties: Pelosi, Schumer, Ryan, McConnell, Trump, Clinton, and Sanders. The lines in

**Size of Contributions: Profiles of American Political Leaders, 2016 Cycle**

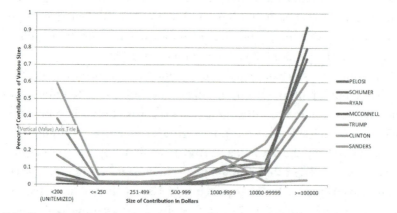

**7.3.** Class will tell.
*Source:* Ferguson, Jorgensen, Chen, 2019.

the graph uniformly take the form of a U, showing that political contributions are either very small or very large. The large contributions at the right end of the line show that most of the money raised by political candidates comes from contributions of $100,000 or more.

The wealthy donors who supported Donald Trump received a $1.5 trillion tax cut in undemocratic haste in early December 2017. Senate Republicans were so desperate to pass this bill that they did not allow other senators time to read the almost 500 pages of the proposed bill filled with hand-written, last-minute alterations. There were no hearings, no evaluation by independent agencies, but ample input from lobbyists.

The tax bill also repealed the compulsory mandate of the ACA, depriving 13 million people of health insurance and raising premiums for those still insured. It ended the tax deduction for student loans, penalizing young members of the low-wage sector trying to move out of poverty. Also included in this tax bill were cuts to Medicare, increased taxes on graduate students, permission for tax-exempt churches to engage in politics, and a definition of the "unborn." This bill is the culmination of decreases in taxes on the rich that have been going on in Republican administrations since World War II. As a result of this tax cut, the tax rate is level for people below the Forbes 400 – the richest people in America – and falls precipitously for the very rich. That is, the top 1 percent of the top 1 percent of the top 1 percent of the population pay taxes at lower rates than all the rest of the population (Saez and Zucman, 2019).

The 2017 tax cut was sold as expansionary fiscal policy that would revive investment and the economy. Recipients of the tax cut need to spend most of their savings for it to stimulate the economy. But, as the consumption function tells us, the proportion of income that people spend falls with their income, and it falls to zero when you consider the very rich Forbes 400. These people and companies sent close to half of their tax savings to foreign tax havens where they would be safe from future taxes. They used the rest of their savings to buy back the stock of their companies. Buying the stock raised the price and spread the gains a little beyond the Forbes 400, but still only to rich people holding these stocks (Zucman, 2015).

These funds were available to repeat the pattern shown in Figure 7.3 in 2020. The rest of the population had been shut out of the election. As you recall from Chapter 3, this was also true in 1896. Although most of us date the origin of money in politics to the Supreme Court decision in *Citizens United* (2010), money was determinative in the previous Gilded Age. The 2020 election was determined by the contest between those upset about the murder of George Floyd and the Forbes 400. The memory of 1896 reminds us that the role of money in politics is lasting in Gilded Ages.

While the effect of money in American politics is not to be ignored, we can see that money is not the whole story. Trump's racism and his willingness to ignore the Blacks and browns suffering from the pandemic that led to his electoral defeat. This is a reminder to the very wealthy that they are not the only people living and voting in the United States.

Finally, in the determinants of electoral success, Putin and the Russians clearly helped Trump to be elected in 2016. The Russian government interfered in the American election to favor Trump's candidacy. They hacked into both Republican and Democratic campaign correspondences, but publicized only the Democratic internal communications. United States intelligence agencies reached these conclusions:

> We assess with high confidence that Russian President Vladimir Putin ordered an influence campaign in 2016 aimed at the US presidential election, the consistent goals of which were to undermine public faith in the US democratic process, denigrate Secretary Clinton, and her electability and potential presidency. We further assess Putin and the Russian government developed a clear preference for President-elect Trump. (Fandos and Barnes, 2020)

Russian interference in the 2016 election was part of a long-run Russian plan to destabilize Western democracies. It was worth investigating thoroughly, but the Administration and Congress were reluctant to look closely at the evidence. With some delay, a Republican Senate Committee confirmed the Russian interference in the 2016 election in early 2020 (Osnos, Remnick, and Yaffa, 2017; Schmidt et al., 2017; Fandos and Barnes, 2020; Sanger and Sang-Hun, 2020; Mazzetti, 2020; US Senate, 2020).

Many observers remember that newspapers throughout the 2016 campaign focused on Hillary Clinton's stolen emails much more than Hillary's proposed programs. President Trump continued his friendship with Putin, and while street demonstrations continued to fill city streets in 2020, Trump invited Putin to a forthcoming meeting of the G-7, the organization of European and American states for international security. President Obama had kicked Putin out of the G-8 when Russia invaded the Ukraine. Manafort, one of Trump's chair of his campaign, was very active in Ukrainian politics, and subsequently went to prison for tax evasion. Even before this escapade, the United States was losing influence with former allies. Trump did not do anything to restrict Russian influence in 2020. And the Russians appear to be active again (Crowley, 2020; Frenkel and Barnes, 2020; Haberman, Cochrane, and Tankersley, 2020; Osnos, 2020; Sanger and Perlroth, 2020).

Russian disinformation is meant to enervate and disorient an opponent, creating generalized distraction and noise that can free the Russian state to act as it wants. The same could be said about Donald Trump, another incoherent political phenomenon, who wished to escape the irksome constraints of values and norms and institutions. How audible, let alone consequential, were Russian efforts to boost claims that mail-in voting leads to fraud when President Trump regularly blared the thesis at deafening volumes? And the combined disinformation campaign of Trump and Fox News about the pandemic was devastating (Yaffa, 2020).

Law enforcement officials never fully investigated Trump's own relationship with Russia. Former deputy attorney general Rod Rosenstein never told FBI chief Andrew McCabe about his decision, leaving the FBI with the impression that the special counsel would take on the investigation into the president as part of his broader duties. McCabe said in a later interview that he would have had the FBI perform an investigation of the president's international entanglements if he had known special council Mueller would not continue the inquiry (Schmidt, 2020).

Trump paid Putin the ultimate compliment, imitating his corruption that made Russia into a kleptocracy. The United States as a result is not far behind. The chief scientist brought in to lead the Trump administration's vaccine efforts for the COVID-19 pandemic, Moncef Slaoui, sat on the board of Moderna, a Cambridge, Massachusetts, biotechnology firm with a $30 billion valuation that is pursuing a coronavirus vaccine. Dr. Slaoui's stock holdings in Moderna jumped from nearly $2.4 million to $12.4 million when the company released preliminary, partial data from an early phase of its candidate vaccine trial that helped send the markets soaring on Monday. Dr. Slaoui was on a contract, receiving $1 for his service, which left him exempt from federal disclosure rules to list his outside positions, stock holdings, and other potential conflicts. And the contract position was not subject to the same conflict-of-interest laws and regulations that executive branch employees must follow.

Dr. Slaoui was not the only Trump administration official who was employed by or owned drug and health care companies. His boss, Alex M. Azar II, the health and human services secretary, was a former Eli Lilly executive. The former commissioner of the Food and Drug Administration, Dr. Scott Gottlieb, moved in and out of government twice, and divested his interests immediately upon assuming the FDA job in 2017. As with Trump's announcements described earlier, this appointment reveals that future progress will help the drug companies more than our country's citizens (Kaplan, Goldstein, and Stevenson, 2020).

This corruption is why small business and minority workers received so little coronavirus help despite the CARES Act Congress passed to aid them. The federal government's $350 billion aid program for small businesses devastated by the coronavirus pandemic was advertised as first-come, first-served. But the funds were disbursed through the largest banks. Customers of Citi's private bank, where the minimum account is $25 million, didn't have to use an online portal to apply for a loan; they could simply submit paperwork to their banker, who put in an application on their behalf. At Chase, the nation's largest bank, nearly all private and commercial banking clients who applied for a small-business loan got one, whereas only one out of every fifteen retail banking customers who sought loans was successful. Loans of more than $1 million made up just 4 percent of those approved, but they sucked up 45 percent of the dollars disbursed (Flitter, Smialek, and Cowley, 2020).

And funds to aid hospitals dealing with urban and Black COVID-19 patients saw their funds given to rich hospital chains with ample financial resources. HCA Healthcare is one of the world's most affluent hospital chains, earning more than $7 billion in profits over the past two years, worth $36 billion and paying its chief executive $26 million in 2019. HCA received about $1 billion in bailout funds from the federal government, part of an effort to stabilize hospitals during the pandemic. Employees at HCA repeatedly complained that the company was not providing adequate protective gear to nurses, medical technicians, and cleaning staff. HCA is on the long list of deep-pocketed health care companies that received billions of dollars in taxpayer funds and are laying off or cutting the pay of tens of thousands of doctors, nurses, and lower-paid workers (Silver-Greenberg and Drucker, 2020).

President Trump attempted to inaugurate his reelection campaign with his first mass rally in months in Tulsa, Oklahoma, a state he won handily in 2016. The rally sputtered badly on Saturday night, June 20, as he found a far smaller crowd than his aides had promised him that filled only about a third of the hall they had rented. He did not wear a mask or encourage any attendees to wear mask, although the organizers made attendees sign away their right to sue the president or the Republican Party if they got sick with COVID-19 coronavirus.

In rambling, grievance-filled remarks, Mr. Trump did not refer to the Tulsa massacre of 1921 that destroyed Greenwood, the Black Wall Street, or to George Floyd, whose murder by a white police officer in Minneapolis in May spurred global demands for racial justice. He also failed to mention Juneteenth, which marks the end of slavery in the United States and fell just a day before his rally. Instead, the president railed about "left-wing radicals" who he falsely claimed were rioting in cities across the country and praised police officers who "get injured, they don't complain. They're incredible" while attempting to stop looters and rioters.

"The unhinged left-wing mob is trying to vandalize our history, desecrate our monuments, our beautiful monuments, tear down our statues and punish, cancel and persecute anyone who does not conform to their demands for absolute and total control," Mr. Trump continued. He was referring to attempts to remove Confederate monuments in the wake of George Floyd's murder, efforts that have support in both parties. He seemed exhausted and discouraged after the rally (Cobb, 2020; Gorman, 2020; Shear et al., 2020).

In contrast to all the bombast, Thomas Apt proposed a way to deal with urban violence that requires that police work with other urban agencies to deal with problems. He argued that urban violence is concentrated among small numbers of people and places. It responds to both negative and positive incentives. And it must be dealt with cooperatively by police, urban renewal, and community rebuilding. The place to start is with dangerous individuals in hot spots, focusing on illegal gun carrying, gangbanging, and violent drug dealing. Defunding the police in this format means increasing cooperation between the police and other social services (Abt, 2019).

President Trump often used military expressions to justify his employment of the military to protect his infamous photo op. He characterized Latino immigrants as an invasion and arguing that we are at war with the coronavirus. It is appropriate to adapt and rewrite the conclusion of President Lincoln's famous wartime speech at Gettysburg during the Civil War that is so important in the history told here. Cash, in *The*

*Mind of the South,* said the Civil War "left the essential Southern mind and will ... entirely unshaken. Rather, ... it had operated enormously to fortify and confirm that mind and will." The Republican Party under President Trump now supports a government of white people, by white people and for white people (Cash, 1941, 103).

That effort was helped by the conservative judges that McConnell forced through the Senate. I characterized McConnell's refusal to confirm Obama's nomination to the Supreme Court in 2016 as a coup in my last book. Now the Senate has confirmed 200 new judges; McConnell even adopted an informal slogan to characterize the effort: Leave no vacancy behind. Republicans focused on the appeals courts, since most of the major binding court rulings occur at that level and the Supreme Court hears a relatively small number of cases. Republicans also indicated they would move to fill any vacancies that occur this year despite their tradition of suspending judicial confirmations late in an election year (Temin, 2017, 97; Hulse, 2020).

I wrote in 2017,

> This refusal to follow the Constitution is an extension of the 2010 redistricting coup ... moved our oligarchic society closer to an autocratic one. If it succeeds in politicizing the court system and restricting the Executive Branch, we will distort greatly or even destroy the division of political power set by the Constitution into three independent branches. (Temin, 2017, 97)

The Trump administration appointed many federal judges from the Koch-supported Federalist Society. When Ruth Bader Ginsburg died just before the 2020 election, Trump nominated another conservative judge to the Supreme Court, Amy Coney Barrett, and insisted that she be confirmed before the election so she could vote for Trump's reelection if needed and against Obamacare in the suit the administration was supporting. The Senate violated its own rules to confirm her in time. Barrett is a conservative appeals court judge and protégée of former Justice Antonin Scalia. It was the first time in 151 years that a justice was confirmed without the support of a single member of the minority party, a sign of how bitter Washington's war over judicial nominations has become (Fandos, 2020).

The Trump administration joined the Supreme Court case, asking it to declare Obamacare unconstitutional. Police unions are preventing Congress from making laws to protect future George Floyds from police harm and supporting Republican candidates. And to return to the coronavirus pandemic, Paul Krugman said the South resembled Brazil in its inability to deal with the virus. These divergent parts of our current difficulties show the extent of the problems created by an administration that was run for the benefit of the very rich and did not do anything for ordinary people – even demonizing Black and brown people to explain their actions. I said we were turning into Argentina in my last book and agree with Krugman, although adding geography to the comparison informs us of the roots of these problems in the Civil War and the 1904 election, both described in this book (Temin, 2017; Krugman, 2020b; Scheiber, 2020; Stolberg, 2020).

The short-run effects of these policies will show up as increased poverty and death rates among poor and minority Americans. The long-run effects will not show up for several years, but may be even larger and more damaging than the short-run effects. Diminishing federal investments in education and social capital were described earlier in this chapter. Changing our focus from the United States as a whole to states exposes the extent of the Trump administration policies.

The problem is that the cost of the pandemic is falling on states more than the federal government. States have supported hospital expansions and enhanced personnel to treat infected people. Unlike the federal government, almost all states need to balance their budgets each year. The pandemic money therefore came at the expense of other state expenditures. The most important of these may well be education. Teachers, no longer well paid, are being fired as school districts run out of money. And during the pandemic, computer learning substituted for class-room teaching. These cost-saving changes reduce the personal contact between students and teachers that is the essence of early and grade-school education. They also omit access from poor and minority households that do not have computers and/ or access to the internet. As noted earlier, personal attention is the key for many poor and minority students to stay in school and achieve educational goals (Zimmerman, 2020).

The pandemic led to a rapid decrease of our national income, a fall moderated for the unemployed by the CARES Act. Just as President Trump was missing in action at the start of the pandemic, he was missing in action as Congress was debating continuing help beyond the July deadlines in the CARES Act. It is as if he is the cult leader hired to lead the evangelicals in voting, but not to fulfill any obligations of his presidency (Haberman, Cochrane, and Tankersley, 2020; Hassan, 2019; Rice, 2020).

The 2020 election turned out to be reminiscent of the 2016 election in its progress as opposed to its outcome. As noted, since Trump had not done anything to cure the COVID-19 coronavirus pandemic, he denied that it was going on during his campaign stops. He ran many massive rallies of his supporters without many masks or social distancing. A study of the illnesses after his rallies concluded his rallies caused more than 30,000 COVID-19 infections and 700 deaths. The fear of voting in person caused many voters to mail in their votes. Trump appointed one of his large donors to run the post office and who slowed down the delivery of these ballots. Trump was very anxious after election day to have the voting over even though he had, perhaps unwittingly, set up the vote count to take time, and all elections have had to wait for a few states, albeit not usually critical ones (Astor, 2020; Graves, 2020; Stolberg, 2020).

Despite all these delays, Trump made haste to claim without any evidence that he won the election. While his opponent, Joseph Biden, was in the lead for several states, the fear was created that Trump wanted to repeat the role that the Supreme Court played in the 2000 election. It stopped vote counting in 2000 as Trump wanted to do in 2020, and it ruled in favor of the Republican candidate. This lie was in line with his campaign claim that Biden would produce violence and mayhem, although the protests that Biden supported were almost entirely peaceful. Trump also claimed that the COVID-19 pandemic was no longer with us, which is why he was not concerned that his rallies would kill hundreds of people (Burns and Martin, 2020; Krugman, 2020d).

States continued counting despite all of Trump's statements and court appeals. The result was mixed. Biden won the presidency, but only after several days' wait due to Republican state legislatures in a few critical states that kept the election officials from counting mailed votes before election day. Trump objected to these delays, but the delays were caused by his party and by the resurgent coronavirus that he had not felt obliged to manage or mention as a problem in his campaign that increased the number of mailed votes. Biden was the tortoise who won the race, while Trump was the hare who went to sleep during the pandemic that framed the electoral race (Hulse, 2020).

Biden achieved a milestone when he chose Kamala Harris as his vice president. He brought the second person of color into the White House, and the first woman. Obama has only one African-American parent, and Harris has one also. But while Obama's other parent was white, Harris' other parent was Asian American. As he took office, Biden accomplished an important deed for integration of minorities into the main stream of government. Blacks wait to see if he can turn this symbolic action into measures that will improve their lives (Eligon and Burch, 2020).

The election results caused disruption in the short run as President Trump refused to congratulate his successor. He did everything he could, from a constant barrage of verbal insults to an appeal to the Supreme Court to invalidate the election. He did not do the normal presidential task of easing the entry of a new president into the various complex aspects of his job. He continued his practice of the last four years of forsaking expectations and making life difficult for anyone who disagrees with him. Republican congresspeople followed Trump's lead and did not reach out to Biden on his victory. McConnell led the Republican charge against the election results (Cochrane, 2020; Fandos and Cochrane, 2020; Haberman and Shear, 2020).

Trump's frequent repetition that the election was stolen echoed the German army's insistence that Germany was stabbed in the back during World War I as described in Chapter 4. While Jews were the villains in the 1920s, voting urban Blacks were Republican villains in 2020 (Snyder, 2020).

Misinformation will not end with Trump's presidency. Voters were bombarded with misinformation before the election, and Trump is clinging to his own construction of reality since the election. The alternate universe that Trump disseminated will make it hard for Biden to attack the nation's problems. For example, his secretary of state,

Pompeo, stated a week after the election, "There will be a smooth transition to a second Trump administration." Michael Beschloss, a prominent presidential historian, affirmed, "We have not seen any president in history lose re-election, refuse to concede defeat and take actions that threaten the abuse of presidential power to keep himself in office." The growth of social media makes it very hard for young people to distinguish truth from fantasy (Baker and Haberman, 2020; Baker and Jakes, 2020; Mazzei and Perlroth, 2020; Orlowsky, 2020).

The continuation of McConnell in the Senate indicates that there will be problems for Biden in the longer run. Biden, who was Obama's vice president must recall Obama's problems with Senate opposition; he probably will live that unhappy experience again. The senators who were so eager to pass the 2017 tax cut for their rich friends will not be enthusiastic about any federal spending to ease the problems of poor Black and brown communities hard hit by the pandemic. And senators will balk at passing other expenditures that will help the whole economy recover from the pandemic recession like infrastructure improvement or aids to states and hospitals. Biden will be able to govern in part by presidential decree as Obama did in his second term and Trump did more recently. He can mandate mask wearing and social distancing in order to combat COVID-19, but he will be hard pressed to provide funds for enforcement (Irwin, 2020).

Income inequality increased during the pandemic, and the problems of inequality endure. The rich are happy to approve measures that benefit working and unemployed people as long as they are not asked to pay taxes to help them. They support education for all, absolutely necessary if the American economy is to continue as a world leader, as long as they are not asked to pay taxes to pay teachers and rehab old school buildings. They may even support ending mass incarceration as long as they are not asked to pay taxes for social and educational help for freed convicts. Unless something radical happens soon, the United States will continue to decline in its world standing (Temin, 2017).

Growing inequality is not limited to America. As in the United States, the incomes of median families in the OECD grew far less rapidly than the incomes of the richest 10 percent in the last thirty years. Middle-class job security also fell, and many middle-class families are highly indebted. A recent OECD report concluded, "[T]he middle class looks increasingly like a boat in rocky waters" (OECD, 2019, 13).

California voters showed that they, like Republicans elsewhere, regard business prosperity more than workers' conditions. They voted to allow the ride-hailing services Uber and Lyft to continue to treat their drivers as independent contractors rather than as employees. When manufacturers and hoteliers did this in the late twentieth century, the effects on workers from not having benefits like healthcare and unemployment insurance was severe. The lack of opportunity for job advances also solidified the class divisions (Conger, 2020).

Biden did his best to change the country's direction when he took office in January 2021, despite Republican gains in Congress and state houses. He promised three items in his acceptance speech after he won the election, and he tried to deliver on them as soon as he could. The first item was the resumption of an appeal to all the population, whatever their politics, to pull together in rescuing us from the divisions caused by President Trump. This included working to decrease the racism of the past four years and carry out the implicit commitment of having Kamala Harris as his vice president. Voters were concerned about police violence, continuing their street protests into voting booths. Police unions have placed large obstacles in front of reform, and Biden tried to work through this tangle by negotiation with the competing authorities. The book by Thomas Abt cited earlier showed one way to approach this problem. He did not advocate "defunding" the police; he instead wanted them to cooperate with social services to reduce urban crime (Abt, 2019; Tavernise and Eligon, 2020).

The second item was for the federal government to be active in fighting the coronavirus pandemic. Biden said in his acceptance speech that he would appoint a task force immediately to present him with a plan that incorporated the ideas that he and Harris had been expressing during their campaigns, and he did so on the Monday after his victory. These ideas include wearing masks, maintaining social distancing, washing hands frequently, and being tested regularly. But Republican governors did not go along with federal directives, slowing their impact.

Federal direction may enable schools to open normally in the fall of 2021. That would mean that most students would lose only a bit more than a year and prevent a generation of young people from being without continuous schooling. That also will help integration as poor Black and brown students suffer the most from schooling over zoom, often lacking computers and access to the internet to participate seriously. And personal contacts with teachers are very helpful for students who grew up in houses without books. But Republican opposition to federal controls delayed many school openings.

Finally, economic recovery can lift the economy out of the pandemic recession earlier if the pandemic subsides earlier. Just reopening bars and restaurants, as Trump advocated prematurely, seemed risky after the resumption of infections from the earlier openings. Other countries faced these problems, and solutions have ranged to subsidizing restaurants as they reopen to rationing entry into various kinds of stores. Wearing masks might be useful even as the pandemic recedes. But cooperation has proved elusive.

The Senate refused to pass any government expenses that would increase the deficit, and many senators would not even consider any tax increases. Biden's attempt to recover from the recession was negated in large part. That will carry over to redistricting that will take place next year and lead to more Republican gains in the future. Democracy, in addition to full employment, is at risk (Krugman, 2020e).

A quite different effect of Biden's victory was that we attempted to rejoin our allies and fellow nations abroad. Biden nullified all of Trump's presidential proclamations, as Trump had nullified all of Obama's proclamations, and rejoined various international organizations, such as the Paris Climate Accord and the World Health Organization. These actions made more sense of our immigration process and our joint coronavirus efforts. They also signaled an attempt to combat global warming. Only time will tell if we can regain some of the international trust we had before Trump took office.

# CHAPTER 8

# Conclusion

## 8.1 HISTORY

I integrated Black and white activities into American economic history in this book. Black people have never been together with other immigrants and have been excluded from American prosperity, growth, and politics after gaining their freedom. My approach is that all men and women of all colors are created equal, but their economic histories in the United States are quite different. The resulting tensions still inform us today.

Blacks were enslaved people who helped white Americans expand their economic activity before the Civil War. The Thirteenth Amendment outlawed slavery after the Civil War, and Blacks began to participate in American politics *en masse* for the first time during Reconstruction. This process met with white resistance, and Black inclusion in the growing economy fell sharply in the Gilded Age that followed. White political ambition for Black participation faded. The Supreme Court negated the application of the Fourteenth Amendment to the rights of freedmen. The age of Jim Crow laws spread in Southern states.

After two world wars, a depression, and the Great Migration, Lyndon Johnson's Great Society in the 1960s echoed Reconstruction. The measures in the second attempt to integrate Blacks into the majority status of the United States induced a reaction that echoes the failure of Reconstruction a century earlier. The Supreme Court encouraged the growth of commerce and industry while it aborted efforts to include Blacks into political and economic activities in both the 1880s and

2010s. The court promoted white economic progress and impeded the integration of most Blacks into this prosperity.

It is worth stressing how much the Gilded Age of the late nineteenth and early twentieth century looks like our current Gilded Age. Everyone remembers robber baron names from the first Gilded Age, from Carnegie to Rockefeller and J. P. Morgan. Their current analogues today are Bezos, Cook, Pichai, and Zuckerberg, who testified before the anti-trust subcommittee of the House Judiciary Committee in July 2020. To those leaders of the electronics age, we need to add a few other oligarchs, like Rupert Murdoch, who started the Fox Network that supports and "informs" Donald Trump, Charles Koch, who sponsored the Federalist Society that supplied Trump's judicial appointments, and Vladimir Putin and his Russian oligarchs, who exert such influence on American politics in our newly international economy. The robber barons of both periods created conditions for the establishment of Jim Crow laws then and the growth of mass incarceration, also known as the New Jim Crow, today.

Each time there was a progressive move toward integrating Blacks into the white economy and polity or help poor people advance, a reaction followed that returned Blacks and poor whites to widespread subservience. This was true in the Gilded Age of the late 1800s, and it is true again in the new Gilded Age of the late 1900s. Blacks made gains toward integration in Reconstruction and in the Civil Rights Movement during postwar prosperity. Some of these gains have lasted, as I have shown, but full integration remains far off because policies even in good times exclude Blacks and benefited whites.

*Time on the Cross* said that slaves were only whipped once a week on large plantations. Critics responded that a whipping every week would communicate to all the slaves on the plantation that they would be whipped if they stepped out of line. The Wilmington, North Carolina, massacre in 1898 and the Tulsa massacre in 1921 have sent the same message to African Americans more recently. If you get too close to us and more like us, we will destroy you. As the authors of *Time on the Cross* reminded us, slaves were investments, not to be wantonly destroyed. African Americans and Latinos can be destroyed now with no loss to mainstream white Americans. No one owns Blacks anymore; it is extraordinary that a century and a half after the Civil War that we should treat Blacks so badly.

These restraints saw African Americans as undifferentiated primitives, but African Americans have always been diverse. Frederick Douglass and Harriet Tubman, who we met in Chapter 1, were extraordinary slaves and ex-slaves before the Civil War. Now we have the Black Elite who were educated in the Civil Rights Movement described in Chapter 5, one of whom, Barack Obama, was elected and re-elected president in recent years. Now we have another elected as vice president.

Between these similar periods came the disturbances of world wars and depression in the early twentieth century. Everyone suffered, but Blacks tried a peaceful way to alleviate their fortunes in the Great Migration. Whites struggled through the violence and created economic and political foundations for the following prosperity, but Blacks were largely excluded from this progress. While some educated Blacks have joined white society, the cost of keeping most Blacks imprisoned and disenfranchised now reduces economic growth in the United States. The new Gilded Age is based on services instead of manufacturing, and demand for workers has fallen. The new robber barons inflame racial prejudice to maintain their political hegemony, while neglecting investment other than prisons for Black and brown people.

## 8.2 PROSPECTS FOR THE FUTURE

We need to start now to include Black and other minorities into our economy and political life. Early education is a very important beginning, but mass incarceration and housing segregation prevent public education from progressing. Both are difficult, but mass incarceration is easier to explain and discuss. The penalty of Blacks using cocaine was designed one hundred times as large as the penalty for whites. One out of three Black men now goes to prison at some point in his life. If young men are in prison, they are not in school, and they cannot advance in educational level. Blacks are more likely to be incarcerated at all levels of income than whites are, and the difference is larger for poor households than for rich ones.

We are in a mass incarceration equilibrium with far greater emphasis on Black prisoners. Very few prisoners were let go in the COVID-19 coronavirus pandemic even though the virus was thriving virulently in the prisons. If the white community is so afraid of drug offenders that they will not free them to save the prisoners' lives, how can we convince the white community to abandon mass incarceration?

It will be hard even to start on this process, as President Obama found out when he wanted to remove the Black bias of our drug laws. He succeeded in lowering the difference between the kinds of heroin preferred by Blacks and whites, but he could not get an equalization of penalties through Congress. The growth of private prisons has increased the opposition to reducing mass incarceration since they increase their profits when they have more prisoners, not – as we want – fewer prisoners. Private prisons have become prominent in the internment of potential migrants to the United States from Latin America. Their political power consequently has increased.

The problem of immigration is fraught with difficulty. Previous administrations tried to separate prisons for immigrants, who are not charged with a crime, from American citizens who have been convicted. The current administration has abolished these differences and ruled that all prisons are alike. Any effort to reduce mass incarceration will be entangled with the problem of immigration. That problem has proven hard to solve for decades.

Finally, prisons furnish employment for white rural workers who no longer are focusing on the farms. These people give support to political parties who continue mass incarceration as no one has been able to promise alternative jobs. This again is a thorny conflict, and new employment for rural citizens is a tall order. It is integrated with all the changes in the economy and the labor force described earlier.

The result of these historical policies is that the United States has been declining in the Social Progress Index since its inception in 2018, and it now is the lowest of the G7 and 28th in the world. For health and education, we are below Argentina. This decline was accelerated by President Trump and by the pandemic he ignored, but it started before he was elected. We will continue to decline unless we change our policies dramatically. Trump was our Peron, and he divided us between Blacks and whites, between political parties and states. His destruction of educational and social capital may become evident soon. As noted already, we are behind in education and healthcare (Lewis, 2009; Alston and Gallo, 2010).

We can learn more about the current status of American Blacks by looking at the median African American. I examine the wealth of median Black and white households where the head of the household has varied education. The median household in the case is the household in the middle; there are just as many households richer than they are as there are poorer than they are. The median African-American family before the Civil War was enslaved and could not accumulate wealth. Various historians have disputed that, as discussed in Chapter 1, but the weight of historical evidence is not on their side. The median African-American household today is not living in Flint, Michigan, with contaminated water supplies, or very involved with mass incarceration. Although today's median African-American household probably has experienced trouble with the police or even with mass incarceration as shown in Figure 6.3.

Table 8.1 records the median net worth of Black and white households for several levels of education. William Darity and his colleagues noted the obvious fact that white households had higher net worth than Black households did at every level of education. As the third column of Table 8.1 shows, the ratio of median incomes at each level, and the ratios of white to Black household wealth at different levels of education are all greater than one. At lower levels of education, the ratios are far larger than one, close to twenty and thirty. I will return to this observation shortly.

**Table 8.1** Household net worth by race and education, ($) 2018

| Education | Whites | Blacks | White/Black | Black/less ed. | White/less ed. |
|---|---|---|---|---|---|
| Post-college | 455,212 | 141,115 | 3.2 | 2.0 | 1.7 |
| College | 268,028 | 70,219 | 3.8 | 3.9 | 2.0 |
| Some college | 135,415 | 18,200 | 7.4 | 2.7 | 1.1 |
| High school | 118,580 | 6,660 | 17.8 | 2.4 | 1.4 |
| Less than HS | 82,968 | 2,775 | 29.9 | | |

*Source:* Darity et al., 2018, 6. Ratios added: white/Black at similar education and wealth increases for more education for both whites and Blacks separately.

We should not make the perfect solution an obstacle for a helpful program. Even if education cannot match white assets at each level, they can improve the relative assets of Black households. Darity and his coauthors are correct that no single measure will equalize racial household assets, but we should support education as a way to improve Black household wealth. Changes in community college treatment of their students has begun to increase graduation from college even while federal policy is racist.

To learn more, I added columns four and five to Darity's table. The entries in these columns show the gain in net worth when households move from one education level to the next level. In the language of economists, these columns show the marginal effect of more education on Black and white households. Note that every entry in the Black column is larger than any entry in the white column. Education helps Black households acquire increased net worth more than it helps white households. Of course, Black median wealth with little or no education is far below the median net worth of uneducated whites.

The entry in the second row in the Black column shows a marginal effect close to four for Blacks graduating college. It is the largest entry in these two columns. This accomplishment permits Blacks to join the Black Elite. "A college education gives students the intellectual capital to tackle high-skill jobs, as well as the social capital to make the connections and build the networks that can lead to success" (Kirp, 2019, 4).

The history recounted here is not optimistic about the length of helpful programs. Reconstruction lasted for only a decade, from 1865 to 1877, and then was replaced by Jim Crow laws. The Civil Rights Movement lasted through the 1960s, but it was decaying even at the end of that decade under President Nixon. In other words, to alter the results shown in Table 8.1, we need to have an integration effort that is more durable than any integration effort in our history.

Fortunately, recent research and experience at community colleges shows that students who had bad education or even served time in jail can be brought up to speed later. Several community colleges across the country have adopted a new motivation. Instead of attracting a good student body, they decided they would work to *graduate* a diverse student body and send students to finish their college experience.

Motivation is key, and the implementation varies between colleges and states. I noted in Chapter 7 that the University of Texas is a prominent example. David Laude, who became provost at Texas during this effort, focused on freshmen who often dropped out. In his words, "If students aren't feeling connected to the university, that someone cares about them, it doesn't matter how many tutoring hours we offer them" (Kirp, 2019, 86).

The University of Texas starts caring about students before they enter college, with information about different colleges to apply to and summer reminders of deadlines for entering students. When students get to college, faculty use data analyses to predict who might drop out. Easy access to clinical psychologists – who have access to the underlying data – reassures students they belong in college and helps them find a desired major. Small sections where students and faculty interact replace large introductory lectures in math and other entry subjects. The performance of all students improved, minority and white, and more Blacks chose to continue into STEM fields. Variants of these approaches have been tried in community colleges across the country, from Florida to Texas and California, and north to New York City and Massachusetts. They all share the focus on students and urging students to study, do well in their courses, and go on to graduate college. This may be the key to furthering integration when we next have a racial equity push from our federal government (Kirp, 2019).

Returning to the lower rows of Table 8.1, the ratios in column three show white households with high school education (or less) have vastly larger net worth than their Black counterparts. Where did this division come from? Mass incarceration is the villain. Recall that the penalty of Blacks using cocaine was one hundred times as large as the penalty for whites. One out of three Black men goes to prison at some point in his life under current conditions, as opposed to one out of seventeen for white men.

If young men are in prison, they are not in school, and they cannot advance in educational level. (As described earlier in Figure 6.3, prisons are very different than schools; while prisons are dominated by orders and control, schools encourage students to explore their interests.) Figure 6.2 shows that Blacks are more likely to be incarcerated at all levels of income than whites, even though the difference is larger for poor households than for rich ones.

The difficulties are illustrated by the dozen years a nineteen-year-old Black rapper, Meek Mill, was kept on probation by a Philadelphia trial judge for carrying a gun. The judge accused the rapper of not following the rules of his probation and sentenced Meek to two-to-four years in state prison over probation violations in November 2017. This action turned this rapper's case into a lightning rod for criminal justice reform. A Pennsylvania appeals court released Meek from prison and granted him bail after serving five months of his sentence. The appeals court removed the trial judge from the case and granted Meek a retrial, in large part because the only witness who testified against Meek in his original case was a police officer later found guilty of lying and theft. The court tossed Meek's original conviction, and Meek committed to work for criminal justice reform to thank the rich Black and white fans who got him out of prison (Allyn, 2019).

To summarize our lessons from Table 8.1, note that every entry in the fourth column, showing all the marginal increases in net worth for Blacks, is larger than all of the entries in the fifth column that show the same for white households. While the gains from college education appear dramatic, the increase in education for children and poorly educated Blacks is even more important.

Congress both raised the minimum wage and expanded it to workers in previously unprotected industries in 1966. This measure reduced the earnings inequality between Black and white Americans by more than 20 percent. This finding suggests that raising and expanding the minimum wage could once again reduce the persistent earnings divide between white workers and Black, Hispanic, and Native American workers whose wealth is compared in the bottom rows of Table 8.1. A focus on raising the minimum wage also might be more politically palliative than trying to raise taxes on rich people. "Though legislation to raise the wage floor would be a universal program in name and application, in practice it would be a remarkably effective tool for racial justice" (Derenoncourt and Montialoux, 2020).

Darity's table reminds me that he was a graduate student at MIT while I was teaching there. We were under pressure from the Carter

Administration to look for Black graduate students in the 1970s. We found a half-dozen of them who needed some individual care to fit into our curriculum. Most of these Black students received their doctorate and went on to have fine academic careers. President Reagan ceased government pressure on the economics department to integrate, and we returned to having an occasional student of color in our program. This example shows that it is possible to help Black students through graduate school, but on the other hand, it shows how brief this experience was.

We faced a confusing problem after a few months. The Black students were attentive and forthcoming in class, but they did very poorly on exams. I and other faculty interviewed the students to find out what was going on. It turned out the graduate students studied in groups. Most study groups in our department were small, and the Black students had a study group of their own. The white study groups had past exams from upper classmen, but the Black students did not know any more advanced students. We got some past exams for the Black students and solved the problem. This is one small example of a problem I have discussed at several points in this history. Black students lack the context of educational activities when they try to advance themselves. These problems require a little tutorial from the faculty, as discussed earlier.

Another example of self-selected study groups comes from school districts across the nation whose buildings were closed in the fall of 2020 due to the COVID-19 coronavirus pandemic. Parents organized "learning pods" – small groupings of children who gathered every day to learn in a shared space, often participating in the online instruction provided by their schools. Parents with low exposure were likely to join pods with families who had similarly low exposure to the coronavirus. This seemingly rational impulse excluded Black and Latino families, who were likely to be infected by the virus. Privileged families that had limited exposure to the virus would not opt into learning pods with children of essential workers. Either we can continue that pattern by retreating into the comfort of our own advantages, or we can act to dismantle racist educational policies (Ebbert, 2020; Goodnough, 2020; Green, 2020).

A historical example comes from Black banking. Traditionally, as I have described, Blacks were excluded from education. They also, albeit free after the Civil War, were unable to borrow from banks run and patronized by whites. When Blacks tried to start banks of their own, they were hampered by the lack of history and variety among their potential borrowers. Commercial banks typically earn money by choosing between loan applicants, but Black banks did not have many options and did not last long. They suffered from the same segregation that plagued our graduate students and current "learning pods."

The absence of Black banking hampered the economic progress of Black communities, and there was always the threat if they got too prosperous that they would suffer the destruction that Wilmington, North Carolina, suffered in 1898 and the Black Wall Street in Tulsa, Oklahoma, suffered in 1921. This inability to progress is part of the reason that Black households at different levels of education have smaller family savings by large margins than whites (Baradaran, 2017).

One form of reparations might be to rebuild Head Start and other early education programs. They have decayed over time, and they would help Black children to grow in diverse directions. There are still the problems of segregated schools, but the community colleges described above may help solidify the gains from early education (Bernstein et al., 2020).

Now return to Isabel Wilkerson's book that said Blacks in the United States are an untouchable caste. This seems to be accurate for the whole sweep of our history. But it does not take account of the history recounted here when two separate groups of people tried their best to raise African Americans to be full-fledged citizens. These efforts were undone by very rich white men, railroad and steel magnates in the late nineteenth century, and financial types in the late twentieth century. The record described here as if ordinary people were and are happy to accept Black people as equals, but rich people – who generally have no personal contact with Blacks – are hostile.

Wilkerson's book contains a lot of history, but it is not a historical narrative like this book. Wilkerson moved back and forth in space from the American South to Nazi Germany and India, and in time from ancient to modern times. Her stories are well told and enjoyable to read, but they are to sell an idea rather than to recount American history. She also ignores the history and promise of universal education that has been stressed here. For example, she said, "Things began to change in the 1960s when civil rights legislation opened labor markets to women." See a fuller description in Chapter 6 of this book. She closes her book with a quick, albeit ambiguous, comparison. She said it would be hard to eliminate the caste system in America, but that Germany eliminated the Nazi caste system after World War II (Wilkerson, 2020b, 182, 380, 383).

We must agree with Wilkerson that Blacks are unwelcome everywhere, even in a liberal community at the end of Cape Cod, Massachusetts. Provincetown is a liberal town that welcomes gay and transgender people cheerfully. But when a female member of the Black Elite – who was a professor at the University of Chicago – entered a beach for a swim, a white woman came rushing out of her waterfront house to tell her she was trespassing. "There were hundreds of people all across the long pile of the beach, but I was not surprised that woman was singling me out and not any of the other people," the professor said. "I was the only person of color on the beach." The professor eventually left the beach after a verbal altercation with the property owner. She later spoke to the police, who, she said, had "absolutely no interest in helping, and no interest in me filing an official report" (Martin, 2020).

That does not mean all rich people, but rather the ideologues that are leading our country now. A brief summary of modern macroeconomics may illuminate this story. Macroeconomics did not exist before World War I. The economic disturbances that appeared at the peace conference induced John Maynard Keynes to create this subfield of economics. He and his friends in the Cambridge Circus assumed that we all wanted to have employment for all workers without excessive inflation. The tumultuous 1970s created distrust of the Keynesian framework since the decade had both inflation and unemployment. This was easily included in Keynesian thought by introducing a supply side to Keynes' demand analysis, but conservatives around the University of Chicago were not happy.

Milton Friedman gave a presidential address at the American Economic Association in 1968 that opposed federal government economic activity. This view had consequences over time in two ways. One way was the theory of austerity. This is the theory underlying President

Trump's refusal to act when confronted by the COVID-19 coronavirus pandemic and again when negotiating with Congress to continue unemployment insurance in August, 2020. The other strand gave rise to two articles that altered business education in the 1970s by Fama and Jensen and Meckling by arguing that financial markets were efficient and that managers should focus on the market more than to production. That is why President Trump put more weight on the stock market than to the hundreds of thousand people dying from COVID-19 (Appelbaum, 2019).

We need to recapture Keynes' concern for all the people, not just business and rich people, not just whites, but also Blacks and other immigrants. The first way to do this would be to have a large economic stimulus to restart the economy after the coronavirus is tamed. Republicans and businesspeople will resist such a Keynesian policy, but – as Christine Romer argued in 2008 – a large stimulus will promote a solid recovery.

It is striking that the United States has the most prisoners in mass incarceration and the most deaths from the COVID-19 coronavirus pandemic. What do these two phenomena have in common? They both demonize and destroy Black communities in the United States. Two of these phenomena originated around 1970 when inequality of income began to increase, and both incarceration and inequality increased steadily over the past half-century. As recounted in this book, racism is a prominent part of the two Gilded Ages, and antebellum African slavery set the United States on this trajectory.

As I argued in my previous book, *The Vanishing Middle Class*, the very rich do not consider poor people important. In the Trump administration, the very rich did not even consider poor and Black people to be members of their community as defined by the US Constitution. They were quite willing to watch hundreds of thousands die from the COVID-19 coronavirus and not do anything. There were few dissidents. George Soros, a prominent international finance mogul who supported freedom fighter supporters in Eastern Europe, announced that his foundation was investing $220 million in efforts to achieve racial equality in America by supporting several Black-led racial justice groups for years to come (Herndon, 2020).

Opposing Soros, Charles Koch and his associates want to declare the Post Office bankrupt and eliminate this staple of American life. Their attack began decades ago and culminated in a 2006 change in the Postal Service law that compelled it to pay in advance for fifty years for health and retirement benefits of all of its employees, and stipulated that the price of postage could not increase faster than the rate of inflation. Between 2007 and 2016, the Post Office lost $62.4 billion, almost 90 percent of that due to prefunding retiree benefits. Prefunding the health benefits of retirees "is a requirement that no other entity, private or public, has to make." As in so many things, this will harm Blacks more than white people" (Bogage, 2020; Graves, 2020; Smith, J., 2020).

Finally, states handle voting in our federal system, and the same budget cuts that are short-changing education also are short-changing voting. People, particularly Black people, are having trouble voting now as they have had in the past. They also have to deal with Trump's lies about mail-in votes. The barriers can come from bad laws as in the past – particularly the 2006 law that threatens the Post Office today – and from hardships that are more recent as well. The new Supreme Court upheld the Florida Republican institution of debt repayments – a poll tax – for voting by ex-felons who had been granted voting rights by a popular constitutional amendment (Baker, M., 2020; Liptak, 2020; Wines and Fausset, 2020).

The result of all this is that the United States has continued to decline in the Social Progress Index, where it is the lowest of the G7 and 28th in the world. We are now at ninety-one for access to quality education and ninety-seven for access to quality healthcare. Argentina, which is 41st in the world, ranks ahead of us for education and healthcare, at sixty-six and sixty-four. Our low scores for education and healthcare are the legacy of slavery. We will continue to decline unless our polices change dramatically. The very rich will prosper, as will the top fifth whose incomes have continued to rise for the past half-century, while the lower 80 percent will see their incomes and social services decline (Social Progress Index, 2020).

Against the force of Jim Crow, Frederick Douglass spoke out for voting rights at the end of the nineteenth century. He had been talking and writing on this subject since the Civil War, and he kept it up as he grew older. Recall his words as quoted in Chapter 3. Now, against a revived Jim Crow society, Stacey Abrams was the first Black woman to run in a major party for governor of a state in 2018. She received more votes than any other Democratic candidate in Georgia, but she was defeated by the Secretary of State who ran against her by refusing to let Black people vote. She now runs an organization named *Fair Fight* to invest in new voters and protect the Black vote. It is sad that a century after Douglass, Abrams has to fight for Black votes all over again. As described earlier, Black economic history repeats itself (Casey, 2019; Abrams, 2020).

# References

Abramovitz, Alan, 2018. *Great Alignment: Race, Party Transformation, and the Role of Donald Trump*. New Haven, CT: Yale University Press.

Abrams, Stacey, 2020. *Our Time Is Now*. New York: Picador.

Abt, Thomas, 2019. *Bleeding Out: The Devastating Consequences of Urban Violence – And a Bold New Plan for Peace in the Streets*. New York: Basic Books.

Acharya, A., M. Blackwell, and M. Sen, 2016. "The Political Legacy of American Slavery." *Journal of Politics*, 78 (3), 621–41.

ACLU, 2020, "COVID-19 Model Finds Nearly 100,000 More Deaths Than Current Estimates, Due to Failures to Reduce Jails." *ACLU COVID-19 Jail Report*, August 8.

Adams, Charles F., Jr., and Henry Adams, 1871. *Chapters of Erie, and Other Essays*. Boston: James R. Osgood and Company

Agee, James, and Walker Evans, 1941. *Let Us Now Praise Famous Men*. Boston: Houghton Mifflin.

Ager, P., 2013. "The Persistence of De Facto Power: Elites and Economic Development in the US South, 1840–1960." Technical Report, Universitat Pompeu Fabra, Barcelona, Spain.

Aizcorbe, Ana M., Carol E. Moylan, and Carol A. Robbins, 2009. "Toward Better Measurement of Innovation and Intangibles." *BEA Briefing*, January. Available at: www.researchgate.net/publication/242498352_BEA_BRIEFING_Toward_Better_Measurement_of_Innovation_and_Intangibles

Alexander, Lewis, and Janice Eberly, 2018. "Investment Hollowing Out." *IMF Economic Review*, 66 (1). Available at: https://ssrn.com/abstract=3162101 or http://dx.doi.org/10.1057/s41308–017-0044-2

Alexander, Michelle, 2010. *The New Jim Crow: Mass Incarceration in the Age of Colorblindness*. New York: New Press.

Allegretto, Sylvia, and Lawrence Michel, 2018. "The Teacher Pay Penalty Has Hit a New High." *Economic Policy Institute*, September. Available at www.epi.org/publication/teacher-pay-gap-2018/

Allyn, Bobby, 2019. "Meek Mill Pleads Guilty to Misdemeanor Gun Charge, Ends 12-Year Legal Case." *National Public Radio,* August 27. Available at www.npr .org/2019/08/27/754769378/meek-mill-pleads-guilty-to-misdemeanor-gun-charge-ends-12-year-legal-case

Alston, Lee J., and Joseph P. Ferrie, 1999. *Southern Paternalism and the American Welfare State: Economics, Politics, and Institutions in the South, 1865–1965.* New York: Cambridge University Press.

Alston, Lee J., and Andres A. Gallo, 2010. "Electoral Fraud, the Ruse of Peron and the Demise of Checks and Balances in Argentina." *Explorations in Economic History,* 47 (2), 179–97.

Alston, Lee J., and Kyle D. Kauffman, 2001. "Competition and the Compensation of Sharecroppers by Race: A View from Plantations in the Early Twentieth Century." *Explorations in Economic History,* 38 (1), 181–94.

Alvarez, Lizette, and Cara Buckley, 2013. "Zimmerman Is Acquitted in Killing of Trayvon Martin." New York Times, July 14.

American Society of Civil Engineers, 2017. *2017 Infrastructure Report Card.* Reston, VA: ASCE Foundation.

Anderson, Carol, 2016. *White Rage: The Unspoken Truth of Our Racial Divide.* New York: Bloomsbury.

Appelbaum, Binyamin, 2019. *The Economists' Hour: False Prophets, Free Markets, and the Fracture of Society.* New York: Little, Brown.

Aptheker, Herbert, 1971. *Afro-American History: The Modern Era.* Secaucus, NJ: Citadel Press.

Apuzzo, Matt, and Steven Erlanger, 2020. "A Black Belgian Student Saw a White Fraternity as His Ticket. It Was His Death." *New York Times,* October 4.

Arnett, Dugan, 2020. "Twice Denied Testing, UMass Amherst Scholar Dies after Long Battle with Coronavirus." *Boston Globe,* May 1.

Ashkenas, Jeremy, Gabriel J. X. Dance, and Gilbert Gates, 2016. "How Donald Trump Uses the Tax Code in Ways You Can't." *New York Times,* October 7.

Associated Press, 1994. "Haldeman Diary Shows Nixon Was Wary of Blacks and Jews." *New York Times,* May 18.

Astor, Maggie, 2020. "We Have Never Had Final Results on Election Day." *New York Times,* November 1.

Autor, David, 2019. "Work of the Past, Work of the Future." *AEA Papers and Proceedings,* 109, 1–32, May.

Autor, David, Claudia Goldin, and Lawrence F. Katz, 2020. "The Race between Education and Technology Revisited." *AEA Papers and Proceedings,* 110, 347–51.

Autor, David, David Dorn, Lawrence F. Katz, Christina Patterson, and John Van Reenen, 2020. "The Fall of the Labor Share and the Rise of Superstar Firms." *Quarterly Journal of Economics*, 135 (2), 711–83, May.

Aviv, Rachel, 2020. "Punishment by Pandemic." *New Yorker*, June 15.

Ayers, Edward, 1992. *The Promise of the New South: Life after Reconstruction*. New York: Oxford University Press.

Bacevich, Andrew, 2016. *America's War for the Greater Middle East: A Military History*. New York: Random House.

Bailey, Martha J., and Nicolas J. Duquette, 2014. "How Johnson Fought the War on Poverty: The Economics and Politics of Funding at the Office of Economic Opportunity." *Journal of Economic History*, 74 (2), 351–88, June.

Bailyn, Bernard, 2000. "Slavery and Population Growth in Colonial New England," in Peter Temin (ed.), *Engines of Enterprise: An Economic History of New England*. Cambridge, MA: Harvard University Press, pp. 253–59.

Baker, Mike, 2020. "The Facts about Mail-In Voting and Voter Fraud." *New York Times*, June 22.

Baker, Peter, 2020a. "Bolton Says Trump Impeachment Inquiry Missed Other Troubling Episodes." *New York Times*, June 17.

  2020b. "Trump Scorns His Own Scientists over Virus Data." *New York Times*, September 16.

Baker, Peter, and Lara Jakes, 2020. "Fighting Election Results, Trump Employs a New Weapon: The Government." *New York Times*, November 10.

Baker, Peter, and Maggie Haberman, 2020. "Win or Lose, Trump Will Remain a Powerful and Disruptive Force." *New York Times*, November 4.

Baker, Peter, Maggie Haberman, Katie Rogers, Zolan Kanno-Youngs, and Katie Benner, 2020. "How Trump's Idea for a Photo Op Led to Havoc in a Park." *New York Times*, June 2.

Baker, Richard B., 2015. "From the Field to the Classroom: The Boll Weevil's Impact on Education in Rural Georgia." *Journal of Economic History*, 75 (4), 1128–60.

Balco, Radley, 2014. *Rise of the Warrior Cop: The Militarization of America's Police Forces*. New York: Public Affairs.

Baradaran, Mehrsa, 2017. *The Color of Money: Black Banks and the Racial Wealth Gap*. Cambridge, MA: Harvard University Press.

Barstow, David, Susanne Craig, and Russ Buettner, 2018. "Trump Engaged in Suspect Tax Schemes as He Reaped Riches from His Father." *New York Times*, October 2.

Barry-Jester, Anna Maria, and Casselman Ben, 2016. "Obamacare Has Increased Insurance Coverage Everywhere." FiveThirtyEight, September 22.

Bates, Beth Tompkins, 2001. *Pullman Porters and the Rise of Protest Politics in Black America, 1925–1945*. Chapel Hill, NC: University of North Carolina Press.

Bator, Francis M., 2007. *No Good Choices: LBJ and the Vietnam/Great Society Connection*. Cambridge: American Academy of Arts and Sciences.

Baum, Dan, 2016. "Legalize It All: How to Win the War on Drug." *Harper's Magazine*, April.

Baum-Snow, N., 2007. "Did Highways Cause Suburbanization?" *Quarterly Journal of Economics*, 122 (2), 775–805.

Bayer, Patrick, and Kerwin Kofi Charles, 2018. "Divergent Paths: A New Perspective on Earnings Differences Between Black and White Men since 1940." *Quarterly Journal of Economics*, 133 (3), 1459–501.

Beck, E.M. and Stewart E., 1992. "Racial Violence and Black Migration in the American South, 1910 to 1930." *American Sociological Review*, 57 (1), 103–16, February.

Bellafante, Ginia, 2018. "Maybe It's Not Taxes That Scare Off Business but Failing Subways." *New York Times*, December 13.

Bellesiles, Michael A., 2010. *America's Year of Living Violently*. New York: New Press.

Berlin, Ira, 2010. *The Making of Africa America: The Four Great Migrations*. New York: Viking.

Berman, Ari. 2017. "Wisconsin's ID Law Suppressed 200,000 Voted in 2016 (Trump by 22, 748)." *The Nation*, May 9. Available at: https://www.thenation.com/article/wisconsins-voter-id-law-suppressed-200000-votes-trump-won-by-23000/

Bernanke, Barry, 1992. *Golden Fetters: The Gold Standard and the Great Depression, 1919–39*. New York: Oxford University Press.

Bernstein, Andrea, 2020. *American Oligarchs: The Kushners, the Trumps, and the Marriage of Money and Power*. New York: Norton.

Bernstein, Jon, Roger Crandall, Bridget Long, and Bob Rivers, 2020. "Invest in the Economy, Invest in Early Childhood Education and Child Care." *Boston Globe*, August 11.

Blackett, R.M.J., 2013. *Making Freedom: The Underground Railroad and the Politics of Slavery*. Chapel Hill: University of North Carolina Press.

Blackmon, Douglas A., 2008. *Slavery by Another Name: The Re-Enslavement of Black Americans from the Civil War to World War II*. New York: Random House.

Blight, David, W., 2018. *Frederick Douglass: Prophet of Freedom*. New York: Simon & Shuster.

Bogage, Jacob, 2020. "The USPS Needs a Bailout. Congress Is Partly to Blame." *Washington Post*, April 15.

Bonczar, Thomas P., 2003. "Prevalence of Imprisonment in the U. S. Population, 1974–2001." U.S. Department of Justice, Bureau of Justice Statistics, August, NCJ 197976.

Bonczar, Thomas P., and Allen J. Beck, 1997. "Lifetime Likelihood of Going to State or Federal Prison." U.S. Department of Justice, Bureau of Justice Statistics, March, NCJ 160092.

Bond, H.M., 1938. "Social and Economic Forces in Alabama Reconstruction." *Journal of Negro History*, 23 (3), 290–348.

Bordewich, Fergus, 2012. *America's Great Debate: Henry Clay, Stephen A. Douglas and the Compromise that Saved the Union.* New York: Simon & Schuster.

Bosman, Julie, 2017. "Michigan Allots $87 Million to Replace Flint's Tainted Water Pipes." *New York Times*, March 27.

2020. "In Flint, a 'Double Challenge' of Water and Virus." *New York Times*, August 19.

Bouie, Jamelle, 2020. "Why Coronavirus Is Killing African-Americans More Than Others." *New York Times*, April 14.

Bound, John, and Richard B. Freeman, 1992. "What Went Wrong? The Erosion of Relative Earnings and Employment among Young Black Men in the 1980s." *Quarterly Journal of Economics*, 107 (1), 201–32.

Boustan, Leah Platt, 2010. "Was Postwar Suburbanization 'White Flight'? Evidence from the Black Migration." *Quarterly Journal of Economics*, 124 (1), 417–43, February.

2017. *Competition in the Promised Land: Black Migrants in Northern Cities and Labor Markets.* Princeton: Princeton University Press.

Bridge, James H., 1992. *The Inside History of the Carnegie Steel Company* (rev. ed.). New York: University of Pittsburgh Press.

Broadberry, Stephen N., 1998. "How Did the United States and Germany Overtake Britain? A Sectoral Analysis of Comparative Productivity Levels, 1870–1990." *Journal of Economic History*, 58 (2), 375–402.

Brody, Richard, 2013. "The Worst thing about Birth of a Nation is How Good It Is." *New Yorker*, February 6.

Bryan, William Jennings, 1896. "Mesmerizing the Masses." July 9. Available at: http://historymatters.gmu.edu/d/5354/

Buettner, Russ, and Charles V. Bagli, 2016a. "How Donald Trump Bankrupted His Atlantic City Casinos, but Still Earned Millions." *New York Times*, June 11.

2016b. "Donald Trump's Business Decisions in '80s Nearly Led Him to Ruin." *New York Times*, October 3.

Buettner, Russ, Susanne Craig, and Mike McIntire, 2020. "Long-Concealed Records Show Trump's Chronic Losses and Years of Tax Avoidance." *New York Times*, September 27.

Buettner, Russ, Mike McIntire, Susanne Craig, and Keith Collins, 2020. "Trump Paid $750 in Federal Income Taxes in 2017. Here's the Math." *New York Times*, September 29.

Burnham, Walter D., 2010. *Voting in American Elections: The Shaping of the American Political Universe since 1788.* Bethesda: Academia Press.

Burns, Alexander, and Jonathan Martin, 2020. "As America Awaits a Winner, Trump Falsely Claims He Prevailed." *New York Times,* November 4.

Bush, George W., 2007. "President Bush Signs 'Improving Head Start for School Readiness Act of 2007' into Law." Available at: https://georgewbush-white-house.archives.gov/news/releases/2007/12/20071212-3.html

Carey, Kevin, 2020. "The 'Public' in Public College Could Be Endangered." *New York Times,* May 5.

Carruthers, Celeste K., and Marianne H. Wanamaker, 2013. "Closing the Gap? The Effect of Private Philanthropy on the Provision of African-American Schooling in the U.S. South." *Journal of Public Economics,* 101, 53–67.

Carson, E. Ann, and Elizabeth Anderson, 2016. "Prisoners in 2015." U.S. Department of Justice, Bureau of Justice Statistics, December, NCJ 250229.

Carter, Susan B., et al., 2006. *Historical Statistics of the United States.* New York: Cambridge University Press.

Casey, Nicholas, 2019. "Georgia Plans to Purge 300,000 Names from Its Voter Rolls." *New York Times,* October 30.

Cash, W.J., 1941. *The Mind of the South.* New York: Knopf.

Cave, Albert A., 2003. "Abuse of Power: Andrew Jackson and the Indian Removal Act of 1830." *The Historian,* 65 (6), 1347–50.

Cecchetti, Stephen G., and Enisse Kharroubi, 2019. "Why Does Credit Growth Crowd Out Real Economic Growth?" *Manchester School,* 87, 1–28 (September). Also, National Bureau of Economic Research Working Paper 25079 and BIS working paper 490.

Cecelsky, David S., and Timothy B. Tyson (eds.), 1998. *Democracy Betrayed: The Wilmington Race Riot of 1898 and Its Legacy.* Chapel Hill: University of North Carolina Press.

Chernow, Ron, 2004. *Alexander Hamilton.* New York: Penguin Press.

 2017. *Grant.* New York: Penguin Press.

Chetty, Raj, and Nathaniel Hendren, 2018a. "The Impacts of Neighborhoods on Intergenerational Mobility I: Childhood Exposure Effects." *Quarterly Journal of Economics* 133 (3), 1107–162.

 2018b. "The Impacts of Neighborhoods on Intergenerational Mobility II: County-Level Estimates." *Quarterly Journal of Economics* 133 (3), 1163–228.

Churchill, Winston S., 1948. *The Second World War: The Gathering Storm.* Vol. 1. Boston: Houghton Mifflin.

Clark, Christopher, 2013. *The Sleepwalkers: How Europe Went to War in 1914.* New York: HarperCollins.

Clarke, Richard A., 2004. *Against All Enemies: Inside America's War on Terror.* New York: Free Press.

Clawson, Dan, and Mary Ann Clawson, 1999. "What Has Happened to the US Labor Movement? Union Decline and Renewal." *Annual Review of Sociology,* 25, 95–119.

Clear, Todd R., 2007. *Imprisoning Communities: How Mass Incarceration Makes Disadvantaged Neighborhoods Worse.* New York: Oxford University Press.

Cobb, Jelani, 2020. "Juneteenth and the Meaning of Freedom." *New Yorker,* June 19.

Cochrane, Emily, 2020. "Top Republicans Are Silent on Biden Victory as Trump Refuses to Concede." *New York Times,* November 7.

Cohan, William D., 2018. "The Billionaire Who Led Sears Into Bankruptcy Court." *New York Times,* October 16.

Collins, Charles Wallace, 1912. *The Fourteenth Amendment and the States: A Study of the Operation of the Restraint Clauses of Section One of the Fourteenth Amendment to the Constitution of the United States.* New York: Springer.

Collins, William J., 1997. "When the Tide Turned: Immigration and the Delay of the Great Black Migration." *Journal of Economic History,* 57 (3), 607–32.

Collins, William J. and Marianne F. Wanamaker, 2014. "Selection and Economic Gains in the Great Migration of African Americans: New Evidence from Linked Census Data." *American Economic Journal: Applied Economics,* 6 (1), 220–52.

Collins, William J., and Marianne F. Wanamaker, 2015. "The Great Migration in Black and White: New Evidence on the Selection and Sorting of Southern Migrants." *Journal of Economic History,* 75 (4), 947–92,

Conger, Kate, 2020. "Uber and Lyft Drivers in California Will Remain Contractors." *New York Times,* November 4.

Cook, Lisa D., 2012. "Converging to a National Lynching Database: Recent Developments and the Way Forward." *Historical Methods: A Journal of Quantitative and Interdisciplinary History,* 45 (2):55–63.

Cook, Lisa D., Trevon Logan, and John Parman, 2018, "Racial Segregation and Southern Lynching." *Social Science History,* 42 (4), 635–75.

Cooper, Helene, 2020a. "African-Americans Are Highly Visible in the Military, but Almost Invisible at the Top." *New York Times,* May 25.

2020b. "The Few, the Proud, the White: The Marine Corps Balks at Promoting Generals of Color." *New York Times,* Aug. 31.

Costa, Dora L., and Matthew E. Kahn, 2003. "Understanding the American Decline in Social Capital." *Kyklos* 56 (1), 17–46.

Cottle, Michelle, 2020. "Ask Not What President Trump Can Do for You." *New York Times,* June 15.

Cottom, Tressie M., 2017. *Lower Ed: The Troubling Rise in For-Profit Colleges in the New Economy*. New York: New Press.

Cramer, Katherine K., 2013. *The Politics of Resentment: Rural Consciousness in Wisconsin and the Rise of Scott Walker*. Chicago: University of Chicago Press.

Cramer, Maria, 2020. "The Great Barrier Reef Has Lost Half Its Corals." *New York Times*, October 14.

Creswell, Julie, 2009. "Profits for Buyout Firms as Company Debt Soared," *New York Times*, October 4.

Crowe, Karen, ed., 1984. *Southern Horizons: The Autobiography of Thomas Dixon*. Alexandria, VA: IWV Publishing.

Crowley, Michael, 2009. "Trump and Putin Discuss Russia's Attendance at G7, but Allies Are Wary." *New York Times*, June 1, 2020.

2020. "Trump Won't Commit to 'Peaceful' Post-Election Transfer of Power." *New York Times*, September 23.

Current, R.N., 1988. *Those Terrible Carpetbaggers*. New York: Oxford University Press.

Dasgupta, Partha, 2007. *Economics: A Very Short Introduction*, Oxford: Oxford University Press.

Darity, William, Jr., Derrick Hamilton, Mark Paul, Alan Alja, Anne Price, Antonio Moore, and Catarina Chiopris, 2018. *What We Get Wrong About Closing the Racial Wage Gap*. Durham, NC: Cook Center on Social Equity, Duke University, April.

Davenport, Coral, 2019. "New E.P.A. Lead Standards Would Slow Replacement of Dangerous Pipes." *New York Times*, October 10.

David, Paul A., 1967. "New Light on a Statistical Dark Age: U. S. Real Product Growth before 1840." *American Economic Association, Papers and Proceedings*, 57 (2), 294–306 (May).

David, Paul A., et al., 1976. *Reckoning with Slavery*. New York: Oxford University Press.

David, Paul A., 1994. "The Dynamo and the Computer: An Historical Perspective on the Modern Productivity Paradox." *American Economic Review. Papers and Proceedings*, 80, 355–61.

David, Paul A., and Peter Temin. 1974. "Slavery: The Progressive Institution." *Journal of Economic History*, 34 (3), 739–83 (September).

1979. "Explaining the Relative Efficiency of Slave Agriculture in the Antebellum South: Comment," *American Economic Review*, 69 (1), 213–18 (March).

2019. "New E.P.A. Lead Standards Would Slow Replacement of Dangerous Pipes." *New York Times*, October 10.

Davenport, Coral, and Kendra Pierre-Louis, 2018. "U.S. Climate Report Warns of Damaged Environment and Shrinking Economy." *New York Times*, November 23.

Davis, Ethan, 2009–2010. "An Administrative Trail of Tears: Indian Removal." *American Journal of Legal History*, 50 (1), 49–100 (January).

Davis, Julie Hirschfeld, and Michael D. Shear, 2019. *Border Wars: Inside Trump's Assault on Immigration.* New York: Simon & Schuster.

Dawisha, Karin, 2014. *Putin's Plutocracy: Who Owns Russia?* New York: Simon & Schuster.

Dean, Edwin R., and Kent Kunze, 1992. "Productivity Measurement in Service Industries," in Zvi Grilishes (ed.), *Output in the Service Sectors.* Chicago: University of Chicago Press. pp. 73–107.

Delpit, Lisa, 2012. *"Multiplication is for White People" Raising Expectations for Other People's Children.* New York: New Press.

Derenoncourt, Ellora, 2019. "Can You Move to Opportunity? Evidence from the Great Migration." Job Market Paper, Harvard University, January 25.

Derenoncourt, Ellora, and Claire Montialoux, 2020. "To Reduce Racial Inequality, Raise the Minimum Wage." *New York Times*, October 25.

Dew, C., 2002. *Apostles of Disunion: Southern Succession Commissioners and the Causes of the Civil War.* University of Virginia Press.

Dewan, Shaila, and Mike Baker., 2020. "Facing Protests Over Use of Force, Police Respond With More Force." *New York Times*, May 31.

Dickerson, Caitlin, 2018. "3,000 Migrant Children Remain Separated From Parents; 100 Are Under Age 5." *New York Times*, July 5.

2020a. "Parents of 545 Children Separated at the Border Cannot Be Found." *New York Times*, October 21.

2020b. "U.S. Expels Migrant Children from Other Countries to Mexico." *New York Times*, October 30.

Donald, David H., 1995. *Lincoln.* New York: Simon & Schuster.

Donohue, John J. III, and James Heckman, 1991. "Continuous Versus Episodic Change: The Impact of Civil Rights Policy on the Economic Status of Blacks." *Journal of Economic Literature*, 29 (4), 1603–643.

Douglass, Frederick, 1894. "Lessons of the Hour." *Metropolitan A. M. E. Church.* Baltimore: Press of Thomas & Evans.

Drucker, Jesse, and James B. Stewart, 2020. "How a Century of Real-Estate Tax Breaks Enriched Donald Trump." *New York Times*, October 30.

DuBois, W., 1992. *Black Reconstruction in America, 1860–1880.* New York: Harcourt Brace.

Duncan, Russell. 1986. *Freedom's Shore: Tunis Campbell and the Georgia Freedmen.* Athens: University of Georgia Press.

Dunning, William A., 1897. *Essays on the Civil War and Reconstruction.* New York: Macmillan.

1901. "The Undoing of Reconstruction." *The Atlantic,* October. Available at: www.theatlantic.com/magazine/archive/1901/10/the-undoing-of-recon-struction/429219/

DuVernay, A., Averick, S., and Barish, H., 2016. *13th* [Documentary]. United States: Netflix.

Dymski, Gary A., 2006. "Discrimination in the Credit and Housing Markets: Findings and Challenges," in William Rogers (ed.), *Handbook on the Economics of Discrimination.* UK: Edward Elgar. p. 220.

Dyson, Michael Eric, 2017, "Charlottesville and the Bigotarchy," *New York Times,* August 12.

Ebbert, Stephanie, 2020. "State to Allow Remote Learning Pods, Kids' Programs Outside Schools." *Boston Globe,* August 29.

Edmondson, Catie, 2020." Senate Kills Broad Curbs on Military Gear for Police, Thwarting Push to Demilitarize." *New York Times,* July 21.

Egnal, Marc, 2010. *Clash of Extremes: The Economic Origins of the Civil War.* New York: Hill and Wang.

Ehle, John, 1988. *Trail of Tears: The Rise and Fall of the Cherokee Nation.* New York: Doubleday.

Ehrlich, Walter. 1968. "Was the Dred Scott Case Valid?" *Journal of American History,* 55 (2), 256–65.

Eligon, John, 2018. "Hate Crimes Increase for the Third Consecutive Year, F.B.I. Reports." *New York Times,* November 13.

Eligon, John, and Audra D.S. Burch, 2020. "Black Voters Helped Deliver Biden a Presidential Victory. Now What?" *New York Times,* November 11.

Ellsworth, Scott, 1982. *Death in a Promised Land: The Tulsa Race Riot of 1921.* Baton Rouge: Louisiana State University Press.

Epstein, Reid J., 2020. "The G.O.P. Delivers Its 2020 Platform. It's from 2016." *New York Times,* August 25.

Epstein, Reid J., and Annie Karni, 2020. "G.O.P. Platform, Rolled Over From 2016, Condemns the 'Current President'." *New York Times,* June 11.

Fama, Eugene, 1970. "Efficient Capital Markets: A Review of Theory and Empirical Work." *Journal of Finance,* 25 (2), 383–417.

Fandos, Nicholas, 2020. "Trump Acquitted of Two Impeachment Charges in Near Party-Line Vote." *New York Times,* February 6.

Fandos, Nicholas, and Julian E. Barnes, 2020. "Republican-Led Review Backs Intelligence Findings on Russian Interference." *New York Times,* April 21.

Fandos, Nicholas, and Emily Cochrane, 2020. "Republicans Back Trump's Refusal to Concede, Declining to Recognize Biden." *New York Times,* November 9.

Farrell, John A., 2017. *Richard Nixon: The Life.* New York: Random House.

Fausset, Richard, and Rick Rojas, 2020. "Where Ahmaud Arbery Ran, Neighbors Cast Wary Eyes." *New York Times,* May 16.

Faust, Drew Gilpin, 2008. *This Republic of Suffering: Death and the American Civil War.* New York: Knopf.

Federal Reserve, Board of Governors, 2020. *Report on the Economic Well-Being of U.S. Households in 2019, Featuring Supplemental Data from April 2020.* Washington, DC. May.

Federal Hospital Insurance and Supplementary Medical Insurance Trust Funds, Board of Governors, 2019. *2019 Annual Report.* Washington, DC.

Feinstein, Charles, Peter Temin, and Gianni Toniolo, 2008. *The World Economy Between the World Wars.* Oxford: Oxford University Press.

Fenoaltea, Stephano, 1984. "Slavery and Supervision in Comparative Perspective: A Model." *Journal of Economic History,* 44 (3), 635–68.

Fenwick, Ben, 2020. "The Massacre That Destroyed Tulsa's 'Black Wall Street'." *New York Times,* July 13.

Ferguson, Thomas, 1995. *Golden Rule: The Investment Theory of Party Competition and the Logic of Money-Driven Political Systems.* Chicago: University of Chicago Press.

Ferguson, Thomas, Paul Jorgensen, and Jie Chen, 2019. "How Money Drives US Congressional Elections: Linear Models of Money and Outcomes." *Structural Changes and Economic Dynamics.*

Ferguson, Thomas, and Peter Temin, 2003. "Made in Germany: The German Currency Crisis of 1931." *Research in Economic History,* 21, 1–53.

2004. "Comment on 'The German Twin Crisis of 1931'." *Journal of Economic History,* 64 (3), 872–76.

Fergusson, Adam. 2010. *When Money Dies: The Nightmare of Deficit Spending, Devaluation, and Hyperinflation in Weimar Germany* (1st [U.S.] ed.). New York: Public Affairs.

Ferling, John., 2007. *Almost a Miracle: The American Victory in the War of Independence.* New York: Oxford University Press.

Fields, Karen E., and Barbara J. Fields, 2012. *Racecraft: The Soul of Inequality in American Life.* New York: Verso.

Finan, Christopher M., 2007. *From the Palmer Raids to the Patriot Act: A history of the Fight for Free Speech in America.* Boston: Beacon Press.

Finch, George A., 1922. "The Revision of the Reparation Clauses of the Treaty of Versailles and the Cancellation of Inter-Allied Indebtedness." *American Journal of International Law,* 16 4 (October), 611–27.

Finkelman, Paul, 2007. "Scott v. Sandford: The Court's Most Dreadful Case and How It Changed History." *Chicago-Kent Law Review,* 82 (3), 3–48.

Fischer, David Hackett. 2004. *Washington's Crossing.* New York: Oxford University Press.

Fitzgerald, M.W., 2007. *Splendid Failure: Postwar Reconstruction in the American South.* Chicago, IL: Ivan R Dee Press.

Flavelle, Christopher, and Lisa Friedman, 2020. "As Election Nears, Trump Makes a Final Push Against Climate Science." *New York Times,* October 27.

Flitter, Emily, 2020. "'Banking While Black': How Cashing a Check Can Be a Minefield." *New York Times,* June 18.

Flitter, Emily, Jeanna Smialek, and Stacy Cowley, 2020. "How the White House Rolled Back Financial Regulations." *New York Times,* November 6.

Fogel, Robert W., 1960. *The Union Pacific Railroad: A Case in Premature Enterprise.* Baltimore: Johns Hopkins Press.

    2003. *The Slavery Debates: A Retrospective, 1952–1990.* Baton Rouge: Louisiana State Press.

Fogel, Robert W., and Stanley A. Engerman, 1974. *Time on the Cross.* Boston: Little Brown.

Foner, Eric, 1988. *Reconstruction: America's Unfinished Revolution, 1863–1877.* New ork: Harper and Row.

    2013. "Foreword," in John Hope Franklin, *Reconstruction after the Civil War* (3rd ed.). Chicago: University of Chicago Press.

    2014. *A Short History of Reconstruction* (updated ed.). New York: HarperCollins.

    2019. *The Second Founding: How the Civil War and Reconstruction Remade the Constitution.* New York: Norton.

Foner, Eric, and John A. Garraty, (eds.), 1991. *The Reader's Companion to American History.* New York: Houghton Mifflin.

Foner, Philip S., 1955. *History of the Labor Movement in the United States, Vol 2. From the Founding of the AF of L to the Emergence of American Imperialism.* New York: International Publishers.

Forbes, Robert P., 2007. *The Missouri Compromise and Its Aftermath.* Chapel Hill: University of North Carolina Press.

Foroohar, Rana, 2016. *Makers and Takers: How Wall Street Destroyed Main Street.* New York: Crown Business.

Franklin, John Hope, 1961. *Reconstruction after the Civil War.* Chicago: University of Chicago Press.

Freeman, Richard B., 1976. *Black Elite: the New Market for Highly Educated Black Americans.* New York: McGraw-Hill.

Frenkel, Sheera, and Julian E. Barnes, 2020. "Russians Again Targeting Americans With Disinformation, Facebook and Twitter Say." *New York Times,* September 1.

Friedman, Lisa, 2020. "E.P.A. to Promote Lead Testing Rule as Trump Tries to Burnish His Record." *New York Times*, September 27.

Gara, Larry, 1964. "The Fugitive Slave Law: A Double Paradox." *Civil War History*, 10 (3), 229–40 (September).

Garcia, Emma, and Elaine Weiss, 2020. "The Teacher Shortage Is Real, Large and Growing, and Worse than We Thought. EPI report, March 26.

Gergel, Richard, 2019. *Unexampled Courage: The Blinding of Sgt. Isaac Woodard and the Awakening of Harry S. Truman and Judge J. Waties Waring.* New York: Macmillan.

Gertner, Nancy, 2020. "Coronavirus Can Mean a Death Sentence to Prisoners." *Boston Globe*, May 5.

Gillette, W., 1982. *Retreat from Reconstruction, 1869–1879.* Baton Rouge: Louisiana State University Press.

Goldin, Claudia, and Lawrence F. Katz, 2008. *The Race between Education and Technology.* Cambridge, MA: Harvard University Press.

Goldstone, Lawrence, 2011. *Inherently Unequal: The Betrayal of Equal Rights by the Supreme Court, 1865–1903.* New York: Walker.

Goodnough, Abby, 2020. "Families Priced Out of 'Learning Pods' Seek Alternatives." *New York Times*, August 14.

Goodstein, Laurie, 2018. "'There is So Much Evil': Growing Anti-Semitism Stuns American Jews." *New York Times*, October 29.

Goodwyn, Lawrence, 1976. *Democratic Promise: The Populist Moment in America* New York: Oxford University Press.

1978. *The Populist Movement: A Short History of the Agrarian Revolt in America.* New York: Oxford University Press.

Gordon, Robert J., 2000. "Interpreting the 'One Big Wave' in U.S. Long-term Productivity Growth," in Bart van Ark, Simon Kuipers, and Gerard Kuper (eds.), *Productivity, Technology, and Economic Growth.* Boston: Kluwer, pp. 19–65.

2016. *The Rise and Fall of American Growth.* Princeton: Princeton University Press.

Gorman, James, 2020. "Top U.S. Health Officials Tiptoe Around Trump's Vaccine Turntable." *New York Times*, Sept. 20.

Grady, Denise, 2020. "Fauci Warns That the Coronavirus Pandemic Is Far From Over." *New York Times*, June 9.

Graham, Howard Jay, 1968. *Everyman's Constitution: Historical Essays on the Fourteenth Amendment, The "Conspiracy Theory," and American Constitutionalism.* Madison: Wisconsin Historical Society Press.

Grant, Ulysses S., 1885. *Personal Memoirs of Ulysses S. Grant.* New York: Charles L. Webster.

Graves, Lisa. 2020. "The Billionaire Behind Efforts to Kill the U.S. Postal Service." *In the Public Interest*, July.

Gray, Kathleen, 2020. "Settlement Money for Flint Water Crisis will Mostly Go to Children." *New York Times*, August 20.

Green, Clara Totenberg, 2020. "The Latest in School Segregation: Private Pandemic 'Pods'" *New York Times*, July 22.

Grossman, Richard S., 2010. "US Banking History, Civil War to World War II," in Robert Whaples (ed.), *Eh,net Encyclopedia*. Available at: http://eh.net/encyclopedia/article/grossman.banking.history.us.civil.war.wwii

Gunderson, Gerald, 1974. "The Origin of the American Civil War." *Journal of Economic History*, 34 (4), 915–50 (December).

Guthrie, Woody, ND. "The Blinding of Isaac Woodard." Available at: www.woodyguthrie.org/Lyrics/Blinding_of_Isaac_Woodard.htm

Gutman, Herbert, and Richard Sutch, 1976. "Sambo Makes Good, or Were Slaves Imbued with the Protestant Work Ethic," in Paul David et al., *Reckoning with Slavery: A Critical Study in the Quantitative History of American Negro Slavery*. New York: Oxford University Press, pp. 55–93.

Haberman, Maggie, Emily Cochrane, and Jim Tankersley. 2020. "With Jobless Aid Expired, Trump Sidelines Himself in Stimulus Talks." *New York Times*, August 3.

Haberman, Maggie, and Eric Lipton, 2019. "'Business as Normal': Pence's Stay at Trump Hotel in Follows a Trent." *New York Times*, September 3.

Haberman, Maggie, and Michael D. Shear. 2020. "Denial, and Resignation, From Trump and a Handful of Aides." *New York Times*, November 7.

Hacker, Andrew, 1992. *Two Nations: Black and White, Separate, Hostile, Unequal.* New York: Scribner.

2020. "With Jobless Aid Expired, Trump Sidelines Himself in Stimulus Talks." *New York Times*, August 3.

Hahn, S., 2005. *A Nation Under Our Feet: Black Political Struggles in the Rural South from Slavery to the Great Migration*. New York: Belknap Press.

Haldeman, H.R., 1994. *The Haldeman Diaries: Inside the Nixon White House*. New York: G. P. Putnam's Sons.

Handlin, Oscar, and Mary F. Handlin, 1950. "Origins of the Southern Labor System." *William and Mary Quarterly*, 7 (2), 199–222 (April).

Harley, C. Knick, 1980. "Transportation, the World Wheat Trade, and the Kuznets Cycle." *Explorations in Economic History*, 17, 218–50.

Harris, Fred R., and Roger W. Wilkins (eds.), 1988. *Quiet Riots: Race and Poverty in the United States: The Kerner Report Twenty Years Later*. New York: Pantheon.

Harvey, George, 2002. *Henry Clay Frick: The Man*. New York: Beard Books, 1928; reprinted.

Hassan, Steven, 2019. *The Cult of Trump: A Leading Cult Expert Explains How Trump Uses Mind Control.* New York: Free Press.

Helper, Hinton Rowan, 1857. *The Impending Crisis in the South: How to Meet It.* New York: Burdick Brothers.

Herndon, Astead W., 2020. "George Soros's Foundation Pours $220 Million Into Racial Equality Push." *New York Times,* July 13.

Hesseltine, William B., 1935. "Economic Factors in the Abandonment of Reconstruction." *Mississippi Valley Historical Review,* 22 (2), 191–210.

Higgs, Robert, 1977. *Competition and Coercion: Blacks in the American Economy, 1865–1914.* New York: Cambridge University Press.

1984. "Accumulation of Property of Southern Blacks Before World War I: Reply," *American Economic Review,* 74 (4), 777–81.

Hilt, Eric, and Katherine Liang, 2020. "Andrew Jackson's Bank War and the Panic of 1837." Paper presented at Harvard University, February 14.

Hinton, Elizabeth, 2016. *From the War on Poverty to the War on Crime: The Making of Mass Incarceration in America.* Cambridge, MA: Harvard University Press.

Historical American Lynching (HAL) Data Collection Project, nd. Available at: http://people.uncw.edu/hinese/HAL/HAL%20Web%20Page.htm

*Historical Statistics of the United States: Colonial Times to 1970,* 1975. Washington, DC: US Government.

Hofstadter, Richard, 1956. *The Age of Reform From Bryan to FDR: Populism, Progressivism, and the New Deal.* New York, Knopf.

Hoffman, Jeremy S., Vivek Shandas, and Nicholas Pendleton, 2020. "The Effects of Historical Housing Policies on Resident Exposure to Intra-Urban Heat: A Study of 108 US Urban Areas." *Climate,* 8, 12. January. doi: 10.3390/cli8010012.

Holt, Charles F., 1977. "Who Benefitted from the Prosperity of the Twenties?" *Explorations in Economic History,* 14, 277–89.

Holt, Michael F., 2008. *By One Vote,* Lawrence: University Press of Kansas.

Huetteman, Emmarie, and Yamiche Alcindor, 2017. "Betsy DeVos Confirmed as Education Secretary: Pence Breaks Tie." *New York Times,* February 7.

Hulse, Carl, 2020. "A Split Decision for Democrats." *New York Times,* November 4.

Hume, David, 2012. *Essays: Moral, Political, and Literary* (Volume 1, Part II, Essay 5). Overland Park, KS: Digireads.

Hundt, Reed, 2019. *A Crisis Wasted: Barack Obama's Defining Decisions.* New York: Rosetta Books.

Irwin, Neil, 2020. "Why the Biden Economy Could Be the Same Long Slog as the Obama Economy." *New York Times,* Nov. 8.

Jacobs, Harriet, 2001. *Incidents in the Life of a Slave Girl.* Mineola, NY: Dover Publications.

Jensen, Michael C., and William H. Meckling, 1976. "Theory of the Firm: Managerial Behavior, Agency Costs and Ownership Structure." *Journal of Financial Economics*, 3, 305–60.

Johnson, Rucker C., 2011. "Long-run Impacts of School Desegregation and School Quality on Adult Attainments." NBER wp 16664.

2019. *Children of the Dream: Why School Integration Works*. New York: Basic Books.

Jones, D.B., W. Troesken, and R. Walsh, 2012. *A Poll Tax by Any Other Name: The Political Economy of Disenfranchisement*. Technical report, University of Pittsburgh.

Josephson, Matthew. 1934. *The Robber Barons*. New York: Harcourt Brace.

Kaplan, Sheila, Matthew Goldstein, and Alexandra Stevenson, 2020. "Trump's Vaccine Chief Has Vast Ties to Drug Industry, Posing Possible Conflicts." *New York Times*, May 20.

Kaplan, Thomas, 2017. "Ads to Amplify His 'Invasion' Claim." *New York Times*, August 5, 2019.

2018. "Trump Is Putting Indelible Conservative Stamp on Judiciary." *New York Times*, July 31.

Karp, Matthew, 2016. *This Vast Southern Empire: Slaveholders at the Helm of American Foreign Policy*. Cambridge, MA: Harvard University Press.

Katznelson, Ira, 2005. *When Affirmative Action Was White: An Untold History of Racial Inequality in Twentieth-Century America*. New York: Norton.

2013. *Fear Itself: The New Deal and the Origins of Our Time*. New York: Norton.

Keefe, Patrick Radden. 2019. "How Mark Burnett Resurrected Donald Trump as an Icon of American Success," *New Yorker*, January 7.

Kelly, Kate, 2020. "The Short Tenure and Abrupt Ouster of Banking's Sole Black C.E.O." *New York Times*, October 3.

Kelly, Kate, Shane Goldmacher, and Thomas Kaplan, 2020, "The Wallets of Wall Street Are With Joe Biden, if Not the Hearts." *New York Times*, August 9.

Kerber, Linda K., 1998. *No Constitutional Right to be Ladies: Women and the Obligations of Citizenship*. New York: Hill and Wang.

Kerner Commission, 1968. *The 1968 Report of the National Advisory Commission on Civil Disorders*. New York: New York Times Company.

Keynes, John Maynard, 1919. *The Economic Consequences of the Peace*. London: Macmillan.

Kim, Sukkoo, and Robert A. Margo, 2004. "Historical Perspectives on U.S. Economic Geography." *Handbook of Urban and Regional Economics*, 4, 2981–3019.

Kindleberger, Charles P., 2005. *Manias, Panics and Crashes: A History of Financial Crises* (5th ed.). New York: John Wiley & Sons.

Kirp, David, 2019. *The College Dropout Scandal.* New York: Oxford University Press.

Kolko, Gabriel, 1963. *The Triumph of Conservatism: A Reinterpretation of American History, 1900–1916.* New York: Free Press.

1965. *Railroads and Regulation, 1877–1916.* Princeton: Princeton University Press.

Koo, Richard C., 2018. *The Other Half of Macroeconomics and the Fate of Globalization,* Chichester, UK: Wiley.

Kopp, Emanuel, Daniel Lee, Susana Musulla, and Suchanan Tambunlertchai, 2019. "US Investment Since the Tax Cuts and Jobs Act of 2017." IMF Working Paper, No. 19/120, July.

Krasner, Larry, 2021. *For the People: A Story of Justice and Power.* New York: One World.

Krause, Paul, 1992. *The Battle for Homestead. 1880–1892.* Pittsburgh, PA: University of Pittsburg Press.

Krotoszynski, Ronald J. 2016. "A Poll Tax by Another Name." *New York Times,* November 14.

Krugman, Paul, 2020a "Trump and His Infallible Advisers." *New York Times,* May 4.

2020b. "America Didn't Give Up on Covid-19. Republicans Did." *New York Times,* June 25.

2020c. "April Was Trump's Cruelest Month." *New York Times,* August 27.

2020d. "The War on Truth Reaches Its Climax." *New York Times,* November 2.

2020e. What's Not the Matter with Georgia?" *New York Times,* November 9.

Kousser, J. Morgan, 1974. *The Shaping of Southern Politics: Suffrage Restriction and the Establishment of the One-Party System.* New Haven: Yale University Press.

Kuziemko, Ilyana, and Ebonya Washington, 2018. "Why Did Democrats Lose the South? Bringing New Data to and Old Debate." *American Economic Review,* 108 (10), 2830–67.

Lamoreaux, Naomi R., 1985. *The Great Merger Movement in American Business, 1895–1904.* New York: Cambridge University Press.

Larson, Kate Clifford, 2004. *Bound for the Promised Land, Harriet Tubman: Portrait of an American Hero.* New York: Ballantine.

Lawrence, Jacob, 1993. *The Great Migration: An American Story.* New York: HarperCollins.

Lazarus, Emma, 1883. *The New Colossus.* Washington, DC: Washington Park Service.

Lehr, Dick, 2014. *The Birth of a Nation: How a Legendary Filmmaker and a Crusading Editor Reignited America's Civil War.* New York: Public Affairs (Perseus Books).

Lemann, N., 2007. *Redemption: The Last Battle of the Civil War.* New York: Farrar, Straus and Giroux.

Levenson, Thomas., 2018. "'Reasonable Doubt' on Climate Change Is Killing the Planet." *Boston Globe,* December 12.

Levitsky, Steven, and Daniel Ziblatt, 2018, *How Democracies Die.* New York: Crown.

Lewis, Paul H., 2009. *The Agony of Argentine Capitalism: From Menem to the Kirchners.* Santa Barbara: Praeger.

Linder, Marc, 1987. "Farm Workers and the Fair Labor Standards Act: Racial Discrimination in the New Deal." *Texas Law Review,* 65, 1354–61.

Liptak, Adam, 2020. "Supreme Court Allows Restrictions on Voting by Ex-Felons." *New York Times,* July 16.

Lipton, Eric, and Benjamin Weiser, 2020. "Turkish Bank Case Showed Erdogan's Influence with Trump." *New York Times,* October 29.

Lithwick, Dahlia, and David S. Cohen. 2016. "Buck Up, Democrats, and Fight like Republicans." *New York Times,* December 18.

Litwack, Leon F., 1979. *Been in the Storm So Long: The Aftermath of Slavery.* New York: Random House.

Logan, Trevon D., 2018. "Whitelashing: Black Politicians, Taxes, and Violence." National Bureau of Economic Research. Working paper 26014 (June).

2020. "Do Black Politicians Matter? Evidence from Reconstruction." *Journal of Economic History,* 80 (1), 1–37 (March).

Logan, Trevon D., and John M. Parman, 2017. "The National Rise in Residential Segregation." *Journal of Economic History,* 77 (1), 127–70.

Logan, Trevon D., and Peter Temin, 2020. "Inclusive American Economic History: Containing Slaves, Freedmen, Jim Crow Laws, and the Great Migration." Institute for New Economic Thinking Working Paper 110 (February). Available at: https://papers.ssrn.com/sol3/papers.cfm?abstract_id=3536068

Lynch, Mona, 2016. *Hard Bargains: The Coercive Power of Drug Laws in Federal Court.* New York: Russell Sage Foundation.

MacFarquhar, Neil, 2020. "In George Floyd's Death, a Police Technique Results in a Too-Familiar Tragedy." *New York Times,* May 29.

MacLean, Nancy, 2017. *Democracy in Chains: The Deep History of the Radical Right's Stealth Plan for America.* New York: Viking.

Maheshwari, Sapna, and Vanessa Friedman, 2020. "The Pandemic Helped Topple Two Retailers. So Did Private Equity." *New York Times,* May 14.

Maier, Charles S., 1988. *Recasting Bourgeois Europe: Stabilization in France, Germany and Italy in the Decade after World War 1.* Princeton: Princeton University Press.

Maier, Pauline, 2010. *Ratification: The People Debate the Constitution, 1787–1788.* New York: Simon & Schuster.

Mandavilli, Apoorva, 2020. "What If 'Herd Immunity' Is Closer Than Scientists Thought?" *New York Times*, Aug. 17.

Mandavilli, Apoorva, and Catie Edmondson, 2020. "'This Is Not the Hunger Games': National Testing Strategy Draws Concerns." *New York Times*, May 25.

Mandle, Jay R., 1978. *The Roots of Black Poverty: The Southern Plantation Economy after the Civil War*. Durham, NC: Duke University Press.

2008. *Democracy, America, and the Age of Globalization*. New York: Cambridge University Press.

Margo, Robert A., 1982. "Race Differences in Public School Expenditures: Disenfranchisement and School Finance in Louisiana, 1890–1910." *Social Science History*, 6 (1), 9–34.

Margo, Robert, 1990. *Race and Schooling in the South, 1880–1950*. Chicago: University of Chicago Press.

Martin, Devin Sean, 2020. "Race-based Incidents Do Happen Here." *Provincetown Independent*, July 16.

Marx, Karl, 1852. "The Eighteenth Brumaire of Louis Napoleon." *Die Revolution*.

Mayer, Jane, 2016. *Dark Money: The Hidden History of the Billionaires Behind the Rise of the Radical Right*. New York: Doubleday.

Mazzei, Patricia, 2018. "Back-to-School Shopping for Districts: Armed Guards, Cameras and Metal Detectors." *New York Times*, August 11.

Mazzei, Patricia, and Nicole Perlroth, 2020, "False News Targeting Latinos Trails the Election." *New York Times*, November 4.

Mazzetti, Mark, 2020. "G.O.P.-Led Senate Panel Details Ties Between 2016 Trump Campaign and Russia." *New York Times*, August 18.

McPherson, James M., 1995. "Who Freed the Slaves?" *Proceedings of the American Philosophical Society*, 139 (1), 1–10, March.

McGuire, Robert A., and Robert L. Ohsfeldt, 1986. "An Economic Model of Voting Behavior over Specific Issues at the Constitutional Convention of 1787." *Journal of Economic History*, 46 (1), 79–111 (March).

Mechem, John Leland, 1924. "The "Pittsburgh Plus" Case." *American Bar Association Journal*, 10 (11), 806–11 (November).

Meissner, Doris, Donald M. Kerwin, Muzaffa Chisti, and Claire Bergeron, 2013. "Migration Enforcement in the United States: The Rise of a Formidable Machinery." *Migration Policy Institute*, January.

Merritt, Keri Leigh, 2017. *Masterless Men: Poor Whites and Slavery in the Antebellum South*. Cambridge: Cambridge University Press.

Mitchell, Michael, and Michael Leachman, 2014. "*Changing Priorities: State Criminal Justice Reforms and Investments in Education*." Washington, DC: Center on Budget and Policy Priorities, October 28.

Mixon, Peter, 2008. "The Crisis of 1873: Perspectives from Multiple Asset Classes." *Journal of Economic History*, 68 (3), 722–57.

Morgan, Edmund, 1975. *American Slavery, American Freedom: The Ordeal of Colonial Virginia*. New York: Norton.

Morris, Aldon D., 1984. *The Origins of the Civil Rights Movement: Black Communities Organizing for Change*. New York: Free Press.

Morrison, Toni, 1987. *Beloved*. New York: Knopf.

Myrdal, Gunnar, 1944. *An American Dilemma: The Negro Problem and Modern Democracy*. New York: Harper and Brothers.

National Park Service, 2019. *About the Homestead Act*. Beatrice, NE: Homestead National Monument of America. September 20.

National Science Board, 2012. "Diminishing Funding and Rising Expectations: Trends and Challenges for Public Research Universities." A Companion to *Science* and *Engineering Indicators*. Available at: www.nsf.gov/nsb/sei/companion2/files/nsb1245.pdf

Neal, Larry, 2015. *A Concise History of International Finance: From Babylon to Bernanke*. New York: Cambridge University Press.

        2020. "Financing the Louisiana Purchase: A Case Study of how Modern Finance Arose During the Truce of Amiens, 1801–1803." Paper presented at the London School of Economics, March 6.

Nobel Prize, 1993. The Sveriges Riksbank Prize in Economic Sciences in Memory of Alfred Nobel 1993. NobelPrize.org. Nobel Media AB 2019. Fri. 27 Dec 2019. Available at: www.nobelprize.org/prizes/economic-sciences/1993/summary

Nordhaus, William D., 2006, "Principles of National Accounting for Nonmarket Accounts," in Dale Jorgenson, J. Steven Landefeld, and William D. Nordhaus (eds), *A New Architecture of the U.S. National Accounts*. Chicago: University of Chicago Press, pp. 143–160.

Obama, Barack, 2007. *Dreams from My Father: A Story of Race and Inheritance*. New York: Random House.

Obama, Michelle, 2018. *Becoming*. New York: Crown.

OECD, 2019, *Under Pressure: The Squeezed Middle Class*. Paris: OECD Publishing. Available at: https://doi.org/10.1787/689afed1-en/

Olney, Martha L., 1998. "When Your Word Is Not Enough: Race, Collateral, and Household Credit." *Journal of Economic History*, 58 (2), 408–31.

Orlowsky, Jeff, 2020. *The Social Dilemma*. Netflix film.

O'Rourke, Kevin H., 1997. "The European Grain Invasion, 1870–1913." *Journal of Economic History*, 57 (4), 775–801 (December).

Osnos, Evan, 2020. "The Folly of Trump's Blame-Beijing Coronavirus Strategy." *New Yorker*, May 10.

Osnos, Evan, David Remnick, and Joshua Yaffa, 2017. "Active Measures," *New Yorker*, February 24.

Overton, Spencer, 2006. *Stealing Democracy: The New Politics of Voter Suppression*. New York: Norton.

Page, Benjamin I., Jason Seawrite, and Matthew J. Lacombe, 2019. *Billionaires and Stealth Politics*. Chicago: University of Chicago Press.

Parsons, Elaine Frantz, 2015. *Ku-Klux: The Birth of the Klan during Reconstruction*. Chapel Hill: University of North Carolina Press.

Patel, Jugal, and Wilson Andrews, 2016. "Trump's Electoral College Victory Ranks 46th in 58 Elections." *New York Times*, December 18.

Patterson, Gerald R., 1982. *A Social Learning Approach, Vol. 3: Coercive Family Process*. Eugene, OR: Castilia Publishing.

Payne, Charles M., 1995. *I've Got the Light of Freedom: The Organizing Tradition in the Mississippi Freedom Struggle*. Berkeley: University of California Press.

Pearlstein, Steven, 2018. *Can American Capitalism Survive? Why Greed Is Not Good, Opportunity is Not Equal, and Fairness Won't Make Us Poor*, New York: St. Martin's.

Pew Research Center, 2011. *Wealth Gaps Rise to Record Highs Between Whites, Blacks and Hispanics*. Washington, DC: Pew Research Center. July 26.

Pfaff, John F., 2017. *Locked In: The True Causes of Mass Incarceration – and How to Achieve Real Reform*. New York: Basic Books.

Philippon, Thomas, 2015. "Has the US Financial Industry Become Less Efficient? On the Theory and Measurement of Financial Intermediation." *American Economic Review*, 105 (4), 1408–38.

Piketty, Thomas, 2014. *Capital in the Twenty-First Century*. Cambridge, MA: Harvard University Press.

Poniewozik, James, 2020. "As Images of Pain Flood TV, 'Where Is Our Leader?'" *New York Times*, June 5.

Prather, H. Leon, Sr., 1998. "We Have Taken a City: A Centennial Essay," in David S. Cecelsky and Timothy B. Tyson (eds.), . *Democracy Betrayed: The Wilmington Race Riot of 1898 and Its Legacy*. Chapel Hill: University of North Carolina Press. pp. 15–40.

Putnam, Robert D., 1993. *Making Democracy Work: Civic Tradition in Modern Italy*. Princeton: Princeton University Press.

Putnam, Robert D., 2000. *Bowling Alone: The Collapse and Revival of American Community*, New York: Simon & Shuster.

Rabin, Roni Caryn, 2020. "Why the Coronavirus More Often Strikes Children of Color." *New York Times*, September 1.

Rabinowitz, Howard N., 1982. *Southern Black Leaders of the Reconstruction Era*. Urbana: University of Illinois Press.

Rable, G.C., 2007. *But There Was No Peace: The Role of Violence in the Politics of Reconstruction.* Chicago: University of Georgia Press.

Rae, Douglas W., 2003. *City: Urbanism and Its End,* New Haven: Yale University Press.

Rajan, Raghuram G., and Luigi Zingales, 2003. *Saving Capitalism from the Capitalists: Unleashing the Power of Financial Market to Create Wealth and Spread Opportunity.* New York: Crown Business.

Ransom, Roger, 2001. "Economics of the Civil War". EH.Net Encyclopedia, edited by Robert Whaples. August 24. Available at: http://eh.net/encyclopedia/the-economics-of-the-civil-war/

Ransom, Roger L., and Richard Sutch, 1977. *One Kind of Freedom: The Economic Consequences of Emancipation.* New York: Cambridge University Press. (2nd ed., 2001).

Raphael, Steven, and Michael A. Stoll, 2013. *Why Are So Many Americans in Prison?* New York: Russell Sage Foundation.

Rassier, Dylan G., 2012. "The Role of Profits and Income in the Statistical Discrepancy." *Survey of Current Business.* February.

Ravitch, Diane, 2017. "The Demolition of American Education." *New York Review of Books Daily,* June 5. Available at: www.nybooks.com/daily/2017/06/05/trump-devos-demolition-of-american-education/

Rediker, Marcus, 2013. *The Amistad Rebellion: An Atlantic Odyssey of Slavery and Freedom.* New York: Penguin.

Remini, Robert, 2010. *At the Edge of the Precipice: Henry Clay and the Compromise that Saved the Union.* New York: Basic Books.

Rice, Susan E. 2020. "Trump Isn't Here to Serve the People." *New York Times,* September 1.

Richardson, Heather Cox, 2020. *How the South Won the Civil War: Oligarchy, Democracy, and the Continuing Fight for the Soul of America.* New York: Oxford University Press.

Robbins, Lionel, 1934. *The Great Depression.* London: Macmillan.

Rosenberg, Matthew, Adam Goldman, and Michael S. Schmidt, 2017. Obama Administration Rushed to Preserve Intelligence of Russian Election Hacking." *New York Times,* March 1.

Rothstein, Richard, 2017. *The Color of Law: A Forgotten History of How Our Government Segregated America.* New York: Norton.

Rousseau, Peter L. 2002. "Jackson's Monetary Policy, Specie Flows, and the Panic of 1837." *Journal of Economic History,* 62 (2), 457–88 (June).

Saez, Emmanuel, and Gabriel Zucman, 2019. *The Triumph of Injustice: How the Rich Dodge Taxes and How to Make Them Pay.* New York: Norton.

Sanger, David E., and Choe Sang-Hun. 2020. "Two Years after Trump-Kim Meeting, Little to Show for Personal Diplomacy." *New York Times*, June 12.

Sanger, David E., and Nicole Perlroth, 2020. "Russian Intelligence Hackers Are Back, Microsoft Warns, Aiming at Officials of Both Parties." *New York Times*, September 10.

Sawyer, Wendy, and Peter Wagner, 2020. "Mass Incarceration: The Whole Pie 2020." Prison Policy Initiative Press Release. March 24. Available at: www. prisonpolicy.org/reports/pie2020.html

Scheiber, Noam, Farah Stockman, and J. David Goodman, 2020. "How Police Unions Became Such Powerful Opponents to Reform Efforts." *New York Times*, June 6.

Schmidt, Michael S., 2020. "Justice Dept. Never Fully Examined Trump's Ties to Russia, Ex-Officials Say." *New York Times*, August 30.

Schmidt, Michael S., Matthew Rosenberg, Adam Goldman, and Matt Apuzzo, 2017. "Intercepted Russian Communications Part of Inquiry into Trump Associates." *New York Times*, January 19.

Schnabel, Isabel, 2004. "The German Twin Crisis of 1931." *Journal of Economic History*, 64 (3), 822–71.

Schuker, Stephen A., 1976. *The End of French Predominance in Europe: The Financial Crisis of 1924 and the Adoption of the Dawes Plan*. Chapel Hill: University of North Carolina Press.

Schwartz, Nelson D., and Michael Corkery, 2018. "When Sears Flourished, So Did Workers. At Amazon, It's More Complicated." *New York Times*, October 23.

Scofield, Jerri-Lynn, 2020. "Paltry Flint Toxic Water Settlement: Let's Not Kill All the Lawyers (at Least Not Some of Them)." *Naked Capitalism*, August 23.

Shaub, Walter M., Jr., 2020. "Ransacking the Republic." *New York Review of Books*, July 2 Issue.

Shear, Michael D., and Maggie Haberman, 2017. "Trump Defends Initial Remarks on Charlottesville; Again Blames 'Both Sides'." *New York Times*, August 15.

Shear, Michael D., Maggie Haberman, and Astead W. Herndon, 2020. "Trump Rally Fizzles as Attendance Falls Short of Campaign's Expectations." *New York Times*, June 20.

Shear, Michael D., Noah Weiland, Eric Lipton, Maggie Haberman, and David E. Sanger, 2020. "Inside Trump's Failure: The Rush to Abandon Leadership Role on the Virus." *New York Times*, July 18.

Silver-Greenberg, Jessica, and Jesse Drucker, 2020. "Nursing Homes With Safety Problems Deploy Trump-Connected Lobbyists." *New York Times*, August 16.

Skidelsky, Robert, 2019. *Money and Government: The Past and Future of Economics.* New Haven: Yale University Press.

Smith, Adam, 1776. *The Wealth of Nations.*

Snyder, Timothy, 2020. "Trump's Big Election Lie Pushes America toward Autocracy." *Boston Globe*, November 11.

Social Progress Index, 2020. Available at: www.socialprogress.org/

Soloveichik, Rachel H., 2010. "Artistic Originals as a Capital Asset." *American Economic Review*, 100 (2), 110–14.

Solow, Barbara L. (ed.), 1991. *Slavery and the Rise of the Atlantic Systems* Cambridge: Cambridge University Press.

Stamp, Kenneth M., 1956. *The Peculiar Institution: Slavery in the Ante-Bellum South.* New York: Random House.

Staples, Brent, 2006. "When Democracy Died in Wilmington, N.C." *New York Times*, January 8.

Stegmaier, Mark J., 1996. *Texas, New Mexico, and the Compromise of 1850: Boundary Dispute & Sectional Conflict.* Kent, OH: Kent State University Press.

Sterling, Eric E. 1999. "Drug Laws and Snitching: A Primer." *Frontline.* Available at: www.pbs.org/wgbh/pages/frontline/shows/snitch/primer/

Stewart, Charles, III, and Stephen Ansolebehere. 2013. "Waiting in Line to Vote." White Paper: US Election Assistance Commission.

Stokes, Melvyn, 2007. *D.W. Griffith's* The Birth of a Nation: *A History of "the Most Controversial Motion Picture of All Time."* Oxford, UK: Oxford University Press.

Stolberg, Sheryl Gay, 2020. "Stanford Study Seeks to Quantify Infections Stemming From Trump Rallies." *New York Times*, October 31.

Stuntz, William J., 2011. *The Collapse of American Criminal Justice.* Cambridge, MA: Harvard University Press.

Sullivan, Paul, 2019. "The Allure, and Burden, of Private Equity." *New York Times*, March 8.

Sundstrom, William A., 1992. "Last Hired, First Fired? Unemployment and Urban Black Workers During the Great Depression." *Journal of Economic History*, 52 (2), 415–29.

Tabuchi, Hiroko, 2018a. "The Oil Industry's Covert Campaign to Rewrite American Car Emissions Rules." *New York Times*, December 13.

　2018b. "The Oil Industry's Covert Campaign to Rewrite American Car Emissions Rules." *New York Times*, December 13.

Tanenhaus, Sam, 2018. "'I'm Tired of America Wasting Our Blood and Treasure': The Strange Ascent of Betsy DeVos and Erik Prince." *Vanity Fair*, September 6.

Tankersley, Jim, and Matt Phillips, 2018. "Trump's Tax Cut Was Supposed to Change Corporate Behavior. Here's What Happened." *New York Times*, November 12.

Tarullo, Daniel J., 2019. "Financial Regulation: Still Unsettled a Decade after the Crisis." *Journal of Economic Perspectives*, 33 (1), 61–80.

Taub, Jennifer, 2020. *Big Dirty Money: The Shocking Injustice and Unseen Cost of White Collar Crime.* New York: Viking.

Tavernise, Sabrina, and John Eligon, 2020. "Voters Say Black Lives Matter Protests Were Important. They Disagree On Why." *New York Times*, November 7.

Teachout, Zephyr, 2014. *Corruption in America: From Benjamin Franklin's Snuff Box to Citizens United.* Cambridge: Harvard University Press.

2020. *Break 'Em Up.* New York: St. Martin's Press.

Temin, Peter, 1964. *Iron and Steel in Nineteenth Century America: An Economic Inquiry.* Cambridge: MIT Press.

1966. "Steam and Waterpower in the Early Nineteenth Century." *Journal of Economic History*, 26 (2), 187–205 (June).

1969. *The Jacksonian Economy.* New York: Norton.

1976. "Recovery of the South and the Cost of the Civil War." *Journal of Economic History*, 36 (4) (December).

1980. "Modes of Behavior." *Journal of Economic Behavior and Organization*, June, pp. 175–95.

1989. *Lessons from the Great Depression.* Cambridge: MIT Press.

2002a. "The Golden Age of Economic Growth Reconsidered." *European Review of Economic History*, 6 (April), 3–22.

2002b. "Teacher Quality and the Future of America." *Eastern Economic Journal*, 28 (Summer 2002), 285–300.

2004. "The Labor Market of the Early Roman Empire." *Journal of Interdisciplinary History*, 34 (Spring), 513–38.

2013. *The Roman Market Economy.* Princeton: Princeton University Press.

2017. *The Vanishing Middle Class: Prejudice and Power in a Dual Economy.* Cambridge: MIT Press.

2018. "The Political Economy of Mass Incarceration: An Analytical Model." *International Journal of Political Economy*, 9 (4), 1–13 (September).

2019. "Taxes and Industrial Structure." *Business History*, 61 (7), 1144–57.

2020. "Finance and Intangibles in Economic Growth: Eating the Family Cow." *International Journal of Political Economy*, 49 (1), 1–24 (Spring).

Terborg-Penn, Rosalyn, 1998. *African American women in the struggle for the vote, 1850–1920.* Bloomington: Indiana University Press.

Thornton, J. Miles, III, 2014. "Challenge and Response in the Montgomery Bus Boycott of 1955–56." *Alabama Review*, 67 (1), 40–112.

Thrush, Glenn, and Maggie Haberman, 2017. "Trump Gives White Supremacists an Unequivocal Boost." *New York Times*, August 15.

Tolnay, Stewart E., 2003. "The African-American 'Great Migration' and Beyond." *Annual Review of Sociology*, 29, 209–32 (August).

Tolnay, Stewart E., and E.M. Beck, 1992. "Racial Violence and Black Migration in the American South, 1910 to 1930." *American Sociological Review*, 57 (1), 103–16.

Tørsløv, T., L. Weir, and G. Zucman, 2018. "The Missing Profits of Nations." NBER Working Paper 24701.

Tough, Paul, 2019. *The Years that Matter Most: How College Makes or Breaks Us*. New York: Houghton Mifflin Harcourt.

Trotter, Joe William, Jr., 2019. *Workers on Arrival: Black Labor in the Making of America*. Oakland: University of California Press.

Trump, Mary L., 2020. *Too Much and Never Enough*. New York: Simon & Shuster.

Tully, Tracey, 2020. "About 20% of N.J. Prisoners Could Be Freed to Avoid Virus." *New York Times*, July 30.

Tully, Tracey, Nate Schweber, and Kevin Armstrong, 2020. "Emotional Reunions Follow the Early Release of N.J. Inmates, in an Effort to Contain the Virus." *New York Times*, November 5.

Tye, Larry, 2004. *Rising from the Rails: Pullman Porters and the Making of the Black Middle Class*. New York: Henry Holt.

US Congress, 1862. *The Pacific Railroad Act of 1862* (12 Stat. 489).

US Department of Health and Human Services, 2015. "Head Start Program Facts: Fiscal Year 2015." Available at: https://eclkc.ohs.acf.hhs.gov/about-us/art icle/head-start-program-facts-fiscal-year-2015

US Department of Labor, Bureau of Labor Statistics, 2017. "Employment by Major Industry Sector." Available at: www.bls.gov/emp/tables/employ-ment-by-major-industry-sector.htm

US Senate, 2020. "Report of the Select Committee of the Senate of the United States Senate on Russian Active Measures Campaigns and Interference in the 2016 Election, Volume 4." U.S. Senate, 116th Congress, First Session. Report 116-XX.

Valelly, Richard M., 2004. *The Two Reconstructions: The Struggle for Black Enfranchisement*. Chicago: University of Chicago Press.

Waldman, Paul, 2017. "Republicans Reach Staggering New Heights of Hypocrisy." *Washington Post blog*. September 6. Available at: http://wapo.st/2iZ6VbD

Wallace-Wells, David, 2019. *The Uninhabitable Earth: Life after Warming*. New York: Tim Duggan Books.

Walker, Donald R., 1988. *Penology for Profit: A History of the Texas Prison System, 1867–1912*. College Station, TX: Texas A&M Southwestern Studies.

Warf, Barney, and Joseph C. Cox, 1996. "Spatial Dimensions of the Savings and Loan Crisis." *Growth and Change*, 27 (2), 135–55.

Watson, J.L., 1980. "Slavery as an Institution, Open and Closed Systems," in J.L. Watson (ed.), *Asian and African Systems of Slavery*. Oxford: Oxford University Press.

Weil, David N., 2014. *The Fissured Workplace: Why Work Became So Bad for So Many and What Can Be Done to Improve It*. Cambridge: Harvard University Press.

Weiser, Benjamin, and William K. Rashbaum, 2020. "D.A. Accuses Trump of Delay 'Strategy' in Fight Over Tax Returns." *New York Times*, July 16.

Weiss, Elaine, 2018. *The Women's Hour: The Great Fight to Win the Vote*. New York: Penguin.

Western, Bruce, 2006. *Punishment and Inequality in America*. New York: Russell Sage Foundation.

2018. *Homeward: Life in the Year After Prison*. New York: Russell Sage Foundation.

Wezerek, Gus, 2020. "Racism's Hidden Toll." *New York Times*, August 11.

Wheeler-Bennett, John W., 1938. "Ludendorff: The Soldier and the Politician." *Virginia Quarterly Review*, 14 (2), 187–202 (Spring).

Wheelock, Daren, and Douglas Hartmann, 2007. "Midnight Basketball and the 1994 Crime Bill Debates: The Operation of a Racial Code." *Sociological Quarterly*, 48 (2), 315–42 (Spring).

Whatley, Warren C., 1990. "Getting a Foot in the Door: "Learning," State Dependence, and the Racial Integration of Firms." *Journal of Economic History*, 50 (1), 43–66.

White, Richard, 2012. *Railroaded: The Transcontinentals and the Making of Modern America*. New York: Norton.

Whitten, David, V., 2001. "Depression of 1893," in Robert Whaples (ed.), *EH.Net Encyclopedia*. August 14. Avilable at: http://eh.net/encyclopedia/the-depression-of-1893/

Widdig, Bernd, 2001. *Culture and inflation in Weimar Germany* ([Online August] ed.). Berkeley: University of California Press.

Wilentz, Sean, 2018. *No Property in Man: Slavery and Antislavery at the Country's Founding*. Cambridge, MA: Harvard University Press.

Wilkerson, Isabel, 2010. *The Warmth of Other Suns: The Epic Story of America's Great Migration*. New York: Random House.

2020a. "America's Enduring Caste System." *New York Times*, July 1.

2020b. *Caste: The Origins of Our Discontents*. New York: Random House.

Williamson, J., 1965. *After Slavery: The Negro in South Carolina During Reconstruction, 1861–1877*. Chapel Hill: University of North Carolina Press.

Williamson, Jeffrey G., and Peter H. Lindert, 1980. *American Inequality: A Macroeconomic History*. New York: Academic Press.

Wills, Brian Steel, 1993. *A Battle from the Start: The Life of Nathan Bedford Forrest.* New York: Harper Perennial.

Wills, Garry, 1992. *Lincoln at Gettysburg: the Words that Remade America.* New York: Simon & Schuster.

Wilson, William Julius, 1996. *When Work Disappears: The World of the New Urban Poor.* New York: Knopf.

Wines, Michael, 2018. "Why So Many Kentuckians Are Barred from Voting on Tuesday, and for Life." *New York Times,* November 4.

Wines, Michael, and Richard Fausset, 2020. "With Census Count Finishing Early, Fears of a Skewed Tally Rise." *New York Times,* August 4.

Winkler, Adam, 2018. *We the Corporations: How American Businesses Won Their Civil Rights.* New York: Norton.

Winston, Clifford, 1998. "U.S. Industry Adjustment to Economic Deregulation." *Journal of Economic Perspectives,* 12 (3), 89–110.

Woodward, Bob, 2020. *Rage.* New York: Simon & Schuster.

Woodward, C. Vann, 1968. *The Burden of Southern History* (enlarged ed.). Baton Rouge: Louisiana State University Press.

1971. *Origins of the New South.* Baton Rouge: Louisiana State University Press.

2002. *The Strange Career of Jim Crow: A Commemorative Edition.* New York: Oxford University Press.

Wright, Gavin, 1978. *The Political Economy of the Cotton South: Households, Markets and Wealth in the Nineteenth Century.* New York: Norton.

1986. *Old South, New South: Revolutions in the Southern Economy Since the Civil War.* New York: Basic Books.

2020, "Voting Rights, Deindustrialization, and Republican Ascendancy in the South." Institute for New Economic Thinking Working Paper Series No. 135. Available at: https://ssrn.com/abstract=3731832

2013. *Sharing the Prize: The Economics of the Civil Rights Revolution in the American South.* Cambridge: Harvard University Press.

Wu, Tim, 2018. *The Curse of Bigness: Antitrust in the New Golden Age.* New York: Columbia Global Reports.

Yaffa, Joshua, 2020. "Is Russian Meddling as Dangerous as We Think?" *New Yorker,* September 14.

Zimmerman, Jonathan, 2020. "What Is College Worth?" *New York Review of Books,* 67 (11), July 2.

Zucchino, David. 2020. *Wilmington's Lie: The Murderous Coup of 1898 and the Rise of White Supremacy.* New York: Atlantic Monthly Press.

Zucman, Gabriel, 2015. *The Hidden Wealth of Nations: The Scourge of Tax Havens.* Chicago: University of Chicago Press.

# Index

Washington, George, 14–15, 220–21
  African immigrants, views of, 15
  Hamilton and, 17–18
Watergate, 209
Watt, James, 9–10, 25
wealth building, 203–4
*The Wealth of Nations* (Smith, A.),
  9–10
Webster, Daniel, 46
Western, Bruce, 192, 239–40
Western Allies, 156–57
Western Europe, 164–65, 194–95, 236
western expansion, 97
Western Passage, 21–22
Westmoreland, William, 176–77
wheat farming, 95–97
wheat prices, 97–98
Whig Party, 45–46, 68–69
Whisky Ring, 89
white Americans, 133
White Citizens Council, 172–73
white economic history, 5, 13, 92
white economy, 106
white flight, 138–39, 170–71, 186–87, 234
white gangs, 86
white newspapers, 72–73
white rioters, 144–45
white society, 26
white Southerners, 59
white supremacy, 121, 172–73, 197

white workers, 10–11
whiteness, 96, 124–25
Whitney, Eli, 23–24
Wilkerson, Isabel, 4–5, 169, 274–75
Williamson, Jeffrey G., 97–98
Wilmington massacre, 144–45
Wilmington "riot," **124–25**
Wilson, Woodrow, 126–27, 135–36, 139–40
Wisconsin, 67–68, 247
women, 24, 34, 144
Woodard, Isaac Jr., 157–61, 171–72
Woodward, Bob, 241
Woodward, C. Vann, 104, 114, 125–26
working class Blacks, 201–2
World Health Organization, 264
World War I, 133–34, 145–46, 161
  Blacks and, 134
  end of, 144
  Triple Entente and, 139–40
World War II, 54, 94, 130, 133–34, 153–54,
  239–40
  beginning of, 156–57
  postwar recovery from, 164–68
  Woodard in, 159–60
Wu, Tim, 236–37

Young Plan, 148–49, 152–53

Zingales, Luigi, 228–29
Zuckerberg, Mark, 3–4